Alone in Japan

Alone in Japan

A Journey to the Future

TOM FEILING

ALLEN LANE
an imprint of
PENGUIN BOOKS

ALLEN LANE

UK | USA | Canada | Ireland | Australia
India | New Zealand | South Africa

Allen Lane is part of the Penguin Random House group of companies
whose addresses can be found at global.penguinrandomhouse.com.

Penguin Random House UK
One Embassy Gardens, 8 Viaduct Gardens, London SW11 7BW

penguin.co.uk

Penguin
Random House
UK

First published in Great Britain by Allen Lane 2026

001

Set in 12/14.75pt Dante MT Std
Typeset by Six Red Marbles UK, Thetford, Norfolk
Printed and bound in Great Britain by Clays Ltd, Elcograf S.p.A.

The authorized representative in the EEA is Penguin Random House Ireland,
Morrison Chambers, 32 Nassau Street, Dublin D02 YH68

A CIP catalogue record for this book is available from the British Library

ISBN: 978-0-241-64091-3

Penguin Random House is committed to a sustainable future
for our business, our readers and our planet. This book is made from
Forest Stewardship Council® certified paper.

Contents

Introduction: Going Back to My Future

I'm not sure what it was that inspired me to go back to Japan. Perhaps the idea came while I was looking through a box of old photos. Three in particular jumped out at me – I'm looking at them again now. They were taken in a photo booth in an amusement arcade in Kabukichō, the biggest night life district in Tokyo, in 1993. The first is a head shot of me, a 25-year-old English teacher coming to the end of a three-year, post-university stint in Japan, an expression of optimism and youthfulness on my face.

It is a real photo, but the other two are not.

The second one shows what my face might look like if it were combined with that of a baboon. It's an early example of digital photographic manipulation – not a very sophisticated one, admittedly, but funny all the same. The third photo is marginally more convincing; it shows me as the software program imagined I would look as an old man. Looking at it 32 years later, it's interesting how far off the mark it was. True, these days, just as the program predicted, I have jowls in the corners of my mouth, but it has made my eyelids too heavy, and the expression in my eyes has lost all its sharpness.

Back then, such a magical device could only have been Japanese. The images it created – pseudo-real, half-fantasy – were the height of technical sophistication, another example of how Japanese tech seemed to be light years ahead of the rest of the world. I'm struck by what passed for fun in the early 1990s, and how quickly image manipulation software has moved on.

More surprising however, is how much Japan has aged. It's not just that it has, in the course of my lifetime, become the country with the oldest average age in the world. It has also become a postmodern country: one that used to pride itself on being at the cutting edge but is now confined to poring over photos of its younger, more vigorous self. But perhaps I'm being unkind; just as the passage of time has forced me to reassess what it means to be middle-aged, so Japan has had to reckon with what it means for a country to stop growing and start ageing.

*

My first experience of Japan began in London in 1990: I was 22, and six months out of the London School of Economics. I was living in a tatty flat in Camberwell, wondering what to do with my life. I hoped for inspiration, but none came. Britain was living through the last years of Thatcherism. Young as we were, the mood was one of bitter resignation. One of my fellow disaffecteds started a band called Past Caring. Friends who could went travelling, dropping out in India or Thailand.

Though I was in no mood to 'chill out', I was stumped for anything better to do. The brighter sparks among my fellow graduates had gone off to become yuppies in the City of London, but for humanities graduates like me it was a scramble to avoid the dole queue. I'd spent the months since graduating in a series of dead-end jobs, not because I wasn't qualified for anything better, but because I had no idea what I actually wanted to do. Clueless, I answered an ad for a sales job that I came across in the back pages of the *Evening Standard* and found myself trying and failing to sell advertising space. Then I tried selling satellite dishes. Finally, I got a steady job as a pest control operative – in common parlance, a rat catcher.

So my ears pricked up when I heard from my friend Sharon. After graduating, she had gone to Japan to work in the JET scheme, which found teaching jobs for graduates in Japanese high schools. Giving English lessons sounded lucrative; apparently, one young foreigner had bought a Porsche after just six months of teaching there. Although I was saddled with student debts, I had a hunger to see the world. I had no prior interest in Japan, but it seemed the only place I might square the circle. Somehow, I scraped together the money for a plane ticket; I started learning Japanese on the flight.

From the moment I arrived at Narita Airport, I was entranced by the sophisticated technology being put to use in Japan. Everything was so comfortable, peaceful and clean! I took an express train from the airport to Tokyo and then another to Ayabe, a little town in the west of the country where I had arranged to spend a week with Sharon before I'd have to find a job. The train glided in and out of the stations so quietly that I missed my stop and slept all the way through to Osaka. After backtracking to Kyoto and changing to a local train to Ayabe, I met up with Sharon and spent the evening relaxing in an *onsen*, one of Japan's many natural hot springs. Warmed through by the water, we donned *yukata* (light cotton bathrobes) and walked down to a lake. The moon shone overhead as snowflakes fell onto the water. It was idyllic. London and its problems seemed a world away.

A few weeks later, I found a job in a language school in Chichibu, a quiet town in the mountains an hour and a half north-west of Tokyo. My students were high school kids, office workers and OAPs. One was a teenage girl who wanted to design toilets for a living. Another worked in a factory making cameras for Canon and told me about the days when the company only made sights for rifles. A third was a *salariman* – a salary man, or white-collar worker – whose parents had arranged meetings with forty prospective brides for him, all of whom had turned him down.

If London was full of the familiar and the contemptible, Japan was bursting with new and delightful things, many of which I couldn't understand and taxed my social scientist's brain. I read everything about Japan I could lay my hands on, from Haruki Murakami's *The Wind-Up Bird Chronicle* to Yukio Mishima's *Forbidden Colours* and John Hersey's *Hiroshima*. I also started trying to figure out why, exactly, everything was so mysterious, poring over books like Ruth Benedict's *Mirror, Sword and Jewel* and Peter Dale's *The Myth of Japanese Uniqueness*.

After six months in Chichibu, I was itching for some excitement, so I moved to Tokyo, and another English-teaching job. It left me with plenty of free time, much of which I spent exploring the city on my bike. The capital was a great place to be a cyclist, for there were no potholes and the tarmac was always fresh. On warm summer nights, cycling around the Imperial Palace and back up through Ueno to Yanaka when there was nobody about, I felt at peace with my surroundings in a way I had seldom known before.

Although most of my Japanese friends chose to live in modern apartments, I moved into a rickety old wooden house. I remember the smell of the tatami mats on the floor, the aged cedar of which the house was built and incense from the local temple. I remember the heat of the summer months, when I would slide open the window and the way the sunlight would illuminate the desk I had in the alcove.

The house was on the edge of Yanaka cemetery, the oldest in Tokyo. Further south was the burial plot of the imperial family, which was surrounded by massive stone walls and seemed to be guarded by crows. Necropolitan Yanaka was far removed from the futuristic fantasy I'd had of the capital, but it was quiet and cheap, and I quickly grew to love Shitamachi – old downtown Tokyo – of which Yanaka was the unofficial capital.

I bought a camera and started taking photos around the city. I wanted to capture it all: bright sunny days, when the light picked out the silvery grey tiles of the temples and the thick straw ropes that hung at the *torii* gates of the shrines around Yanaka cemetery. Diminutive gardens set around moss-covered rocks and outsized stone lanterns. But also scenes from the hyper-modern city: vast building sites, acres of plate glass stretching into the sky, the neon lights of Shinjuku, and rows of office workers sitting rapt in front of pachinko machines. The contrast between the ultra-modern and the ancestral was unremarkable to most Japanese, but I found it endlessly fascinating. This, I felt, was what I had been looking for: a dose of another country's history, to be sure, but also a dose of the future that, in time, awaited us all.

★

I spent another couple of years living in Tokyo, but gradually I grew hungry for new experiences and left Japan. Eventually, I ended up back in London, where, for a time, I was able to keep up a connection. I found work coordinating shoots for Japanese TV companies when they came to the UK to produce inserts for their variety shows, and spent several years putting together programmes about whatever took the producers' fancy: Enid Blyton's childhood home; the Paisley Rocketeers, pioneers of space flight; the bus routes in London that *don't* use red double-decker buses. TV audiences were all agog at the promise of 'internationalization' in those days, and despite the Japanese economy having gone into recession in 1992, there was still plenty of money sloshing around.

In time, however, the money dried up, the TV crews stopped coming and the jobs became fewer and further between. My curiosity took me elsewhere again, and my Japanese language skills grew rusty. As years became decades, the time I had spent in Japan became a distant memory, only kept alive by photos in albums I hardly ever looked at, and old friends I heard from only occasionally.

Then, in the summer of 2017, a year shy of my 50th birthday, I found myself at a loose end. By then, I was living in London again, but I had none of the baggage that keeps people tied to a city. My work was freelance, erratic and badly paid. I was single and had no kids to look after, and most of my friends had either moved on or were busy with their own jobs and families. Suddenly, I didn't feel at home in London any more. So after 24 years away, and on something of a whim, I decided to go back to Japan. Moving there had got me out of a rut as a young man; perhaps it would do the same for me now that I was middle-aged.

I got ready for the trip with a mix of excitement and trepidation. I had completely forgotten how to speak Japanese, so I bought a standard *kanji* book and started studying the Chinese characters at the heart of the written language again. I applied to join a course at a Japanese language school in Tokyo. It was in Okachimachi, just south of Yanaka, the neighbourhood where I had once lived. The tuition fees were a bit of an outlay, but I figured I could just about afford a year-long course. Once my language skills were back up to speed, I'd see about finding a job.

I had stopped following news from Japan years ago, but all the same I knew that it was not the same country I'd left behind in

1993. It was no longer the most dynamic country in Asia – quite the opposite, in fact, for after the bubble economy burst in the early 1990s, it had gone into the first of several 'Lost Decades'. Economic growth had flatlined, as had wages and living standards, and there still seemed to be no end in sight.

*

It was close to midnight on a rainy night in late November when I arrived back in Ueno from Narita. I had breezily assumed it would be easy to find my hostel from the station, but I soon got lost in the warren of alleyways that run east from the Yamanote line. It was very picturesque, in a shop-worn, post-war kind of way, the brightly coloured lights reflected in the puddles and the old wooden houses huddling in the shadow of the railway tracks. I passed the back door of a tiny ramen restaurant, where the chef was tipping hot water from a huge cooking pot down the drain, getting ready to shut up shop for the night. I tried to ask him for directions, but the words got scrambled on the tip of my tongue, and when I asked him to repeat his reply, he just bolted back into his kitchen.

The next day, Tokyo was full of tourists, and nothing was familiar. The city might as well have been in deep fog. I was overwhelmed by the vastness of the subway map, and this made me feel sad, for I had once felt completely at home here. Now I was just another gormless sightseer, dithering at the self-service ticket machine in a cheap noodle restaurant, trying to figure out what I wanted to eat and how to order it. When I had left in 1993, I had been able to read the newspaper, albeit haltingly. Twenty-four years later, I struggled to decipher the two alphabets – *hiragana* and *katakana* – let alone read *kanji* characters. As for the spoken language, I remembered the basic greetings and a handful of useful adjectives – *tsugoi* ('great'), *kakoii* ('cool') and *kawaii* ('cute') – but that was about it.

I had a week to kill before I could move into my new place, so I spent some time reacquainting myself with my old stomping ground. Yanaka: magic word, password to precious, distant memories. When I'd lived there, no one had paid much attention to the neighbourhood. It was full of old things – temples, shrines, houses and people – that were of little interest to most Japanese people back in the early 1990s. However, things had changed. The glitzy accoutrements that people had clamoured for when the economy was booming had started to look a bit naff. Now they valued authenticity: the old neighbourhoods that had managed to survive the years of breakneck economic growth, and the craftspeople who lived in them; the modest, the home-grown and the overlooked.

This made Yanaka – which had always been a repository of traditional culture, and a collective memory bank of sorts – highly valuable. Educated young hipsters had piled in, opening artisanal bakeries and upmarket handicrafts shops selling mementos to day trippers. Foreign tourists, who were now coming to Japan in record numbers, loved the neighbourhood too.

I went back to the old house where I had lived in the 1990s, but it had been pulled down and replaced with something more convenient: an anonymous-looking modern building, clad in tough plastic weatherboards. All that the old place had had in the way of washing facilities was a copper sink at the top of the stairs, which I'd shared with the three other tenants. When I'd wanted to have a bath, I'd gone to the public bathhouse, or *sento*, over the road. I had been looking forward to a soak with the old men of Yanaka, so I was galled to discover that, like my old house, the *sento* had been knocked down and replaced with a block of flats.

The gentrification of Yanaka meant that I could no longer afford to live there, so a week after my return I moved into a tiny room in a share house. It was in Matsudo, a quiet, nondescript dormitory town, like hundreds of others in the commuter belt of the vast conurbation, but I liked it well enough, for the time being at least. Officially, Matsudo wasn't even in Tokyo, but the commuter trains travelled even faster than I remembered, and it only took 15 minutes to cover the ten miles back to Ueno.

Every morning, I took the train from Matsudo to Ueno, changed onto the Yamanote line, and travelled two stops south to Okachi-machi, where I spent the next four hours in class. The courses at my

Japanese language school were surprisingly popular, mainly with Chinese students. I was the oldest student in my class, and probably the entire school. I spent my afternoons poring over grammar exercises and memorizing *kanji*.

In the evening, I would take a train to Otemachi, in the heart of Tokyo's financial district, where I taught English conversation classes to office workers.

It stung a little to go back to a job I thought I had left behind for good, but I was full of forward momentum. Besides, I had little choice. The last last time I'd lived in Japan, I had seen little of the country apart from Chichibu and Tokyo. This time, I wanted to have a proper look around, and to do that I would have to save up some money. I was amazed to discover that there had been practically no inflation in the 24 years I had been away, but travelling in Japan still wasn't cheap.[1]

*

Gradually, I began to recover the fragments of what I remembered of Tokyo, pulling them up as if through muddy water, back into the clear light of day. By travelling the subway, and walking its streets and alleyways, I pieced the map of the city back together in my head. One day, I walked down Shōwa-dōri from Ueno Park, over the old bridge at Nihonbashi to Tokyo station. The following day, I walked around the inner moat of the Imperial Palace, the huge, unknowable green space in the centre of the city. I joined the throng of tourists streaming across the pedestrian crossing in Shibuya, which had been branded 'Scramble Crossing' as part of the tourist-friendly redevelopment of the neighbourhood. I gawped at the acres of *kawaii* merchandise on display in Harajuku, and come the evening, I wandered the glowing streets of Kabukichō, with its hostess clubs.

In some ways, nothing had changed. The skyscrapers housing the country's biggest corporations were as imposing, and their topiary gardens as immaculately pruned, as I remembered. The sheer wattage of the city's lights was as impressive as ever and the cars streaming past were as spotlessly clean as they had been. The taxi drivers still wore gleaming white gloves, and the city's transport system remained a wonder of efficiency, punctuality and extraordinary cleanliness.

But as weeks became months, and I started to zoom in on the little details of the lived-in city beyond the sights, the signs of an economy that had gone off the boil became inescapable. Some of the changes were for the best: there was no longer any need for the station attendants to squeeze commuters onto overcrowded trains like sardines, and the necktie was no longer obligatory for office workers. But other changes were more disconcerting. The *salarimen* still dressed in standard-issue black and grey, but their suits looked shinier, as if the straitened times had forced them to ditch the cotton and wool for polyester and acrylic. And they seemed less driven and more introspective than I remembered.

I noticed subtle changes in the city's shops, too. When I had lived in Japan as a youngster, I had loved designer clothes, but I could never afford to buy anything. This time round, the streets of Shibuya and Shinjuku were crowded with second-hand shops, some of which were selling excellent designer garb, and I was able to kit myself out in some top-notch cast-offs. This was quite a change: in the good old days of the early 1990s, nobody would have dreamed of buying second-hand goods. When Japan was the richest country in the world, things were always brand new, and when a new model came onto the market, Japanese consumers threw away their top-of-the-range VCRs, hi-fis and Walkmans without a second thought.

★

I wrote to old friends at the addresses I had for them without much expectation of getting a reply. I had fallen out of touch with most of them before the advent of the internet and email and, sure enough, each letter was returned to sender. The only friend I had stayed in touch with, and knew where to find, was Atsushi Hiranuma. He still lived in Chichibu, the town where I had spent my first six months in Japan in 1990.

Atsushi had challenged the lazy stereotypes I brought to Japan from London. He didn't work in an office, and he had none of the martial qualities I associated with workaholic 'Japan Inc.'. After days spent teaching English and studying the dreaded *kanji*, I would spend my evenings in his shed-cum-studio, warming my hands over the stove while he broadcast his nightly radio show. Towering over the turntables was the biggest record collection I had ever seen, covering every imaginable genre from Northern Soul to Ghanaian Highlife, Brazilian Tropicalia to Algerian Rai. Since his equipment had a range of only half a mile, he could have counted his listeners on the fingers of one hand, but he enjoyed playing MC, and I was happy to get a musical education.

'Come up for the weekend,' Atsushi said when I emailed him. In Chichibu, I found him a little diminished. His musical tastes had mellowed as much as they possibly could: he now only listened to English folk singer-songwriters from the 1970s, none of whom I'd heard of. Sitting on the tatami mats in his front room, imbibing the familiar scent of straw and cedar, I was struck by how quietly he played his music.

We soon found ourselves looking through old photos, among them some from the trip to London he had made with his then-girlfriend. They had eloped there because her family disapproved of their relationship, partly because he was poor and partly because his mother was a member of Soka Gakkai, the cultish Buddhist off-shoot beloved of Westerners like Tina Turner. They had decided to get married at the Japanese Embassy in London and, since their trip coincided with one of my own trips home, I had been best man.

I asked Atsushi if he and his partner Yoshiko ever went abroad on holiday these days. 'No,' he said, 'although I'd like to visit some Asian countries.' I said that if they ever thought about going back to London, they would be welcome to stay at my place, but intuition told me that there would be no return trip. 'There are too many terrorists in Europe,' he said, though I also detected something like disappointment in their previous trip. London, I sensed, had not been as feisty or as glamorous as they had hoped. British people's clothes looked like their carpets, Atsushi had said at the time, and Yoshiko had been shocked by the state of our teeth.

On Sunday morning, before I caught the train back to Tokyo, Atsushi took me for a drive to have a look at Mount Buko, the sacred mountain that overlooks Chichibu. It has been revered as a Shinto deity for millennia, and offerings are still made to it at the annual winter festival. On our way back down the mountain, which was shrouded in early morning mist, a deer bounded out of the trees, and ran across the road in front of us. It occurred to me that, aside from crows and pigeons, I had never seen a wild animal in Japan before. Of course, that said more about how little I'd actually seen of the country in the three years I had lived there than it did about the country itself. All the same, the deer gave me a precious glimpse of another, long-overlooked side of Japan, one that existed long before its people and their farms, factories and roads came along, but was marginalised in the rush for economic development.

Atsushi was less thrilled; like all Japan's mountain communities, Chichibu was at the sharp end of the process of mass ageing afflicting the country, he said gravely. Now that the humans were growing older and fewer, the animals were getting bolder.

★

I had another insight into the challenges facing a country with an ageing population the following weekend, when I went in search of Reiko, a long-lost friend of a friend. She would be in her 70s by now, my friend had told me, and she was worried about her. I had agreed to go and check on her, and when I confessed to Atsushi and Yoshiko that I was concerned my Japanese still wasn't good enough to hold a conversation, they offered to come with me.

Reiko lived in Tendai, a neighbourhood about 40 minutes from Tokyo station by train, and then another ten minutes on a monorail from Chiba. Gliding over the rooftops in a capsule was an amazing way to travel. Atsushi and Yoshiko said they'd spent the previous evening rehearsing what they were going to say when they got to Reiko's house. 'It is important to get the tone right, because a lot of Japanese people won't open the door to someone they don't know,' Yoshiko explained. The crime rate in Japan was still famously low, but con men preying on the elderly had become a big issue in the time I'd been away.

We got to Reiko's house, and Yoshiko rang the intercom. It had a camera, so she could see us, but we couldn't see her. When she answered, Yoshiko explained who she was, introduced me, and said that my friend was worried about her. Reiko said that she didn't want to talk to us and hung up. Yoshiko rang the buzzer again, and did some more explaining, most of which I couldn't follow. This time, Reiko said that she had been in touch with my friend and was planning to go to England in May. Then she hung up again.

And that really was that, so we walked back to the monorail station. Atsushi wondered if Reiko might be senile. She had seemed frightened – maybe she was paranoid? 'Japan is ageing fast,' he told me. 'It's not just that the elderly cost a lot of money once they start getting ill and need to be looked after.' That was a financial problem, he explained, to which Japan's bureaucrats were happy to devote their considerable reserves of mental energy. Costs could be calculated, forecasts made and action plans devised. 'The real problem is the terrible loneliness that many elderly people live with. There are millions of old people like Reiko in Japan.'

When we got back to Tokyo, Atsushi and Yoshiko left to catch a train back to Chichibu and I went to the nearest branch of Doutor to have a cup of coffee. I found a seat next to an old woman who was folding napkins. She had stacks of them in her bag, which she pulled out and restacked one by one, making sure the edge of each napkin was lined up precisely with the edge of the next, like a slow-moving human cash-counting machine.

It was a pointless exercise, because the napkins went back into her bag in exactly the same condition that they came out of it, but it kept her hands busy while she mulled over whatever it was that was preoccupying her. Her lips were wet, partly because she was continually mumbling to herself, and partly because she didn't have any teeth. She was completely self-contained and didn't look up once. Finally, she put the last of the stacks back in her bag, picked up one of the napkins on the table and blew her nose very thoroughly.

Should I have been concerned for her? She didn't seem to think so, and neither did the other customers, but the question stayed with me as I travelled back to Matsudo. It occurred to me that Atsushi had put his finger on two of the biggest changes I had noticed since returning to Japan: the onset of mass ageing and a vague but inescapable sense of loneliness. They seemed to be connected to the sense of decline I detected wandering the streets of Tokyo.

When I was growing up in the 1980s, Japan was a beacon, lighting the way to a high-tech future. That is the role it had played in the Western imagination from the time of the Tokyo Olympics in 1964, when Japan Railways unveiled the *shinkansen*, the fastest train in the world, and Westerners started to come to terms with the fact that Japan was not just catching up with, but surpassing us. Thereafter, Japan became a screen on which to project our brightest hopes: a land where scientific and technological progress was endless and even a disaffected humanities graduate from the UK like me could find his feet.

This time around, things didn't feel quite so hopeful. Yes, there were more escalators and elevators than I was used to seeing in London, more shiny surfaces and a lot more cuddly toys. But Japan was no longer the confident, forward-looking country I remembered, and every time I ventured out of the centre of Tokyo, it was noticeable how much poorer, older and lonelier people seemed.

*

Increasingly, alongside studying Japanese and teaching English, I spent my time reading about the demographic transformation underway in Japan. As the months rolled by, and I settled back into life there, the implications of what I was reading only grew more worrying. I was staggered by what I learned. Slowly but surely, the demographic transformation was changing everything, from the savings rate to the country's rural wildlife, food consumption to road building. Across the country, schools were closing for want of pupils, and robots were being drafted in to lead funeral services.

Old people first outnumbered children in Japan back in 1995, and they have effectively been taking over from the working population ever since. According to the National Census of 2020, the number of people aged between 15 and 64 declined by 11 million since the millennium, while the number of over-65s increased by 14 million.[2] In 1950, just 5 per cent of Japanese people were over 65.[3] By 2021, that number had reached 28 per cent, giving Japan the highest proportion of OAPs in the world.

In the years to come, the overall *number* of over-65s is not forecast to increase much more, but because the total population is shrinking, they are going to account for an ever-larger proportion of it. By 2070, over-65s are expected to make up 38 per cent of the population.[4]

How has this come to pass? Mass ageing is the consequence of a potent cocktail of demographic changes – a low mortality rate, long life expectancy and a low birth rate – all three of which are particularly marked in Japan. Life expectancy has risen, the mortality rate has fallen and, perhaps most importantly, Japan's birth rate has been exceptionally low for the past fifty years. In 2024, the number of babies born in Japan fell below 680,000, a drop of 5.7 per cent on the previous year and the lowest figure recorded since record-keeping began more than 120 years ago.[5] Miho Iwasawa, a demographer at the National Institute of Population and Social Security Research (NIPSSR), says that in all likelihood, by 2070, fewer than 450,000 babies will be born every year.[6]

Japan is not alone in facing these problems. Its fertility rate – the average number of children born per woman – currently stands at 1.3, but plenty of other countries have a lower fertility rate, among them Italy, Spain, Ukraine and Bosnia (and perhaps even more surprisingly Jamaica and Thailand).[7] What makes Japan particularly noteworthy is that its fertility rate fell below 2.1 children per woman, the rate needed to maintain a stable population, in 1974, long before any other country.[8] Because Japanese women started having fewer children before anyone else, their country started seeing the consequences before other countries did.

Japan is the canary in the coalmine, and it is fast running out of air. The twenty-first century is going to be an era not just of mass ageing, but also endless population decline for Japan. Its population has been falling since 2011, and the speed of decline accelerates with every passing year. The population shrank by 644,000 in 2021, 730,000 in 2022 and 837,000 in 2023.[9] That is the equivalent of losing a city the size of Glasgow or San Francisco every year.

In 2025, the population stands at 124 million. It is expected to decline by a further 5 million in the 2020s, 6 million in the 2030s, and 7 million in the 2040s. By 2070, it will in all likelihood have fallen to 87 million. Such a dramatic fall in numbers will take Japan back to where it was in 1953.[10] The most extreme forecast expects the population to fall to 45 million by 2100, which is what it was in 1900.[11]

Poring over these statistics put me in mind of watching a car conk out and roll back down the hill it has just climbed. Japan is gathering speed on its way back down. It is going to pass its former self on the way, but in far worse shape than it was. Population decline is not a benign process, and its consequences are only going to grow more dire with the passage of time.

★

An ageing population would not be a problem if people kept working until they died, but we are not robots and, at some point, we have to retire. If a third of the population stops working and draws a pension from the age of 65, and then goes on to live to 85, their pensions are going to be prohibitively expensive for the government. And if they spend the last 20 years of their lives in poor health, their medical bills will be prohibitively expensive too.

The sheer cost of providing pensions and medical care for an ageing population is what most frightens governments across the developed world. Just look at the UK's National Health Service: when it was founded in 1948, there were around a quarter of a million people in Britain in their late 80s or older. On average, people in this age group require six to seven times as much health spending as those in the prime of their lives, but in those days they made up such a small proportion of the population that their medical bills were manageable. Today, there are more than 1.5 million Britons in their late eighties or older, and there are predicted to be almost 6 million by the end of the century.[12]

You can see why Elon Musk has warned that the impending population crash is the single biggest problem the world faces.[13] It is no accident that this warning came from the man credited with taking electric vehicles into the mainstream; one of the oft-overlooked effects of an ageing population is a lack of innovation. Historically, those aged 30–44 have been society's innovators. The proportion of Europeans of working age began shrinking in 2000, so it follows that Europe is likely to become less innovative just when it needs to find solutions to a host of challenging new social problems.[14]

Without innovation, the only way to arrest economic decline will be to work longer and harder. As the number of humans on the planet shrinks, 'human capital' – our accumulated knowledge and skills – will have to increase to compensate for our declining numbers. The internet and AI suggest ways forward, but, so far, neither has created the breakthroughs in transport, energy generation and food production needed if humanity is to continue to thrive in an era of shrinking workforces and rising social security budgets.

Aside from the drag on living standards, another knock-on effect of a low fertility rate is mass solitude. Having resisted the pressure that traditionalist families and communities put on them to settle down and make babies, huge numbers of young people are going to mature and grow old alone. Declining fertility rates mean smaller families, and that means children born today are going to grow up with fewer relatives, while more adults are going to grow old without having the pleasure of seeing grandchildren come into the world to take their places.

Smaller families also mean fewer family members to look after the elderly when they are no longer able to look after themselves (which will put even more pressure on public and private providers of long-term care for the elderly). The world is not ready for the scale of the loneliness and isolation that lie ahead. The internet and social media might be preparing us for a future in which we enjoy more distant connections, and fewer immediate ones, but it is far from clear that humans can thrive in such a world.

★

I spent many months studying Japan's demographic travails. Slowly, I realized that I had been mistaken. Yes, the economy was in long-term decline, but that didn't mean that Japan no longer had anything to show us about the future. It *was* still giving the world a glimpse of things to come. But it was no longer a beacon. It was a warning.

The twenty-first century is going to be one of more old people and fewer young people. Japan is the first rich-world country to enter this phase of mass ageing and shrinking numbers, but plenty of other countries are inadvertently following its lead. By 2030, 20 per cent of Americans will be 65 or older, with the same proportion or higher in thirty-four other countries.[15] By 2040, 28 per cent of people in the rich world will be over sixty-five, the same proportion as in Japan today, and by 2050, over sixty countries will be classed as having large elderly populations.[16]

Demographers will tell you that this process is already well advanced. In 2018, the world reached an ominous milestone: for the first time in human history, the number of over-60-year-olds reached 1 billion. Even more striking, they outnumbered children under the age of five, also for the first time in history.[17] By the end of this century, we can expect there to be 2.4 billion people over the age of 65 on the planet, compared with just 1.7 billion under the age of 20.[18]

By most measures, the enormous human population of the world is a great achievement, a result of sustained efforts to harness medical technology to preserve and extend human life. The stratospheric rise in human numbers on planet Earth since 1950 is not down to rising birth rates, but to increasing life expectancy and falling rates of infant mortality. The number of the world's children who die before reaching their fifth birthday has fallen to an all-time low and is currently less than half what it was even in 1990.

But longer lives and fewer infant deaths can only boost numbers so far. If a population fails to reproduce itself, sooner or later, numbers will start to fall. In 2024, not a single country in the developed world had a fertility rate above the replacement level of 2.1.[19] By some calculations, countries with 'lowest low' fertility rates, such as

Japan, Germany and Italy can expect to see their populations shrink by 30 per cent with every passing generation.[20]

Below-replacement-level fertility rates are becoming the norm outside the rich world as well. Statistics from the United Nations Population Division show that the global average woman now gives birth to two children, down from five in 1950.[21] Less than 10 per cent of the world's people live in countries with high fertility rates, most of them in Africa.[22] Even countries that had high fertility rates a generation ago now have rates that are going to stop population growth in its tracks. The fertility rate in India, for example, currently stands at 2.0 and is continuing to fall.[23]

This is still news to most people, which is hardly surprising. Five decades ago, Paul Ehrlich's bestselling book *The Population Bomb* sparked global fears of 'mass starvation' on a 'dying planet' because of overpopulation. Until 2024, the United Nations was warning that the population of the world would rise to 11.2 billion by 2100. That year, however, it revised its population estimates, and it now expects the population of the world to peak at about 10.3 billion in the mid-2080s before starting to fall.[24]

On learning that that the population of the world is going to fall, the response of many people in the rich world is likely to be one of surprise, closely followed by relief. After all, most of us are aware of the burden that a booming human population has put on the planet's finite resources. The fear of climate change is already leading significant numbers of couples to have fewer babies; apparently, one in five female climate scientists says she plans to have no children or fewer children because of the climate crisis.[25] Ask a friend if they believe a declining population to be a problem, and they will likely pause for thought, and then give a hesitant 'No.' However, that is naive in the extreme. The implications of population decline are profound, and we are only beginning to understand the scale of the challenges it creates.

Yet most of us don't even realize it's happening. Demographic decline is a huge story, but because it is happening in slow motion, it is hard to see it unfolding. Think of how the proverbial frog reacts to finding itself in a pan of hot water. Because the temperature only rises gradually, it never experiences the shock that would bring it to its senses, and by the time it comprehends that it is being boiled alive, it is too late. Mass ageing is an existential threat, but that doesn't make it newsworthy. In the age of the 24-hour news cycle, it is always going to be pushed off the front page by more dramatic events.

Japan – where the ageing process is most advanced – remains an eminently peaceful and relatively prosperous country, but there are those who have tried to raise the alarm. One such person is Japanese journalist Masashi Kawai, whose book *Mirai no nenpyō* (which means 'chronology of the future') became a bestseller in 2017. By his reckoning, Japan is literally in need of new blood, for its hospitals will start to run out of blood donations in 2026. If doctors want to continue making blood transfusions, they will have to start soliciting for donations overseas. By 2030, the shortage of IT workers will be so severe that Japan's high-tech society will no longer be sustainable, and by 2033 the government will be so strapped for cash that it will no longer be able to maintain the infrastructure in rural areas. By then, one in every three houses will be unoccupied and much of the country will have become uninhabitable. Kawai's gloomy forecast takes the reader up to 2070, when he expects the uninhabited regions of Japan to be invaded by an unnamed 'land-hungry foreign power'.[26]

★

I had come back to Tokyo without giving much thought to how long it would take to learn to read, understand and speak Japanese again. As the enormity of the task dawned on me, I realized I would need to stay for a couple of years, at least. But what kept me in Japan for the next five years was my growing fascination with its demographic quandary. Rapid population decline is proving to be an intrinsic part of post-industrial societies, just as rapid population growth was an intrinsic part of industrialization and modernization. It is a problem that gets to the heart of modernity and its contradictions, and one that all of us will be wrestling with, sooner or later. And it is, perhaps, a unique social issue in that it sees the 'macro' forces of economics and politics collide with the most intimate aspects of human experience: desire, hope and the search for meaning.

I was determined to make sense of what was happening in Japan, and what is now coming for the rest of us. What is life like in a country beset by advanced mass ageing and population decline? Why are these changes happening and what can – and should – be done about them? How do Japanese people – the rich and the poor, the elderly and the young – feel about living in a shrinking country? And what can other countries learn from the Japanese experience?

As I found my feet in Japan again after 24 years away, I became increasingly driven to find answers to these questions. In the process, I would travel the length and breadth of the country and meet people from all walks of life. What they told me was surprising, chastening and often inspiring.

N

RUSSIA

HOKKAIDŌ

• Sapporo

• Hakodate

• Aomori

Morioka •

• Akita City

Sea of Japan

• Sendai

• Fukushima

• Niigata

Snow Country

HONSHŪ

• Chichibu

Japan Alps

Kanazawa •

Tokyo

Yokohama •

• Kamakura

Mount Fuji ▲

Izu Peninsula

L. Biwa

• Nagoya

Kyoto •

Kobe •

• Ōsaka

Inland Sea

Hiroshima •

SHIKOKU

PACIFIC
OCEAN

• Fukuoka

KYŪSHŪ

Nagasaki •

Kagoshima •

0   100   200 miles

0   100   200   300 km

The City

I.

Tokyo: The Life Cycle of a
Post-Growth Megacity

I dare say Japan's demographic problems pass most of Tokyo's foreign visitors by. It is easy to be enthralled, as I was in my first weeks back, by its neon-lit streets and towering skyscrapers, and the myriad ways in which Japan turns our expectations of old and new, East and West on their heads.

More than that, it's just all so pleasant, peaceful and liveable. As well as being the biggest city in the world, Tokyo is arguably the only big city that really works. Even its least prosperous neighbourhoods are well built and well maintained, unemployment is low, strikes practically unheard of, and the crime rate is among the lowest in the world. Japanese people do not die of gunshot or knife wounds, and women can walk home late at night without fear of being attacked.

If a city is a living, breathing organism, the Japanese capital is a supremely healthy creature. Even at the famous Shibuya Scramble crossing at rush hour, you can take a lungful of air without fear of having a coughing fit. Traffic jams are so unusual they make the evening news, there is no speeding and nobody sounds their horn.

How have Japanese city planners succeeded where so many others have failed? It's partly down to a collective appreciation of orderliness and cleanliness, but also to a love of systems. Building and maintaining railways, highways and distribution networks is not just a strength, it's a national obsession. Tokyo's trains are fast, cheap and punctual, and it is the love of systems that explains how the biggest urban railway network in the world runs so smoothly.

Underlying the efficiency and orderliness of Tokyo's urban plan is a remarkably cohesive society. People are unstintingly polite and

3

respectful of one another, and the authorities do what authorities are supposed to do. There are public toilets wherever you would hope to find one, and they are not covered in bombastic scribbling or holes in their doors where somebody has punched them in anger at who knows what.

Mystifyingly to a visitor from the United Kingdom, there are also no litter bins – and yet the streets are spotlessly clean. This is partly attributable to the legions of elderly men and women who sweep the street outside their house every morning, but it is also down to a different way of thinking. The attitude seems to be that litter bins pander to the wrongdoer. If you want to put an end to littering, the last thing you should do is supply people with litter bins. People should take responsibility for their litter, instead of assuming that it's the state's job to clear up after them, like a bunch of scatter-brained children.

*

As I mentioned in the Introduction, Japan's demographic crisis might be its Achilles heel, but it rarely makes the news. Academics, government researchers and policymakers have been warning of the long-term consequences of a low fertility rate for decades, and the government has been promising to do something about it for almost as long. Perhaps this lack of urgency is down to the ageing process being least apparent in Tokyo, the pristine city where most of the country's politicians, journalists and policymakers live.

Tokyo certainly looks like a thriving modern city. Since I last walked the streets nearly 30 years ago, the centre of the city has been transformed by the urban redevelopment projects of its cash-rich corporations and property developers.* In 2014, the 247-metre-high Toranomon Hills skyscraper development in central Tokyo opened to great fanfare. Featuring retail outlets, premier office spaces, luxury private residences and a high-end international hotel chain,

---

* In the early 1990s, the over-inflated property market imploded, dragging the economy into a recession that the government has been struggling to shrug off ever since.

it was the latest in a string of integrated skyscraper developments. Soon after completing Toranomon Hills, the developer revealed plans for ¥1097 billion ($10 billion) of investments in skyscrapers in central Tokyo over the following decade.

These developments have helped to maintain Tokyo's status as the ever-evolving frontrunner among the world's great modern cities. Wandering the manicured boulevards of Aoyama and Omotesando, it is easy to get lost in the perpetual present and put the gloomy predictions of the country's demographers out of mind.

For most of its post-war history, Japan has widely been considered a success story. Over the course of the half century between 1955 and 2005, GDP per capita grew by a factor of 30.[1] Even in the third decade of the twenty-first century, Japan continues to rank among the top ten countries in the world according to all three dimensions of the United Nations Human Development Index (health, education and standard of living). Clear-sighted industrial policy, high educational achievement and good healthcare, supported by a hardworking labour force, have created a society that affords its members an exceptionally high level of economic and social wellbeing.

Few Japanese die in the first precarious months after birth, enjoying as they do one of the lowest infant mortality rates on earth. Politically, they live in a peaceful, stable and open environment largely free of coercion. Fatal traffic accidents have been steadily declining and medical research into coronary heart disease and cancer, the two leading causes of death in Japan, is making good progress. There are lots of public health campaigns, and the elderly follow doctors' advice diligently. Broadly speaking, people stay active and eat well, and consequently enjoy good health for longer than anyone else in the world.

Japan's universal healthcare system gives everyone regular, free check-ups, as well as high-quality, low-cost medical treatment when illness, age or infirmity eventually catches up with them. Its long-term care insurance system is among the most generous in the world, subsidizing between 70 and 100 per cent of the cost of care for the elderly, depending on income.[2] Thanks to these subsidies, Japanese people are considerably healthier than Americans. And yet, despite their considerable cost, Japan spends only half of what the United States spends on healthcare per capita.

You might imagine that the capital of the oldest country in the world would look old. Far from it: thanks to a mania for scrapping and rebuilding, the average age of the buildings in Tokyo is just 28, which is far younger than the average age of its inhabitants: 44.[3] Walking Tokyo's pristine streets, in thrall to its futuristic buildings, is like spending time with Dorian Gray: captivating for as long as you can put the old man in the attic out of mind.

Still, residents of Tokyo are, on average, younger than those of any other prefecture in Japan, because young people are moving to the capital in search of work and education as never before. These days, migrants from the country's towns and villages bypass the provincial cities and head straight for the giant conurbations. As a result, an 'urban implosion' is underway, as the population becomes ever more concentrated in Tokyo, Yokohama, Osaka and Nagoya. Together, these four cities are home to more than half the country's people.[4]

We are schooled to think that there is something inherently progressive about mass urbanization, but the more time I spent in Tokyo, the more signs I saw of its looming decline. Look past all the imposing buildings, and go into individual houses and apartments, and the demographic crisis is plain to see. Despite the city's shimmer and relative affluence, Tokyo's residents have the fewest babies in the country.[5] The capital is dependent on fresh recruits from the countryside to sustain itself, but with the countryside losing its ability to bear and raise children, it has stopped functioning as a seedbed for young workers. That means that Tokyo will soon start to shrink as well.[6]

Cycling around the city centre on weekday afternoons, basking in the unchanging blue of the winter sky, it felt great to be back. But like the ever-youthful Dorian Gray and the wrinkled portrait he keeps hidden in his attic, Tokyo is all front. As soon as I headed into the outlying neighbourhoods, I couldn't help feeling that I was wandering the vast, abandoned set of a film shot in the late 1980s.

6

When a population starts shrinking, you see it first in suburbia, as the demand for housing weakens, driving down land prices. In some of Tokyo's suburban wards, the housing market is already faltering, with vacant family homes not selling at any price. Even in the central wards, prices are forecast to decline by more than 60 per cent by 2040.[7] Yutaka Okada, a senior economist at the Mizuho Research Institute, expects even Japan's largest cities to hollow out in the years ahead. 'Popular areas will survive, but it would not be surprising if areas that are not so popular will have a lot of vacant houses and turn into slums,' he said in an interview with the *Asahi Shinbun*.[8]

You don't have to go far from the city centre to see these 'not so popular' districts. One example is Sunamachi, an easily overlooked residential neighbourhood close to the waterfront in Tokyo Bay. I went back there one afternoon in a fit of nostalgia; during my first stint in Tokyo, I had taught English conversation classes at the community centre. Wandering the pedestrianized shopping street 24 years later, the sense of dereliction was overpowering. Apart from a solitary supermarket, all the shops were shuttered. Most of my students had been young mums and high school students, but this time around, bar a few hardy OAPs pulling shopping trolleys, the main street was deserted, as was the community centre.

Another example is Takashimadaira, a residential neighbourhood in Itabashi-ku, a ward in north-west Tokyo. Its huge housing blocks were built in the 1960s, when the economy was booming, drawing young people from the countryside into the cities. They were built for young families, but are now full of ageing parents, many of whom live alone. As they die, their flats are left empty, creating pocks in the urban fabric that will only grow bigger in the years to come.

The process of ageing and shrinking is even further advanced outside Tokyo. It has become particularly acute in Osaka, where 17 per cent of homes are vacant, but shuttered shopping streets and abandoned homes are on the rise in smaller cities like Kyoto, Kobe and Fukuoka as well.[9] Hiroshima has long been famous for its wonderful night-time view over the bay, but its elderly residents are dying, and as their homes are abandoned, the lights are going out across the city.

*

For the first few months, aside from catching up with my old friend Atsushi, I didn't have much to do in terms of socializing. People were polite enough, but I found it hard to make new friends. So every so often, like British expats the world over, I would head to the nearest British pub. One night, I found myself in one near Shibuya station. For the first beer or two, I wasn't doing much apart from propping up the bar. I watched the landlord, a Londoner called Paul, get into a barney with a Japanese man after asking him to help a very drunken member of his group. 'You should look after your friend,' Paul said. 'This is not your country,' the guy slurred back at him, before staggering out, colliding with various pieces of furniture on the way. Paul rolled his eyes and stuck his nose back in his newspaper.

Sitting next to me was a Canadian called Scott. He said he worked for a multinational recruitment consultancy and had been in Japan for 15 years. I asked him how things had changed in the country in that time. For years, things had not been much different, he said: he had got used to the general sense of inertia that characterizes Japan's government and its largest corporations. 'Even after three decades of next to no growth, and the shock of the earthquake and tsunami that struck Fukushima in 2011, the fundamentals of working life stayed the same,' he told me. However, all that changed in 2019, when Prime Minister Shinzo Abe reformed the immigration law, making it easier for companies to hire skilled foreign workers. 'The pace of change has picked up dramatically in the past year,' he enthused. 'Japan is becoming a really interesting place to be again.'

I reflected on what Scott said. Since my return, I had noticed a lot more foreign faces on the street, even in lowly Matsudo. But most of them were doing low-wage jobs: young Chinese convenience store workers, Filipinos pushing elderly Japanese people in wheelchairs, West Africans digging trenches and laying cables. There was also more acknowledgement of the presence of Korean and Chinese people, perhaps not those on permanent residents' visas, who have been living in Japan for generations, but those coming as tourists with money to spend. There were more tax-free shops, and more foreign-language signs in the stations – in English, Korean and Chinese, and sometimes Nepali and Vietnamese as well.

I wondered how the new arrivals felt about living and working in Japan. When I had first lived in Tokyo, few tourists could afford to visit, resident foreigners were few and far between and discrimination against Koreans was rife. A Japanese friend had told me about a Korean woman he had seen lose her temper in a busy restaurant near Shinjuku station. One of the staff had done something to upset her, and she'd laid into him, the restaurant and the entire country for being arrogant racists, and demanded that they pay Koreans some respect. She had then stormed out, leaving the staff to stare at the floor in embarrassed silence. But what was most memorable was the manager's reaction: after the woman left, he took a handful of salt and scattered it over everything she'd been in contact with, as if hoping to purify his establishment of her polluting language. In his eyes, the Korean woman was not a justly aggrieved victim of discrimination, but a vengeful spirit.

Needless to say, I was not subject to the same discrimination, or the same superstitions. Japanese society has always treated white foreigners differently. In the early 1990s, when Japan was enjoying one of its periodic dalliances with 'internationalization', learning English, watching European arthouse films and taking holidays in New York, London and Paris was the height of urbane sophistication. We like to celebrate the sophisticated fruit of this hybridization, but for every Ryuichi Sakamoto or Yoji Yamamoto, there were ten country bumpkins revelling in the power of the yen, who saw internationalization as little more than a chance to treat the world as a giant dressing-up box.*

---

* Ryuichi Sakamoto (1952–2023) was an Oscar-winning composer and founder of the Yellow Magic Orchestra. Yoji Yamamoto (born 1943) is a pioneering fashion designer known for his avant-garde tailoring.

On New Year's Eve 1993, I paid ¥10,000 (£45 in those days) to get into Gold, which was at the time the city's most fashionable nightclub. I remember walking into the club and being momentarily surprised to find that everyone in there was Black – before quickly realising that they were just Japanese kids with Afro perms and perma-tans. The fad for Black American music gave me some interesting insights into Japan's own special relationship with the United States. While auto workers in Detroit were setting fire to Toyotas and Nissans in protest at what they regarded as unfair trading practices, Japan's newly minted tycoons were buying up Hollywood movie studios, and Japanese kids were spending silly money on original Motown 45s.

There were always critics of this love of the United States, simmering away on the back burner, even in the years of plenty. On Sundays, I would often see the *yakuza* (the Japanese version of the Mafia) parading around Ueno in black military vehicles, flying the rising sun flag of the Imperial Japanese Army and blaring out wartime marching songs to crowds of indifferent shoppers. I had a taste of Japanese nationalism a few times myself. Coming back from a weekend trip to the seaside with a girlfriend, an elderly man in a coffee shop at Shinagawa station had asked her why she was dating a white man. 'We fought a war against people like him,' he told her. She glowed with indignation, but kept her mouth shut in deference to the older man.

Japanese nationalism was rarely belligerent in the early 1990s, to white people at least, but *Nihonjinron* – ideas about what makes Japan unique – was pervasive and never-ending. As the first Asian country to join the club of wealthy nations, a sense of exceptionalism was understandable. Back in 1990, many commentators believed that it was only a matter of time before Japan overtook the United States to become the largest economy in the world. The old men at the helm of the Liberal Democratic Party (LDP), which has run the country for almost all of the last 70 years, liked to put Japan's extraordinary economic growth rates down to its ethnic and cultural homogeneity, the team spirit animating the nation's loyal workers and the devoted housewives and mothers who kept the home fires burning.

The picture that Scott painted – of corporations hungry for skilled foreign workers and a government under pressure to open up to mass immigration – showed me just how much the country had changed since the economic meltdown of 1991. 'The number of foreigners working in management jobs is rising fast,' he told me. 'Opening up to foreign competition is putting pressure on Japanese managers. Contrary to the stereotype of the hyper-efficient Japanese worker bee, many of them are not actually very good at their jobs.' Like it or not, Japan could no longer afford to go it alone.

*

Just as the impact of a faltering fertility rate is primarily economic, so too are its origins. Japan's demographic problems are bound up with the economic stagnation it has endured for the last three decades. This is because the nuclear family – the modern way of making babies – was built on middle-class prosperity; without middle-class prosperity, nobody wants to make babies any more. To understand how and why, you have to appreciate the shadow of its former self that Japan has become.

With the rise of China, it has become easy to forget the economic 'miracle' that Japan pulled off in the post-war years. When Emperor Hirohito surrendered to the Americans in 1945, four-fifths of Japan's ships, a third of its industrial machinery, and nearly a quarter of its rolling stock, cars and trucks had been destroyed.[10] Western experts held a dim view of Japan's prospects. The World Bank pronounced that the country was not ready to start producing steel products, let alone cars, and that it should stick to manufacturing textiles.

The Japanese government proved them wrong. It showed how a state could use industrial policy to build an advanced economy much faster than Western experts deemed possible for a country as poor as Japan was in 1950. It did this by identifying the industries common to the advanced economies of Europe and the United States, giving subsidies and access to cheap credit to Japanese companies working in those sectors, and encouraging them to learn from foreign technology. By partnering an active state with the economic discipline of privately owned corporations, the government spearheaded a process of export-led industrialization, while adroitly avoiding the creation of a graveyard of white elephants, as happened in many other developing nations.[11]

Japanese firms started out exporting cheap toys, bicycles and textiles, but quickly moved into electronics. The Americans were not impressed. Days before the outbreak of the Korean War in 1950, US President Harry Truman's special envoy, John Foster Dulles, advised the Japanese government to concentrate on exporting things like cocktail napkins.[12] But then came the Korean War, in which the American army turned to Japan for supplies of food and armaments. This gave the Japanese economy the shot in the arm it needed and between 1950 and 1973, economic growth averaged an unprecedented 10 per cent per year.[13]

It took some time for the West to update its perceptions of Japan. As late as 1962, French president Charles de Gaulle referred to the Japanese prime minister, Hayato Ikeda, as 'that transistor salesman'. However, two years later, Japan's economy overtook the French economy in size. It overtook Britain in 1967, and became the second largest economy in the world when it surpassed West Germany in 1968.[14]

James Abegglen is credited with being the first American to try to understand the secret behind Japan's phenomenal growth rates. In his book *The Japanese Factory*, which came out in 1958, he wrote: 'The Anglo-American notion that all is owed the shareholder has no currency in Japan. The primary stakeholders in the *kaisha* are its members, the employees.'[15]

It was this sense of all being in it together that allowed for the creation of a mass middle class in Japan. When the economy was doing well, Japanese people liked to think they had succeeded in creating a meritocratic society. Cabinet Office surveys show that from the mid-1960s onwards, over 90 per cent of people identified as middle class.[16]

This was the idea behind *Nihonjinron* – that Japanese people were the same as one another, yet different to any other nationality – and it had tremendous appeal. In the late 1980s, when Japan was at the

peak of its economic power, studies showed that ideological differences, which typically pit a conservative establishment against a
left-wing opposition, were less marked in Japan than in any other
advanced industrial country.[17]

How did this happen? After all, before World War Two, the
majority of Japanese people were either workers or peasants. The
state had mobilized them to go to war by appealing to their nationality, not their social class, and nobody was under any illusion that
Japan was an egalitarian or meritocratic country. Power was in the
hands of the country's *zaibatsu* – giant industrial conglomerates
like Mitsui, Sumitomo and Mitsubishi. Whether you looked at land
ownership, university education or living standards, there was no
escaping that Japan was a thoroughly elitist society.

However, that all changed during the seven years that the United
States occupied Japan after the war. The Americans were convinced
that Japanese militarism had its origins in the country's feudal social
structure. They saw feudalism everywhere and were determined to
uproot it. They broke up the *zaibatsu* and the aristocrats' landed
estates, and embarked on an ambitious land-reform programme,
in the belief that a nation of smallholders would be more likely to
uphold the supposedly peaceful norms of parliamentary democracy.

These reforms made for a more equitable distribution of income
and wealth. After the hardship Japanese people had endured during
the war, the shame of defeat and the bitter recrimination of the
post-war period, they began to enjoy the sweet taste of success
again. It was still faint, and largely confined to the cities, but over
the course of the 1950s, incomes began to rise, not just for the elite,
but for everyone.

The middle-class ideal was personified by the rise in the late 1950s
of the *salariman*, a white-collar worker, typically for one of Japan's
large corporations or the state administration. Sociologist Takehiko
Kariya describes this ideal as follows:

One attends a first-class *juku* [cram school], passes through first-
class middle and high schools and enters a top university. If one has

achieved this, then one can enter a first-class company and have a happy life. In Japanese post-war society, this success story has been drummed into the people and spread as a life plan into every last corner of society.[18]

This middle-class ideal resonated with Japanese people because, for a growing number of them, it was realizable. Thanks to a merito-cratic education system, a man could get a well-paid white-collar job regardless of his social origin. He also benefitted from the life-time employment system that big companies introduced during the country's high growth period in the 1950s and 60s as a way of attracting and retaining the best university graduates. The emphasis was on loyalty, not performance, and wages rose only gradually, but what the *salariman* lost in remuneration, he made up for in security and stability. A job was for life, and with this as his foundation, he could go on to enjoy the lifestyle that went with material prosper-ity: a modern apartment, a stay-at-home wife and a family.

Over the course of the five decades after 1945, Japan went from being a nation of mainly blue-collar workers and peasants to a nation of white-collar workers. Hard work was rewarded with the security of a steady job, and seniority was rewarded with more responsibil-ity and higher pay.[19] As more young men joined the ranks of the *salarimen*, older office workers were promoted into the managerial class, creating a virtuous circle. With lifetime employment, upward social mobility and the novelty of mass consumerism, everyone felt they were better off than their parents' generation.

Crucially, the fertility rate in 1964 was a perfectly sustainable 2.1 children per woman.[20] That year, Japan became the first Asian country to join the Organisation for Economic Cooperation and Development (OECD). In 1971, the OECD declared that, compared to the advanced economies of the West, Japan was indeed a merit-ocracy, a society in which educational success was all you needed to attain financial security and social status.[21] As a consequence, income distribution was more equal than in other rich world countries.

Thereafter, Japan became a model for other countries to admire, even emulate. For a country always keen (and sometimes desperate) to earn the respect of the West, this was a hugely gratifying achievement. Japan had officially arrived, and the bitter shame of military defeat, poverty and occupation was confined to the history books. More importantly, the Japanese people had done it together.

★

That was the official version of events and it largely tallied with the Japan I remembered from my first time living there. Give or take the odd son of a tycoon or daughter of a motorcycle gang member, Japan really had seemed a meritocratic society. But things had changed a great deal while I had been away. Over the last three decades, Japan has seen some of the weakest wage growth in the developed world. Between 1991 and 2022, the purchasing power of the average Japanese salary barely changed and, these days, Japanese workers only earn about three-quarters as much as their counterparts in other developed countries.[22] With both income inequality and poverty rates above the OECD average, the image of a homogeneous middle-class society has evaporated.[23]

A foreign observer might be tempted to ask whether, in a Rip-Van-Winkle land of no inflation, it really matters if incomes don't rise? But stagnation doesn't mean that nothing happens. Companies still want to see profits rise, and when they don't, they feel compelled to cut costs. Most of them still honour their commitments to their older employees, but they are gradually ditching the system of lifetime employment, cutting the number of graduates they hire, and instead taking on more irregular and part-time workers. These workers are known as *freeta*, a portmanteau of the English word 'freelancer' and the German word *arbeiter*, meaning 'worker'. They work in irregular, part-time or temporary jobs, often without guaranteed hours or any of the benefits associated with work other than a wage.

By 2012, 38 per cent of all employees were *freeta*, and this rose to 50 per cent among workers between the ages of 15 and 24.[24] This might have worked as a short-term solution to a temporary recession, but economic growth rates have been stagnant for three decades now, and a growing number of people who became *freeta* when they were 18 or 19 are still there after 20 years or more. It is one thing to work in a 7-Eleven while you're a teenager, but quite another to be doing the same job in your late 30s.

This is how Japan's Lost Decades have spawned a 'lost generation'. On joining the labour market, the well-educated heirs to their parents' high expectations found themselves cut adrift from Japan Inc. Unlike in the West, wealth has not been sucked up into the upper echelons, but news of cash-rich corporations posting record profits doesn't go down well with workers struggling with stagnant wages and rising prices.

There is a widespread sense that income disparities are growing and the country's middle class is being whittled away. Many *freeta* gave up hope of joining the middle class long ago, and even employees in regular, full-time work are not immune to the malaise of impermanence. The sense of all being in it together has gone. Until incomes stopped rising in the early 1990s, over 90 per cent of Japanese people identified as middle class. By 2006, this had fallen to 54 per cent, and 37 per cent considered themselves lower class.[25] Japan has gone from being a country where anyone could join the middle class, to one in which everyone is worried about falling into the ranks of the *freeta*.

The mass disappointment and estrangement this has caused is unprecedented. In 2011, sociologist Masahiro Yamada wrote an essay called 'The Young and the Hopeless' in which he warned that the normalization of irregular work was having a disproportionate impact on young people, not just economically but socially. According to Yamada,

> The old system has stopped functioning. In its place has been created a sort of economic apartheid in which the winners are protected by the rules of the old system while the losers are pushed out into an ultra-precarious new world . . . Powerful social forces simultaneously condemn young people for lacking ambition, while seeking to enslave them without much prospect for fulfilling, balanced lives.[26]

It is hardly surprising that the fertility rate has fallen as the number of *freeta* has risen. It is not easy to settle down and raise a family when your job is badly paid and precarious. Getting married and raising a family require job security and a reasonable salary. Moving from job to job, *freeta* are a bad bet for anyone looking to lend money. Many of them can't pass the background check to rent a flat, much less get a mortgage. Most women don't want to marry a *freeta*. That is why, when you look at men aged between 30 and 34, you find that 60 per cent of those in regular work are married, but only 27 per cent of those in irregular work.[27]

★

The night I spent talking about immigration with Scott in the British pub in Shibuya gave me an unexpected insight into Japan's demographic woes. Opening the doors to immigrants was, it seemed, one important aspect of a broader reckoning with the huge social crisis unfolding in Japan, as its birth rate drops, its population ages and its workforce shrinks. Foreboding stuff, but I shared Scott's excitement at the pace of change and the embryonic multicultural society taking shape in Tokyo. Perhaps there was an upside to this story, after all.

With such thoughts, and the effects of several pints of Guinness swirling around my head, I quite lost track of time, and when I next looked at the clock it was half past midnight. If I was going to make the last train to Ueno, I would have to run. That I did, but by the time I had weaved my way past the hordes of drunken commuters heading for Shibuya station and dashed up the stairs to the Yamanote line, the taillights of the last train to Ueno were receding down the track.

So I decided to walk. It was a bit of a stretch, maybe 7 miles, but it would take me through Roppongi, where I could have another drink, down to Akasaka and then around the Imperial Palace, which were all interesting places. By the time I got to Ueno, the trains would be running again, and I could catch one back out to Matsudo.

I sallied forth from Shibuya station, got my bearings from a street-side roadmap, and headed into the forest of steel, concrete and glass to find Roppongi-dōri. I was glad of the chance to walk the streets by night. Night walking was a habit I had often practised the last time I lived in Tokyo. I liked the sense of communion with the city it gave me. In daylight hours, the city wasn't mine, but by night the buildings took on a personality of their own, as if they'd spent the daylight hours absorbing the humanity coursing around them. Once emptied of people, I could pretend that the city was welcoming me back.

This time, however, it wasn't: no sooner had I climbed the steps to the elevated walkway over Meiji-dōri than I was lost. I had been expecting a short uphill walk from Shibuya, which I knew to be set in a valley, but that aside, I had no idea of the lie of the land I'd be walking. As often happens in Tokyo, the elevated expressways, and the multi-storeyed jumble of buildings that surrounds them, conspired to confuse any sense of the topography I was passing through. Still, it was a good feeling, being a stranger in a huge, hyper-modern city. I watched taxis shoot under the walkway I was standing on and listened to the booming sound of the traffic rushing along the expressway overhead. Finally, I got my bearings, and had another stab at Roppongi-dōri.

Not far up the slope from Shibuya I came to a bar built into the embankment on one side of the road. I paid the cover charge and went inside for a drink. It was a cool little spot, patronized by a mixed crowd of Japanese and European – or possibly Latino and American – youngsters, among them some beautiful girls. The DJ was playing some excellent house music and I soon found myself shuffling. It had been so long since I was on a dance floor, my feet and legs took a while to relearn the lexicon, but gradually I began to move more fluently.

I was looking forward to staying long enough to limber up properly, but the place soon filled up, and before long I had been shuffled up against the tables on the edge of the dance floor. By the time I'd finished my drink, the place was heaving, and I found myself relegated to a darkened corner next to the toilets.

I spent a minute or two bobbing from foot to foot, wrestling with a growing sense of purposelessness. For the first time in a long time, I thought of home. This is why I left Brixton, I said to myself. I had found myself looking for fun in old haunts one too many times. They had been full of people doing the same old thing, 20 years after the event, and the newer spots were full of young people who looked straight through me. I remembered the long walk ahead and headed back out onto Roppongi-dōri.

★

It was fitting, I suppose, to feel totally free at one moment and completely alone the next, at the end of an evening discussing the gig economy and the rise of the *freeta* with an expat personnel manager in central Tokyo. Did the label fit me, I wondered? After all, I was single, and a freelancer. But I didn't feel any affinity with the precarious, lonely lifestyle that Scott had described.

Perhaps that's because *freeta* is such an ambiguous term. While it generally refers to those on irregular contracts, it can also be used to refer to people who have deliberately chosen to work on their own terms, often in their own space. In their own quiet way, many young Japanese people – even the ones in full-time, regular employment – are telling Japan Inc. that they are no longer prepared to abide by the rules. They don't want to work overtime or go drinking with their colleagues after work. Nor do they want to be transferred to a company branch on the other side of the country, far from their friends and families. They are unwilling to sacrifice their personal lives to work, as their parents' generation did. They have a new value system and are not interested in what most employers are offering, even if they do pay a steady wage. In short, they want a better work–life balance.

When the coronavirus pandemic came along, it showed young people that it was possible to work from home and, even after restrictions were lifted, a lot of 'quiet quitters' decided not to go back to work. Instead, they opted to take part-time or freelance work, often related to their personal interests. As ever, the Japanese media was quick to latch on to this trend, spawning an array of new buzzwords to describe the search for meaning outside the old nine to five: *jibun rashisa* ('being true to oneself'), *jiko jitsugen* ('self-actualisation') and *jibun sagashi* ('search for self').

Ironically, this quest for personal freedom has been played out against a backdrop of rising dependency on the previous generation. In his essay 'The Young and the Hopeless', Masahiro Yamada points out that 80 per cent of unmarried Japanese between the ages of 18 and 35 still live with their parents. He calls them 'parasite singles'.[28]

Parasite singledom has its roots in the 1980s, when the children of the baby boomers came of age. When they left school, many of them went on to university, but continued to live in the family home. Even after they graduated and got jobs, they carried on living at home because they could see no reason to leave. They were invariably being looked after by a mother who was a full-time housewife and financially supported by a well-paid father. Most of them did not help out with the housework, let alone pay rent or bills, and they all had their own room in which to develop a sense of freedom and autonomy. Because they didn't have to pay for food or lodging, it left them with lots of spending money and no one to spend it on apart from themselves.

This set-up was particularly liberating for young women because it allowed them to focus on their careers. It was also great news for the nation's manufacturers, who got to sell lots of one-person, one-product stuff. By then, Japan's mass consumer market had reached saturation point. Every family had a house, car, TV and all the domestic appliances they could wish for. This spelled trouble for the country's giant consumer-electronics firms, so they started pushing the idea that it was no longer enough that every household should have a TV; every member of the family needed her own set too. Telephones sprouted extra handsets so the kids could talk to their friends in private, and Mum got her own little car to go to the shops in.

Their grandparents, whose generation had hauled Japan to prosperity in the post-war years, were not impressed. They called the younger generation *dokushin kizoku* – 'single aristocrats' – because they combined their dependence on other people with a newfound sense of entitlement.

Parasite singledom is bad news for the next generation as well, because it discourages people from having families of their own. Parasite singles spend their twenties single. Some of them get married, albeit later than previous generations, but plenty of them never do and spend their entire lives living with their parents. The parasite single might want to get married, but not enough to sacrifice the standard of living his or her father provides. They want a meaningful relationship, and if that means spending their 30s waiting for the right person to come along, so be it. But this is the crux of dependency disguised as freedom. Dependency on your parents is bound to affect your attitude to adulthood: when the only yardstick by which you can measure your worth is the one created by your parents, you are likely to have a highly subjective, inherently exaggerated view of your own value.

Stuck in a state of perpetual adolescence without the means to become independent adults, a generation of young Japanese has effectively become futureless. Ensconced in their rooms, they have plenty of time and space to consider the possibility that they have become too demanding and sulky to attract a partner, lacking any of the experience of fair dealing and compromising needed to make a relationship work.

★

At least that wasn't where I was at, I reassured myself. I walked down Roppongi-dōri to the crossing at Nishi Azabu. I remembered there used to be a bar on the corner called the Red Shoes, but I couldn't see any sign of it. It had been a glamorous spot. I'd been there for drinks with a girlfriend, Sachiko, a handful of times. I hadn't known her for long and can't remember how we met – or why we had stopped meeting. The details of the various brief relationships I had in my early 20s, so vivid and intense at the time, seem to be the first to be forgotten.

I'd found Sachiko on Facebook a few years previously. She had married a Frenchman, had three kids and was working for an NGO in Kuala Lumpar. I'd scrolled through her photos, as you do. Family pictures, a nice house with a pool, probably in the kind of globalized enclave where you can buy almond croissants and flat whites. I'd felt the shame that comes with snooping on a one-time friend's private life – and then the boredom you feel on realizing how uninteresting most people's private lives are. It's a particularly twenty-first-century kind of disappointment.

2.

Overwork: The Life of a Salariman

My teaching job was at an English language school in Otemachi, a neighbourhood in the heart of Tokyo's financial district that epitomizes the kind of country that many Japanese would like to live in in the twenty-first century. Everything was new and pristine: the tarmac on the roads was fresh, the skyscrapers gleamed, and nothing was unplanned, uncontrolled or unauthorized. Not that I saw much of Otemachi from the school, for it was situated in the windowless basement of an office building in the labyrinth of underground walkways that radiate out from the station.

The last time I'd lived in Tokyo, when the country was still rich and 'internationalization' was all the rage, learning English had been fashionable. This time around, my students seemed markedly less excited about learning the world's lingua franca. Most of them were office workers, and were studying English only reluctantly, having been sent to the school by their HR departments in preparation for doing business with foreign clients.

They wanted to be able to read invoices and financial reports, and were rather apprehensive at the prospect of having to make small talk with foreign colleagues. When I was training to be an English teacher, I was told that Asian language-learners tend to prize accuracy over fluency – they might not say much, but what they do say is invariably correct. My experience has largely born this theory out: most of my students were accustomed to rote learning and had only studied English as a written language.

At first, they were a bit wary of the new-fangled approach to language learning whereby they were simply expected to *talk* to their teacher for an hour. Talking about themselves didn't come easily and many of them clammed up in my presence. I was never sure if this was down to shyness or a desire to keep me at arm's length, but I was a determined listener, and gradually they opened up about their jobs and families.

Most of my students were men, and they gave me plenty of insights into the gender-segregated culture of modern Japan. Most of them were in regular, full-time employment, with wives and children. They were reluctant to criticize their employers and seemed to know remarkably little about their wives' and daughters' lives. Perhaps I shouldn't have been surprised: in Japan, the influence of Confucius on social norms – what passes for common sense – cannot be underestimated, and among those norms is respect for (male) authority. Confucianism also puts great store by filial piety, but my students' relations with older people seemed more ritualistic than heartfelt. When I asked them about their grandparents, they talked about annual visits to small towns in distant regions, interspersed with the occasional phone call.

Above all, I was struck, as I had been when I taught English in Tokyo in my early twenties, by my students' stoical attitude to work. They rarely spoke about it with enthusiasm or pleasure and seemed completely resigned to lives of drudgery. The only consolation was the kinship they felt with their colleagues, cemented over drinks every Friday evening, when the *izakaya* (pubs that also serve food) of Otemachi heaved with men in white shirts turned garrulous for a night. Come Monday morning, I would often ask my students what they'd done at the weekend, and they would say that they'd spent the entire time asleep. Sleep was akin to a hobby: a private pleasure, described in the same terms that British people might use to talk about knitting or walking the dog.

Working life is still not good, even for the dwindling ranks of *salarimen* in regular, full-time employment. Companies still count on their loyalty and willingness to work hard, and most employees accept that their work will be unlimited in terms of hours, duties and location. This might seem unduly passive to Western sensibilities, but you have to consider the importance of the group in

Japanese culture. In the UK, many people regard bunking off work early to spend the afternoon in the pub as a canny way of cocking a snoop at one's employers. In Japan, it is seen as an act of supreme selfishness, because it requires one's workmates to work harder. Such is Japanese workers' reluctance to be a burden to their colleagues that, on average, they only take half of the days off they are entitled to. There have even been cases of employers compelling staff to take time off in order to comply with their legal obligations.

Work is a vicious circle. On the one hand, people feel dissatisfied with their working lives; on the other hand, they are constantly being exhorted to work harder. What for, they might wonder? Until the economy went into long-term stagnation, overwork was part and parcel of living in a consumer society. Many individuals worked overtime to save up the money they needed to pay mortgages and buy consumer durables. But in an era of permanent stagnation, dwindling savings and declining living standards, that promise rings hollow.

Members of the older generation like to believe that they are working hard for the sake of the nation. But the relationship between hard work and national prosperity is complicated. While many Japanese people work long hours, that doesn't always mean that more work is being done. Labour productivity is not especially high in Japan and simply exhorting everyone to work harder is not going to do much to raise it. But an exhausted workforce, raised in a culture of deference to authority, finds it hard to call for change. No wonder my students seemed just as tired out as their parents' generation had back in the 1990s.

Once or twice, I asked one of my students about *karōshi*, the Japanese word for 'death through overwork'. As with so many of the aspects of Japanese society I found interesting, it was something they discussed only reluctantly and with some embarrassment. In theory, a Japanese working day is 8 hours, a working week is 40 hours and overtime is not permitted. However, employment law is riddled with loopholes that make limits on working hours practically meaningless.[1]

According to the Ministry of Health, Labour and Welfare, in 1987, the year the ministry first recognised the term, there were twenty-one cases of *karōshi*. The death toll only increased in the 90s, by which time there were over 1,000 cases every year (and that doesn't include the many employees who took their own lives rather than admit they couldn't cope with their workloads).[2]

Much of the blame for Japan's demographic crisis has to lie with the culture of overwork. It can be no coincidence that the fertility rate first dropped below replacement level in 1973, the year that overwork became a scourge in Japan.[3] That was the year of the international oil crisis, a time of mass lay-offs and extended working hours. But there's a difference between the 1970s and today, which makes the low fertility rates of the twenty-first century harder to explain. Back then, the fact that men were chained to their desks and had no time to see their families was not seen as an obstacle to having kids. These days, women expect to spend more time with their husbands, and to share domestic duties – particularly if they are in employment themselves. Meanwhile, many men claim to be too busy to maintain a relationship.

Politicians were wringing their hands over the issue of *karōshi* in the early 1990s and they were still wringing them when I came back 24 years later. When Shinzo Abe became prime minister for the second time in 2012, he promised to remedy the two biggest problems with the Japanese way of work, the first being the yawning pay gap between regular and non-regular workers, and the second, the country's dangerously long working hours. Abe regarded them as obstacles to greater gender equality in the workplace, which he saw as the key to raising the birth rate.

His hope was that higher wages and better employment prospects would encourage people to have more children. If the fertility rate could be pushed up from 1.45 to 1.8, this would ensure that Japan's population wouldn't fall below the magic 100-million mark.* His

---

* In the pre-war years, Japanese politicians often exhorted women to have more children so as to raise the population to 100 million, and the number still seems to have talismanic significance. The figures cited here are from Shinji Kojima, Scott

concern was not so much the growth of irregular employment per se, but the pay gap between regular full-time workers and irregular part-timers. He proposed to give *freetas* a modest improvement in pay, in return for which employers would be given free rein to drive their workers to become more productive.

Unfortunately for Shinzo Abe, events got in the way of this gradualist approach. In 2017, the government was forced to award compensation to the family of Matsuri Takahashi, a 24-year-old employee of advertising giant Dentsu who had thrown herself from the roof of a company dormitory. Prior to her death, Ms Takahashi had suffered months of overwork, sleep deprivation, and harassment by her bosses. With headlines of another case of *karōshi* splashed across the front pages, Abe sought to mollify public anger by vowing to tackle excessive overtime.

Among the remedies he came up with was No Overtime Day: one day a week, typically a Wednesday, when employees were urged not to work overtime. Japan's corporate titans paid lip service to the PM's idea, but most of them did not put it into practice, perhaps because they felt insulted by the idea that their employees might have better things to do with their time than work. Reluctant to let their staff go home, some companies scheduled semi-compulsory drinks with colleagues on Wednesday evenings. Some workers resented No Overtime Day too, because any work not completed by the close of business on Wednesday still had to be done, either by taking work home or by doing even more overtime on another day.

In fairness to the Abe government, there was some improvement after he vowed to reduce Japan's brutally long working hours. In 2004, the proportion of employees working for more than 60 hours a week had stood at 23 per cent; by 2020, it had dropped to 11 per cent.[4] However, the problem is far from fixed. Japanese workers still average about two hours' overtime a day, and a fifth of them still put in more than 50 hours a week.[5]

North and Charles Weathers, 'Abe Shinzō's Campaign to Reform the Japanese Way of Work', *Asia Pacific Journal* Volume 15, Issue 23, Number 3, 20 November 2017.

This is unlikely to change any time soon, as business leaders are strongly opposed to enhanced regulation, and, notwithstanding the window dressing of employment law, they do not regard labour relations as a matter for politicians. In 2011, Toyota's managing director, Takehiko Ijichi, spoke for many of Japan's corporate titans when he said, 'Unless we can quickly get a system introduced in which young people can work without concern for time, Japanese manufacturing will be in big trouble. Restrictions on overtime and other labour regulations are fetters on growth.'[6]

Fortunately for the titans, bar the occasional scandal, the government is generally happy to take a 'hands-off' approach to negotiations between workers and management, and does little to enforce the law or punish wrongdoers. It is an irony of Kafkaesque proportions that, despite widespread and blatant violations of the law governing overtime work, the inspectors from the Ministry of Health, Labour and Welfare responsible for enforcing those laws are themselves seriously overworked. One MHLW inspector was in the habit of carrying a datebook, in which he recorded the time he clocked in and clocked out of the office. He wanted his wife to have evidence she could use in court if ever she had to sue the ministry for his death through overwork.

★

You can't put all the blame for the falling fertility rate on people being too busy to have children. After all, most married couples in Japan still have two children.[7] The problem is that in the post-growth era, the rise of the *freeta*, combined with the perennial problem of overwork, has created profound unpredictability in people's lives, making them less able to commit to marriage in the first place.

Japanese people are not alone in choosing to have fewer, or no children. The same story is playing out in rich countries the world over. Improved education for women, combined with greater access to contraception go a long way in explaining the decline in global fertility rates. 'The brain is the most important reproductive organ,' says Wolfgang Lutz, a demographer at Vienna's International Institute for Applied Systems Analysis. 'Once a woman is socialised to have an education and a career, she is socialised to have a smaller family. There's no going back.'[8]

Another key factor driving the decline is urban living. When young people leave the countryside for the city, the pressure from families and communities to settle down and make babies grows weaker. In its stead, the opinions of friends and co-workers, who are largely indifferent to one another's reproductive choices, become more important. Around the world, people are moving to cities at a rapid rate. Until 2007, most of the world's people lived in rural areas, but that year, for the first time in human history, the balance tipped in favour of city living. Three decades from now, we can expect two-thirds of the world's people to be living in urban areas.

Even in this context, Japan is a highly urbanized country. In 1950, just 53 per cent of the population lived in urban areas, but by 2015 this had increased to 90 per cent.[9] But does that explain why Japanese women are choosing to have fewer children? In trying to explain Japan's declining fertility rate, the most significant factor is the declining marriage rate. In 2022, Japan registered just 4.1 new marriages per 1,000 inhabitants, a huge drop from the 10 per 1,000 it registered in 1970.[10] In Japan, at least, no marriage means no children. Very few people have kids outside marriage, and even cohabiting between unmarried couples is dogged by bureaucratic disapproval.

To find out more about the treacherous relationship between work and marriage in Japan, I arranged to meet a young *salariman* called Yusuke Morimura. He was married with a young daughter and worked for a bank in Osaka. He was a hiking buddy of a friend of a friend of mine, and I figured that dashing between the gleaming skyscrapers of corporate Japan and the lonesome peaks of the Japanese Alps might give him an interesting perspective on the dramatic changes taking place in his country.

Yusuke was coming to Tokyo on business, so we agreed to meet in Ginza. In the early 1990s, Ginza had been the most expensive neighbourhood in the most expensive city in the most expensive country in the world. Those were the days when it was said that the grounds of the Imperial Palace were worth more than the entire state of California. However, returning to Ginza, it was clear that that was then and this was now. The streets were still lined with expensive designer shops, but most of those carrying shopping bags were Chinese tourists, some in fur coats and diamante heels, making the most of a weak yen.

As part of my 'back to the future' schtick, I had arranged to meet Yusuke in the Café Paulista, which opened in Ginza in 1911, making it Japan's oldest coffee shop. The Paulista has a close connection to Brazil, and not just on account of its name, which is a reference to the natives of São Paulo. It was founded by Ryo Mizuno, a Japanese émigré who played a leading role in helping Japanese to move to Brazil in the early decades of the twentieth century. Once there, many of these migrants started working as coffee farmers, and as an expression of its gratitude the Brazilian government supplied Mizuno with free coffee.

To sell it, he decided to set up a coffee shop in Ginza, and he went on to open a further twenty-three cafés all over Japan, making Café Paulista one of the first coffee-shop chains in the world. In the 'miraculous' years of high economic growth after World War Two, thousands of coffee shops proliferated across Japan, most of them modelled on the Café Paulista template. They reached their apogee in the late 1980s, just before the economy crashed, and these days are considered twentieth-century dinosaurs. Young coffee drinkers prefer the stripped-back, brightly lit aesthetic of big modern chains like Starbucks.

I recognized the archetype as soon as I walked into the place, and the mellow sound of bossa nova hit my ears. The staff, dressed in black and white, bowed to me unsmilingly, which made me feel like a visiting CEO. The interior seemed to date from the late 1980s, when Tokyo was the centre of the known universe and tasteful decor was all about muted tones of beige, brown and ochre. It was supposed to evoke the sophistication of Europe – leather seats, wooden panelling and pseudo-classical mouldings on the ceiling – but it could only have been Japanese. Everything, from the rubber plant to the chandelier to the milk, was fake, a celebration of artifice and a tribute to the ingenuity of the nation's scientists.

An old-school coffee shop is a place for quiet time with oneself, away from the pressures of the workplace. Some customers came with acquaintances, of course, but they took care not to let their conversation disturb the other patrons. Mid-morning, there was only a handful of other customers, and save for the hum of the air conditioner and the odd rustle of a newspaper, the place was silent. The headlines were not good that morning. When I had returned to Tokyo, Toyota was the last of Japan's multinational giants still in the world's top fifty companies, but its stock price had fallen so much that it had just dropped off the list.

Yusuke came in, all smiles and apologies for being late. He was dressed in standard *salariman* garb: dark blue suit, white shirt and black shoes, polished to a high shine. He was 34 and had been sent to his bank's Osaka branch by the head office in Tokyo, a practice of moving staff around that Japan's office workers have come to regard as normal. 'I'll come back to Tokyo for good at some point,' he said with a good-natured smile.

He was lucky, in that the bank had allowed his wife and daughter to accompany him to Osaka; many workers spend years living apart from their families. 'My wife and I have been married for five years. We have a daughter, so there's the three of us. I always wanted to have kids.'

When I put it to him that it was becoming rare to see little children in Tokyo, he inclined his head to one side, a gesture of non-commitment I recognized from times I had broached a tricky subject with one of my students. I tried a different tack. Thinking about his friends and colleagues, did he feel that being a parent was normal, or had it become a privilege reserved for the lucky few? He bridled at this idea. 'It's not rare for people my age to have kids. It's normal.'

On the train on the way to Ginza, I had given a woman a hand carrying a buggy up a flight of stairs. She had thanked me profusely, which made me think that giving a hand to a woman with a young child was unusual. Did he think Japan was a child-friendly country? 'That's a difficult question,' he said with knitted brows. 'Maybe Japan is not a country that helps its children to realize their dreams. But you can live here quite comfortably without doing anything much, so in that sense, it is a kind country.'

Yusuke's wife was a nurse. Because their daughter was only two, she worked part-time, but still found it hard to combine her job with being a mother. 'I think she will keep working part-time. Money isn't such a worry for us that she has to work full-time.'

I told Yusuke about a survey I had just read, in which Japanese women said they expected to have fewer children than they'd really like. When asked why, the most frequent answer they gave was that 'childbearing and education are too expensive'.[11] I put it to Yusuke that one reason for the dearth of children in Japan was the cost of raising them. There were childcare and nursery fees to think about, and then the cram schools that parents send their kids to after school, not to mention the cost of sending them to university for four years. Did all those bills give him cause for concern?

Yusuke was too polite to scowl, but I thought I detected a hint of scorn playing on his lip. 'I don't think the declining birth rate has much to do with money,' he said. 'I certainly don't worry about the cost of raising my daughter.' By now, I was kicking myself for thinking that an interview with a banker would give me any insight into the financial challenge of raising a family in post-growth Japan.

Of course, like all parents, Yusuke wanted his daughter to be happy and do well, but the probability of this is largely determined by the economic environment in which she grows up. In most rich-world countries, educational success is still regarded as the surest way to secure a well-paid job and financial security, but achieving it can be off-puttingly expensive. In Japan, the cost of bringing up a child until they graduate from university is about ¥20 million (£100,500) for a child that goes through the state education system and ¥30 million (£150,750) if they go to a private school and a private university. That is the price of a small flat in a provincial city.

In the past, when only boys went to university, the cost was easier to bear, but these days parents have high expectations for girls' education too. A survey conducted by public broadcaster NHK in 2018 asked parents what level of education they hoped their daughters would attain. Sixty-one per cent said, 'university level'. Although this figure has been rising steadily since the 1980s, Japan remains a laggard in this regard, being one of only three industrialized countries that still send more men than women to university (the other two are South Korea and Turkey).[12]

The popularization of higher education goes a long way in explaining why families in Japan are having fewer children. As the value society places on having an education has gone up, so has the amount of time and money young people spend getting one. Plenty of conservative commentators interpret the declining fertility rate as a sign of egocentricity or child-hating among potential parents, but the opposite may be true. I suggested to Yusuke that low fertility rates might be partly a result of an obsessive consideration for children. Given the high cost of bringing them up, and the care and vigilance required, you can see why most couples choose to have just one or two.[13]

Yusuke listened politely, but he clearly wasn't impressed. 'It's true that these days more people want to send their kids to university, but there are scholarships for them. And there are still plenty of people who aren't thinking about sending their kids to university. They aren't put off by the cost of having them.

'Single women might say a lack of money is putting them off getting married and having kids, but that's all front – *tatemae*,' he went on. 'In fact, having a child is cheaper than it used to be. Single women just want money from the politicians, so they complain.'

Didn't he have any sympathy for working women struggling to combine a career with raising a family? He admitted that plenty of companies don't make life easy for female employees who want to keep working after having kids. 'But they can leave their kids with their parents,' he said dismissively. 'I just don't think the cost is what is putting women off having children. It's about the time and effort it takes to raise them.'

I had come across this tendency to blame workshy women for the declining fertility rate before. It was a mainstay of the old-timers' critique of mollycoddled, shopaholic youth. It seemed to me deeply unsympathetic, but I was getting used to seeing the outline of an iron fist under the velvet glove. Yusuke made his case without a hint of rancour, but I found him pretty inflexible when it came to gender equality.

I asked him if he thought working culture in Japan was stopping people from having children. Now that Japan was rich, couldn't its people afford to work less and spend more time with their families? He mulled this idea gravely. 'In Japan, people used to respect those who worked hard. In big companies, you had to work hard to get promoted. Things have changed, but you still have to do what your boss tells you to do, and a lot of bosses are like Donald Trump – they don't let their employees leave work early.'

Yusuke might have been a bit old-fashioned, but he wasn't dogmatic about his beliefs, and I daresay he had worked hard to get where he was. I asked him what he thought a constructive response might be. 'I think the birth rate would probably rise if only men went out to work and women stayed at home.' Oh dear. I was hoping he would say something illuminating. Instead, he was just parroting a line that routinely gets trotted out in Japan's stodgier newspapers.

'But in other countries, companies make it easier for women to combine work and motherhood,' I said. I left the point dangling, hoping he would get it, but the best he could manage was a non-committal, 'I see.'

'The declining birth rate is not just down to the cost of education,' he went on. 'A much bigger factor is that people are delaying getting married. Sometimes they're 35 before they get married, and 40 before they even think about having kids.'

This was a good point. Many people plan to get married and have kids but keep deferring it. In 1955, the average age of first marriage was 26 for a Japanese man and 23 for a Japanese woman. By 2020, it had risen to 31 for a man and 29 for a woman.[14] Delayed parenthood is creating unplanned childlessness on a huge scale.

Probe the reasons for the delay in getting married and having kids and many young people will say that they aren't ready to take on the responsibility that comes with parenthood. There are so many other things they would rather do while they're still young. Youth is about freedom and fun, and, for many people, having kids is neither. As well as the search for pleasure, young people – fearful of the precarity of the *freeta* lifestyle – are also prioritizing education and their careers over starting a family. Spending more time in the education system means that by the time they have a stable career and the financial resources they need to start thinking about having kids, it is often too late. Even after finding a suitable partner, they may find that they are no longer able to have kids.

As Yusuke said, 'Once a woman starts having kids over the age of 30, the risk goes up. If she hasn't had a kid by the age of 30, there is a 50 per cent chance that she never will.'[15] He and his wife had been determined not to fall into that trap. 'My wife was only 25 when we got married. She has an older sister who can't have kids, and I think that when she heard that, it pushed her into having kids young.

'What a lot of people don't understand is that both the declining birth rate and the rising average age of marriage are related to the divorce rate,' he went on. 'In the old days, if a couple wanted to get divorced, all the neighbours knew about it. Their families didn't want to make a bad impression, so they would do all they could to stop them getting divorced. That doesn't happen any more.

'People are more individualistic these days, and they are not that bothered about what the people around them think any more. If someone has got to the stage where they hate their partner, they just split up with them.' This had the ring of truth about it too; Japan might still be a stiflingly conformist country, at least when seen through Western eyes, but social norms have lost a lot of the power they used to hold over people's behaviour.

'Men and women are both much fussier about their marriages, and they often can't see the point of staying together.' I took this 'fussiness' to be a reference to the veritable chasm between men's and women's expectations of one another. On the face of it, gender roles within marriage have been transformed by the millions of Japanese women who go out to work every day. In 2018, nearly 90 per cent of respondents to an NHK opinion poll agreed that 'fathers should commit to household work and take part in child-rearing'. When the survey was first conducted in 1973, only half of respondents had felt that way.[16]

However, while growing numbers of Japanese people expect men to shoulder more responsibility for domestic work, and more men at least pay lip service to the idea, most husbands still spend much less time doing childcare and household chores than their counterparts in other rich countries. From a traditional *machista* point of view, housework is women's work; if a woman loves her husband, she will do it herself, whether she has a full-time job or not.

Could it be that, in spurning marriage, Japanese women are staging a subconscious 'birth strike' against outdated sexist attitudes? Looking at the low fertility rate in her own country, this is certainly what Italian feminist Mariarosa Dalla Costa concluded. Dalla Costa and Selma James, co-authors of the classic *The Power of Women and the Subversion of the Community*, are credited with launching the 'domestic labour debate'. If housework were paid, they argued, the economy would collapse. Instead, it has been relegated to the status of a 'love token' and devalued by its supposed femininity.

One day, I had asked one of my students how much help she got from her partner around the house. 'Japanese men *are* supportive,' she had replied. 'They always say, "Oh, I'll support you when you have kids." But they mean financially. Even younger guys don't do any housework. It's hardly surprising – their fathers are their role models, and they didn't do any housework either.'

I asked Yusuke if he ever did any vacuuming or washing. 'No,' he admitted. 'We men might say we should help out more around the house, but we don't.'

'What about cooking?' I asked. It was one of the oddities of eating in Japan that every chef I had ever seen in a restaurant had been male, while every meal I had eaten in someone's home had been prepared by a woman. 'Do many Japanese men cook at home?'

'No, not many – more than in other Asian countries, but less than in Europe. We are very individualistic. We prefer to go out drinking.' He said this without a trace of bragging or triumphalism, as if it were just part of the division of labour – or at least it used to be, before women started going out to work and expecting their husbands to help out more around the house.

*

After my meeting with Yusuke, I left Café Paulista and walked up Shōwa-dōri towards Akihabara. I thought about what he had said. I liked him – he was friendly and had done all he could to find common ground. But I couldn't help wondering how many working women would be prepared to live with such an old-fashioned young man. In his defence, his attitudes were completely typical. Most of the Japanese men I'd met had grown up with the idea that being a good husband has nothing to do with helping out with the housework and childcare, and that the best a man can give his family is material abundance. Indeed, this has become the hallmark of a happy family, and a successful man.

The traditional understanding of masculinity was part of a reciprocal agreement between husband and wife, whereby he devoted himself to making a living and staying in his boss's good books, while she focussed on running the household and overseeing the children's education. A woman might spend a few years working in an office, but only in order to meet a well-paid man. Once they had found one another and got married, she was expected to sacrifice her career to her children.

On the face of it, this set-up favoured men, for while husbands got to enjoy the community of the workplace, wives became isolated in their nuclear households. However, the life of a housewife wasn't without its benefits. In return for surrendering her public life, a woman got to rule the household. In the years of high growth, more than 90 per cent of men turned over all of their income to their wives on payday.[17]

Back in 1987, Japan's best-known feminist, sociologist Chizuko Ueno, pointed out that one thing Japan never imported from the West was what she called its 'couple culture'. When a Western woman got divorced, she often lost her social life, which was invariably bound up with her partner's. Not so in Japan, where women have always had social lives of their own. Wives were not expected to appear with their husbands at social events or entertain their husbands' friends at home. Compared to their Western counterparts, Japanese couples tended to have more stable relationships, albeit at the cost of living in separate worlds. Sharing less, there was less room for tension, and the divorce rate was lower.

This understanding of family life, along with the *salariman*, the job for life and the 2LDK apartment, was part and parcel of the middle-class ideal that came to dominate the popular imagination in the post-war years.* The nuclear family was certainly a good way of keeping male workers fed and watered while producing children. But it also caused serious pathology. Men who, despite living under the same roof, spent most of their time glued to their desks at work tended to fall out of touch with their families. In their absence, families became mother-dominated, characterized by an intensely close relationship between mother and child. Raised by their mothers, it was only to be expected that many children of baby boomers reserved their affections for them.

Quite aside from the *mazakon* ('mother complex') this engendered in the male psyche, the refusal to see women as anything other than mothers-in-waiting has had a disastrous effect on women wanting a career. Japanese kids might have been better disciplined than Western children, but their obedience came at the cost of women sacrificing themselves to motherhood. Old people were better cared for too, though, again, the price was paid by women, who were expected to show filial piety to both their own and their husbands' parents.

While this vision of the happy nuclear family benefitted men, arguably the biggest winners were Japan's multinational companies. Chizuko Ueno explained the connection between the male-dominated

---

* In Japan, 2LDK is a common term used to describe the layout of a two-bedroom apartment with a combined living, dining and kitchen area.

workplace and the timidity of the workforce like this: 'Sexual segregation excludes women from the public sphere; women seek power in the domestic sphere as mothers; a dominant mother produces a dominated son; and a dependent son becomes a concerned man who shows loyalty to a group.'[18]

You can see the appeal, at least for men and the corporations they work for: in return for the men's unquestioning loyalty, the company offered them the same intense concern they had come to expect from their mothers. All they had to do was put in the hours and toe the line. No wonder, then, that in spite of the faltering of Japan's corporate juggernauts, the culture of loyalty to your employer has stubbornly persisted, at least among men lucky enough to have regular, full-time jobs.

★

Akihabara had changed a great deal in the 25 years I had been away. In the good old days, when the Japanese economy was still bubble-shaped, and Japanese electronics makers dominated the world, 'Electric Town' had been an outsized display case for their latest offerings. I remembered the main street as being lined with dozens of consumer-electronics retailers selling hi-fi stereos, Walkmans and VHS recorders, while the back alleys were a warren of tiny workshops, where men in manila-coloured work coats sold electrical parts.

Back then, the billboards looming from the rooftops had carried adverts for products made by Sony, Panasonic and Sharp, all of them 'Made in Japan' by a workforce dedicated to manufacturing. Now the shops lining Shōwa-dōri were selling toys, game consoles and computer software, or had been converted into maid cafés, and the billboards were advertising the latest anime series on Netflix.

When I'd left Japan in 1993, the very idea that a day would come when Japanese brands no longer dominated the global consumer-electronics market was unthinkable. How did the bottom fall out of consumer-electronics manufacturing in Japan? After all, at the advent of the internet age, Sony, Toshiba and Sharp had been well placed to capitalize on the booming demand for laptop computers and smartphones. Indeed, some Japanese manufacturers were producing mobile phones capable of surfing the internet a decade before Apple came up with the iPhone.

But they failed both to market their innovations abroad and to radically rethink their designs, and their mobile phones were gradually eclipsed by smartphones made elsewhere. As a result, the household names of the internet age are not Sony, Toshiba or Sharp, but American companies like Google, Amazon and Apple. Meanwhile, the market for consumer electronics and durables is dominated by South Korean companies like LG and Samsung, which churn out everything from flatscreen TVs to vacuum cleaners. These days, Samsung's annual profits are larger than those of the top fifteen Japanese electronics makers combined.

For a time, some Japanese commentators argued that this needn't matter. The name on the box might have been that of an American or Korean company, but many of the high-tech components inside their products were still made by Japanese companies. The world's consumer electronics were no longer 'Made in Japan', but they still had 'Japan Inside'. Unfortunately, that argument no longer holds water. Japanese manufacturers' share of DRAM semiconductor production worldwide dropped from 76 per cent in 1987 to just 3 per cent in 2004. Their share of production of the liquid-crystal displays used in phones and TVs made an even more dramatic nosedive, going from 100 per cent in 1995 to just 5 per cent in 2005.[19]

Japanese commentators have put this retreat down to the 'Galapagos Syndrome', arguing that the Japanese market has become isolated from the global marketplace, and is being supplied by manufacturers content to create products that only appeal domestically.* Japanese society had become closed-minded, they said, its

---

* When Charles Darwin went to the Galapagos Islands, he encountered flora and fauna that had evolved independently from mainland South America. The term Galapagos Syndrome was coined to describe the way that Japanese mobile phones developed into products quite unlike those available in the rest of the world.

people too rigid and uncreative to adapt to the demands of the twenty-first-century global market.

Walking the streets of Akihabara, that felt too gloomy an assessment. I couldn't help thinking that Japan has adjusted remarkably well to life in its post-industrial era. Though they are no longer the market leaders, Japan's big electronics makers are still in business. They might have shifted their manufacturing to countries with lower labour costs, but they still have an unrivalled reputation for quality and can still count on the loyalty of a huge domestic market.

Besides, manufacturing prowess is less important than it was a generation ago. Consumer electronics are not as valuable as they were in the 1990s, and many of their functions have been incorporated into laptops and smartphones. These days, the real money is being made in software, not hardware. Games makers like Sega and Nintendo are worth more than the company that makes the TV you play their games on. Japan's consumer-electronics manufacturers might not feature in the top ten any more, but the companies that produce its games, anime and manga are world beaters.

This switch from material production to intellectual creation, from the tangible to the intangible, is good for the 'Cool Japan' brand, which pays rich dividends through the tourism business. Before Covid grounded international flights, the tourist trade was a rare success story in the post-growth era, with the number of foreign visitors to Japan rising to 34 million a year in 2018. In 2023, 25 million visitors came, and the government is hoping to increase this to 60 million a year by 2030.[20] Many of them flock to Akihabara hoping to find not consumer electronics, but games, comics, and the youth culture that inspires them.

What is remarkable is not just the amount of money to be made from games and comics, but, as the billboards of Shōwa-dōri attested, the volte-face whereby Japan has gone from being the world's biggest exporter of consumer goods to an economy dependent on its cultural cachet. What often gets overlooked is that the appeal of the Cool Japan brand is grounded in the demographic changes that have taken place over the last quarter-century. Cool Japan's most valuable innovations are those that appeal to the imagination of the solitary, single consumer.

A good example is *Pokémon,* which has been called the global kids' craze of the 1990s, and is still going strong today. The game's designer, Satoshi Tajiri, was born in 1965 in a suburb of Tokyo not yet overrun by the automobile age. As a child, he was an avid bug collector, and spent his free time roaming the fields next to his house with his friends, collecting, cataloguing and exchanging insects. As they grew older, however, the fields were bulldozed to make way for suburban housing, and their parents and teachers conspired to deny them any free time to spend with one another. When a video arcade opened nearby, Tajiri transferred his love from bugs to *Space Invaders,* and after leaving school he set up his own games company.

He was concerned by the tendency towards atomization, not only in gaming – where increasingly complex games kept players in a state of solitary fixation – but in everyday life. He saw that children were being overly regimented at school and spending more time alone. He set about creating a game that would make them more sociable, while 'tickling their memories of the past', by recreating something of pre-industrial Japan in the 'post-post-industrial' landscape of virtual gaming. He hit on the idea of creating a virtual version of bug collecting for kids who no longer had access to fields or the free time to hang out with their friends. He secured financing from Nintendo and set about designing the software for a game he called *Pokémon,* or 'pocket monsters'.

The main character, also called Satoshi, is stuck at the age of 11. He has no father and sees his mother only occasionally, so he has to rely on himself and his steadfast *pokémon* companion Pikachu. The pocket monsters are as peculiar as they are cute, with a variety of weird powers just waiting to be discovered and collected. The first game alone had 151 monsters, and each subsequent game has added more, so the process of acquiring monsters is endless.

To my mind, what is most notable about *Pokémon* is that, far from being your typical all-conquering macho hero, Satoshi is just a lonely little boy. His creator considers the most important aspect of *Pokémon* to be its 'gorgeous implications for communication'. Tajiri devised a cable that allowed two Game Boys to hook up. Instead of competitive matches between two players, the new technology let them share intelligence they'd gained through playing. Given the huge amount of information needed to progress through the game, they had to trade with one another, and this opened a channel for friendship.

Nintendo launched *Pokémon* for the Game Boy in 1996, and it quickly became a huge hit with Japanese kids. The virtual social life it offered them was a source of fun and comfort all too often denied them by their parents and teachers. By 1998, the game was selling around the world, inspiring a craze that the American press called 'Pokemania'. *Pokémon* expanded to incorporate cartoons, films and merchandising, and by 2003 it had become a multinational media empire, racking up $15 billion in global sales.

Arriving at the tail end of Japan's first Lost Decade, *Pokémon* was the best thing to hit the Japanese business world since the economy nosedived in the early 1990s. Its prominence in a market long dominated by American cartoon characters was a particular cause for celebration. Describing the pride he felt on seeing *Pokémon* soft toys selling in the US, one Japanese reporter was even moved to compare it to the pride Japanese people had felt when Sony, Sharp, Panasonic and Toshiba first became global brand names in the 1970s.[21]

*

From Akihabara, I carried on walking up Shōwa-dōri to Ueno, where I was due to attend my first 'Meetup', a conversation club where Japanese people could practise their English, and foreigners their Japanese. It was held in a branch of Hub, a chain of British-style pubs that had done away with the peculiarities of British-style bar service. Rather than massing at the bar and hoping to catch the bartender's eye, you had to form a line to order a drink. They even brought your Guinness to your table, so you didn't have to stand at the bar while you waited for it to settle.

I had some time to kill before the Meetup began, so I read my book. The *Penguin Parallel Text of Short Stories in Japanese* was an effective way to learn the language, if a bit difficult. An Indian man at the next table asked me if he could take a picture of the front cover, as he thought his daughter might like it. 'Her reading and writing of Japanese are very good,' he said proudly.

Sarjit was a diamond merchant. 'Business is bad,' he told me gloomily. 'Japan is only heading in one direction. The government is spending lots of money to make the place look nice for the Olympics, but once they are over, there will be nothing to do but draw the curtains and prepare for a bumpy downhill ride.'

Sarjit's eyes were fringed with long lashes, and they bulged when he opened them wide. He had a soft, fleshy double chin that swung when he tipped his head back to toss a peanut into his mouth. 'I am proud of India,' he went on. 'We are working hard and getting rich – unlike the Japanese. Of course, they still go through the motions of working hard. But if you don't have a family to support, what motivation do you have?'

Sarjit had been in Japan for 20 years, and he had had enough of the place. 'China is the place to make money from diamonds these days. But once you have kids, it's hard to just up sticks and move somewhere else,' he lamented. He asked me if I was married or had kids, and it occurred to me that for the first time since arriving back in Japan, I was being made to feel inadequate for being single and childless. It would appear that in India, as in the UK, there is an assumption that we all couple up and settle down in time. But as well as being a wonderfully well-mannered place, Japan is one in which being single and childless is nothing out of the ordinary.

Sarjit finished his nuts and began chewing tobacco flavoured with saffron. It must have been what made him smell so nice. In my experience, Japanese people tended not to smell of anything, as perfume is generally considered a bit *hade* ('flashy'). He was also wearing lots of rings on his fingers, unlike Japanese men, who don't much go in for adornment.

'Do you have many Japanese friends?' I asked him. 'Oh yes,' he said, scowling at the very thought of them. Fellow jewellers, I supposed, who had learned to keep their rambunctious foreign colleague at arm's length. Where he did share common ground with many Japanese people was in his dislike of China. 'Very crude, uneducated people,' he said with a vigorous shake of the head that sent a ripple cascading through his double chin. It was nice to watch: smooth and plump, like a ripe peach.

Sarjit also had unkind things to say about Kim Jong Un, the leader of North Korea (whom he called Park), the sexual inadequacy of Japanese men and a host of other topics I either had no interest in or didn't feel qualified to talk about. Living in a country as polite and modest as Japan, it was easy to forget about all the opinionated, ill-informed people in the world. With these words sweating on the tip of my tongue, I made my excuses and headed for the toilet.

When I got back, there was no sign of Sarjit, and the language exchange had begun. I soon found myself talking to a Japanese guy who asked to be called Jay. His English was good; he'd learned it at college in California, he said. He worked for a company that helped Japanese students get into colleges in the United States. I was still thinking about the changes I'd seen in Akihabara, so I asked him why he thought Japan had lost the preeminent position it once held as a maker of computers and mobile phones.

'Foreign companies like Samsung and Apple are successful in the US because Americans like things simple,' said Jay. 'Japanese manufacturers produce primarily for the domestic market, and Japanese consumers like more complicated appliances.' It was a neat explanation, flattering the supposed complexity of the Japanese mind, while suggesting that even when Japan's electronics makers dominated the marketplace, they were destined to lose market share at some point, because Japanese people struggled to think in the simplistic terms used by the rest of the world.

By way of revenge, when it came time for us to switch from

English into Japanese, I asked Jay to teach me some of the cheery vocabulary of population decline. What was the Japanese word for 'ageing society', I asked him. *'Kōreishakai,'* he said impassively. 'Communities on the brink of extinction'? *'Genkan shūraku.'* How about 'lonely death'? *'Kodokushi,'* he muttered.

We were rescued from Japan's gloomy prospects by the young woman sitting opposite us. Yumiko was talking to a young computer engineer who wanted some tips on finding a girlfriend. When I asked her if she was married herself, she nodded and looked at the gold ring on her finger. 'How long have you been married?' I asked her. 'Three years. It's a long time,' she said wistfully. I was reminded of what Yusuke had said about the rise of the 'fussy couple' and their willingness to throw in the towel when things get difficult.

I asked Yumiko if young people felt any pressure to have kids, knowing that their country's population was in decline. 'No,' she said, 'but young people aren't very interested in politics.' 'But isn't a declining population a problem for Japan?' I asked. 'Maybe,' she said, 'but there are so many fun things to do in Tokyo. Who wants to have kids?'

I might have asked Yumiko more about the population crash looming over Japan, but I don't think she was very interested. The Meetup was a place to meet new people, foreign and Japanese, not dwell on the country's social problems. But I sensed there was something else at play too: young people like Yumiko are picking up mixed messages from the sated, post-growth times they are living in. On the one hand, they feel that they have arrived in the future; on the other, they are being told that the game is up, and their country is doomed. Whichever is true, they are responding by turning inwards and focussing on themselves. It's a rebellion of sorts, but a quiet, non-confrontational one, more akin to a mass shirking of the duties and responsibilities that the post-war generation so readily accepted.

3.

The Working Women of Otemachi

One of the regulars at the English-language school where I taught was Haruko, a woman in her late 30s who had taken over as head of her family firm, a small manufacturer of traditional Japanese-style shoes and handbags. She was more open to chatting than most of my other students, and we had a number of fascinating conversations. Quite aside from the difficulty she had had earning the respect of her workforce, most of whom were middle-aged men, she told me she had also struggled to convince them to embrace modern tastes. Their customers were ageing and dying, she told them. If the firm was to survive, they would have to ditch the old styles and start exporting – hence her taking a crash course in conversational English.

When Haruko heard about my interest in Japan's demographic quandaries, she told me about a woman working at a private child-care centre in Aichi prefecture who had been reprimanded for getting pregnant 'before it was her turn'. Her employer had set up 'shifts' for when the female staff were permitted to conceive and chided her for 'selfishly breaking the rules', on the grounds that her colleagues would have to take on her workload while she was on maternity leave.

I discovered that bullying women into delaying childbirth happens in plenty of other workplaces too. In 2017, a 26-year-old employee of a cosmetics company in Tokyo was told that she would only be allowed to have a child when she was 35. Her supervisor had mapped out childbirth schedules in an email to the company's twenty-two female employees. 'Work gets backed up if four or more people take time off at the same time,' she warned them. 'Selfish behaviour will be subject to punishment.' The employee in question, who was in her second year of marriage and had fertility issues, told the *Mainichi Shinbun*, 'I am already having trouble getting pregnant. Are they going to take responsibility if I put off getting pregnant and lose the chance to have children?'[1]

It was Haruko who introduced me to Akiko, a friend of hers who worked for an American real estate company in Otemachi. One evening after work, I met up with Akiko in a crowded beer hall near Otemachi station. We spoke English, which was a rare opportunity for her; although her husband was British, they only spoke Japanese together. They had two daughters of 11 and 9 and she had lots to say about the challenge of combining a career with motherhood, and the outdated attitudes of Japan's menfolk.

'Even now, my dad doesn't care about my career. When my husband became a professor at his university, my dad gave him an expensive bottle of sake. My husband felt a bit uncomfortable, and reminded him, "Your daughter is doing really well too." But he didn't listen. He's just happy that his daughter is the wife of a professor,' she said with a laugh. Doesn't it make you feel angry? I asked her. 'It's beyond anger. I have got used to being treated like that by my dad.'

'Before I met my husband, my dad used to worry about me still being single in my late 20s. One day, he brought me a photo from a professional matchmaker – a *nakōdo*. It was of a guy who was in the Self-Defence Forces. I was surprised, but that was his way of showing his kindness. He thought that being a soldier was a really stable job. It was an "If you marry him, you won't have to work" kind of thing.'

Akiko's mother and father had had an arranged marriage. 'My mum was 29 at the time. She worked for Tokyo Bank, which in those days was the only bank in Japan that handled foreign currencies. The working environment was really international, but even there, she came under pressure to get married from her colleagues.' In those days, there was a phrase that a woman was like a Christmas cake – no use after the 25th.

Couldn't her mother have taken some time off to have a child, and then gone back to work, I asked her. 'She certainly wanted to keep working', she told me, 'but at the time the bank didn't want a woman over 30 working there. 'Historically, it's pretty recent for women to do the same jobs as men, so she didn't have any role models. Women didn't have equal opportunities back then. The Equal Employment Opportunity Law was only passed in 1985.'

Westerners have been expressing shock at how male-dominated Japan is for a long time. Women make up just 1 per cent of senior managers, about 4 per cent of boardroom directors and 10 per cent of politicians in the lower house.[2] 'Even today, it's hard to find a woman executive at a Japanese company and because the management are all men, all the rules are decided by men. They put a lot of pressure on their staff not to take time off, but even if a mother wants to work, she comes under the opposite pressure. They're too generous to married women. They always say, "Don't work too hard."'

Before she got pregnant, Akiko had had a good job working for an American private equity fund. 'My colleagues were really supportive,' she said, 'even the Japanese men. Maternity leave depends on the company, but you get six weeks after the child is born, and a year of childcare leave after that.' Japan's national insurance scheme paid her two-thirds of her salary for the first six weeks, and after that she received payments equivalent to 70 per cent of her salary from the labour insurance.

The problem, Akiko said, was not the management, but her colleagues. 'Taking maternity leave means more work for other members of staff, so everyone gets really stressed out. There's nothing they can do about it, but when the person they get in to cover her is a single woman, or a woman who doesn't have kids, I think they feel frustrated that they have to support someone else's kids.'

By law, both parents are entitled to a year of parental leave. Yet, notwithstanding the assurance that taking paternity leave needn't limit their career options, few new fathers take paternity leave.[3] Even men who do take it find that, on returning to work, the long hours they are expected to put in make it impossible for them to raise their children jointly with their partners.

The bottom line is that someone has to prioritize the children and sacrifice their career, and invariably it is the woman. In Japan, almost two-thirds of women drop out of the workforce after the birth of their first child.[4] This isn't because they want to: three-quarters of university-educated women say they would like to go back to work after giving birth. However, only 43 per cent are able to do so. This compares unfavourably with the situation in the United States, where 73 per cent of new mothers are able to land a job.[5]

Leaving new mothers with no choice but to drop out of the work-force is patently unfair, and it is becoming increasingly unpopular. According to a poll conducted by NHK in 2018, a clear majority believes that a woman should go back to work after having a child, with just 8 per cent of respondents saying that she should stay at home and focus on raising her children.

Forced to choose between having a career and starting a family, it is hardly surprising that plenty of women, despite having had a taste of the financial independence that comes with a higher education and a successful career, decide that they would rather marry a man wealthy enough to allow them to leave the workplace and become a stay-at-home housewife. In a study of Japanese women's changing views on work and marriage, sociologist Kumiko Nemoto inter-viewed a successful woman called Yukari, who said that she would only ever marry a man with a higher salary than her own, and even welcomed the idea of 'doing 70 per cent of the housework' if she met such a man.

Nemoto also spoke to a single woman called Lisa, a 38-year-old assistant editor who admitted that she felt both shame and resent-ment about not being married. 'I think the biggest winner in this society is the housewife who marries a man with the "three highs" [high income, physical height and higher education]. They have lunch in Ginza and only have to worry about private school for their kids.'[6]

What's it like for mothers once they return to the workplace, I wondered. Are Japanese companies supportive of women who have to leave work early to pick their kids up from nursery? Do nurseries appreciate that sometimes parents have to work late? 'It depends how much you earn,' said Akiko with a shrug. 'Everything can be solved by money, so if you're a rich couple, you can use your resources.'

Akiko was lucky in this regard, as she had only ever worked for American companies. 'I changed job six years ago, and now I am working for a real estate company. At the job interview, it didn't matter that I had kids. Even the executives, who are American, took six months paternity leave. The Japanese guys really freaked out!' She chuckled.

What about government policy? The government had just announced another raft of policies to tackle the declining fertility rate. Did she think they would make any difference? 'The government has to make the companies change. The politicians pass new laws, but they do nothing to make sure that companies obey them,' she said with a snort of derision. 'And because there are no penalties, the companies just ignore them.'

Akiko's scepticism is borne out by bitter experience. It was a thrilling moment when the Japanese prime minister vowed to raise the number of female managers at private companies to 30 per cent within the next seven years. But that PM was Junichiro Koizumi, and he made that commitment in 2003. Ten years later, Shinzo Abe made the same promise, also with a seven-year deadline, and in 2023, yet another prime minister, this time Fumio Kishida, vowed to do the same. With such a lousy track record, sceptics could be forgiven for concluding that the LDP – which has governed the country for most of the post-war period – has no real interest in achieving gender equality in the workplace.[7]

★

Until not so long ago, practically all Japanese mothers were full-time housewives. Like Akiko's mother, they received little encouragement to continue working after childbirth, for there were no employment opportunities for married women once they were in their 30s and 40s, and the term 'part-time worker' didn't even appear in official labour statistics.[8]

Women with children only started to join the workforce in the recession that Japan was thrown into by the oil crisis of 1973. Thereafter, most new mothers stayed at home until their child turned three, and then got a part-time job. They did so not because they wanted to pursue a career or become financially independent of their husbands, but in order to earn the extra money they needed to pay for their kids' *juku* (cram school). It is one of the ironies of Japanese women's 'liberation' from housewife-dom that they only left the family home in order to better fulfil their roles as mothers.

Whatever their motives, their husbands did not like to see them go out to work, since men being the sole breadwinners was what the division of labour was all about. Still, this worked to women's advantage, because while his income went into the household kitty, once the fees for the *juku* had been paid, the money she earned was hers to spend as she saw fit. This set-up worked perfectly well until the stock-market crash of the early 1990s. Thereafter, the economy *really* tanked, along with living standards, and suddenly children became unaffordable unless both parents went out to work.[9]

In the last decade alone, more than 3 million Japanese women have joined the workforce. They are overwhelmingly concentrated in lowly professions: retail, office jobs, care-giving, nursing and hospitality. Half of all working women are in irregular or part-time work, and because many of them are mothers, the proportion only rises with age.

The creation of this largely female precariat is a result of efforts by Japanese firms to create a more flexible workforce, and dovetails with the government's efforts to raise productivity and thereby revive Japan's sclerotic economic growth rate. In the rush to expand the workforce, the government seems to have overlooked the intimate relationship between how working women are treated – both in the workplace and at home – and Japan's declining fertility rate. A day spent doing precarious, unrewarding work for an unsympathetic boss, followed by an evening tending to a demanding partner and kids is hardly an appealing prospect. Perhaps that explains why fewer Japanese women than ever are getting married, let alone having children.

When Japan's first census was conducted in the 1920s, only one in twenty people was still unmarried by the age of 50. Marriage was the norm, and it remained so for the next 70 years. In the 1990s, however, this started to change and, by 2015, 23 per cent of men and 14 per cent of women remained single at the same age. Forecasters at the NIPSSR expect this to rise to 33 per cent of men and 20 per cent of women by 2040. Factor in those who get married but become separated from their spouse by divorce or death, and we can expect that, by then, half of the adult population will be single by the time they reach 50.

The rise of singledom is most marked among the young. In 1975, half of men aged 20 to 34 were unmarried; by the millennium, this had risen to 68 per cent. The rise was more dramatic still among women, going from 32 per cent in 1975 to 56 per cent in 2000. This is partly down to the tendency to delay marriage until later in life – but that only tells part of the story. The proportion of unmarried people began to rise after the Equal Employment Opportunity Law came into effect in 1985. This boosted the number of female graduates in the corporate sector, where salaries were higher. Inspired by their example, a growing number of young women migrated from the countryside to the cities in search of higher education and better paid work. Many of them struggled to find husbands who met their expectations. Meanwhile, their older brothers, many of whom had stayed in their hometowns to inherit the family business or farm, were struggling to find wives. Increasingly, both siblings went into middle age single.

The decline in the marriage rate may also be down to fewer people than ever feeling they *should* get married. According to an NHK poll conducted in 2018, a record 68 per cent of respondents agreed that 'a person does not necessarily have to get married'.[10] As the social pressure to get married has eased, it has become a more active choice. Unfortunately, marriage is not exactly a popular choice in Japan. In the United States, 67 per cent of women believe that married people are happier than unmarried ones; in Japan, only 50 per cent think so, and young women are even less keen on the idea.[11] According to a survey conducted by the NIPSSR, 90 per cent of young women believe that 'staying single is preferable to what they imagine marriage to be like'.[12]

This is despite the fact that studies have shown marriage generally has positive effects for both men and women. Kazuhisa Arakawa, author of *Chō soro shakai* ('super solo society') is a leading researcher of the shift towards singledom and solo living. According to a survey he conducted, about 80 per cent of married people in their 40s say that they are happy, which is a much higher rate than among unmarried people of the same age.[13] Married people also live longer, healthier lives than single people (although this only holds true for people in happy partnerships; bad marriages often mean frequent conflicts, which are not good for your mental or physical health).

In spite of their misgivings about marriage, the Sixteenth Japanese National Fertility Survey, published in 2022, indicated that over 80 per cent of young men and women would like to get married at some point in their lives.[14] When asked why, both sexes mentioned a desire for children, emotional fulfilment and social validation.[15]

Interestingly, however, while a clear majority of women want to get married because they want (or feel they should have) children, most of them don't associate marriage or childbearing with romance and are rarely seduced into marrying a less-than-bankable partner. 'Better financial prospects' is women's number one reason for marrying and when you look at women's financial prospects, you can understand why. In 2005, only 43 per cent of unmarried women in the workforce were in full-time work, with the rest working as part-time, temporary or contract workers.[16]

Having children outside marriage is still rare in Japan. One of the main reasons for the fall in the number of marriages in Japan is women's inability to find a suitable partner. Unofficially, a man has to be earning upwards of ¥5 million (£25,125) a year to be considered a good catch. Unfortunately, the average annual income for a man is ¥3.96 million (£19,899), and the marriage rate decreases noticeably among men earning less than that.[17]

Another factor in explaining the declining marriage rate is that, while getting a good education and a well-paid job enhances a man's marriage prospects, it has the opposite effect on a woman's. The university enrolment rate for women has risen rapidly in recent years and hit 52 per cent in 2021 (it is 58 per cent for men). If male and female graduates paired up, all would be well, but male graduates tend not to be as picky about their partner's income as their female counterparts. Most men are happy to marry a woman whose income is lower than their own, and many feel threatened by a woman who earns as much or more than he does. This leaves female graduates with a significant shortage of men to choose from.[18]

The consolation prize is that the better salaries that come with higher education give women a measure of financial independence, and this allows them to defer marriage until the right man comes along. The problem is that the standards by which young women judge a potential husband have risen in line with improvements in their own earning potential. Mr Right doesn't always arrive on time, and sometimes he doesn't show up at all.

★

The irony is that, until the 1980s, Japan had one of the highest marriage rates in the world: 97 per cent of men and 98 per cent of women got married at least once in their lifetime.[19] Most of these marriages were arranged after an *omiai* (a formal marriage interview). Arranged marriages gave people little in the way of choice, but plenty in the way of security. As long as you had a steady job and your parents had access to a matchmaker, there was usually someone out there for you.

The number of so-called love marriages only surpassed the number of arranged marriages in the late 1960s, but even then, most of them weren't exactly freely chosen. They were *shokuba kekkon* ('workplace marriages') which invariably began when the head of department took his team out for a drink after work and, with varying degrees of subtlety, played the role of matchmaker. This was all part of the fatherly interest that companies took in their employees' wellbeing. A young man got a job for life, on a gradually rising escalator that took him through the pay scale, plus someone to hold his hand when a young woman in the typing pool took his fancy. She, meanwhile, was expected to focus on playing the role of good wife and mother.

Only after 1990 did freely chosen marriages become the norm.[20] This was partly because, with the decline of lifetime employment, fewer young people had a steady workplace to go to (or at least one where they could expect to spend the rest of their lives). It was also down to the empowerment of women that followed passage of the Equal Employment Opportunity Law in 1985. Young women became more assertive and started thinking about marriage in a more egalitarian way. As we've seen, a potential partner's income is still important, but the traditional reasons for getting married – 'economic security' and 'attaining social recognition as a mature person' – were no longer enough. Young women expected support, respect and intimacy from their partner. Traditional arranged marriages were often between older men and younger women, but as women's expectations of their partners changed, the number of same-age couples began to rise.[21]

This might all sound positive, but plenty of young men were completely flummoxed by these changes. They were already worried that, in financial terms at least, they had a lot less to offer a woman than their fathers had when they were young. Now they were being told that their fathers' manly banter was a form of *sekuhara* – sexual harassment – and that they should provide their partners with 'mental security' and 'mutual support'.

Although arranged marriages are no longer the norm, there is still plenty of work for the modern matchmaker, guiding communication between clients and prospective partners, with the goal of pushing them towards marriage. Together with her husband, Kiyomi Nakanishi runs an umbrella organization for matchmakers called the Japan Matchmakers' Cooperative (Nihon Nakōdo Kyōkai). As a matchmaker herself, she often plays chaperone to her clients on their first dates, and says she has been party to some painfully awkward encounters. Many of her male clients lack consideration for their would-be partners, while others are just too shy to say much. In some cases, conversational difficulties arise from the man's self-absorption, or his preoccupation with work matters. Women typically want their partners to be ambitious and assertive, she tells her clients, but they also want them to make an effort to be attractive, personable and interesting, and to show them some respect.[22]

Even assuming a young man and woman hit it off, the next obstacle they face is the thorny issue of family. In Japan, most marriages still depend on the mutual consent of their respective families (this hasn't changed since my friends Atsushi and Yoshiko's day). A woman who marries the eldest son of the family is expected to look after his parents, as well as her own, when they are old. Many women are no longer prepared to do this. They want to pursue a career and build a life with a supportive partner, not play nursemaid to his ageing parents.

Another factor deterring women from getting married is the persistent taboo surrounding cohabitation. Families tend to disapprove of trial runs. However, while traditionalists might frown upon living together before marriage, it is a crucial testbed for a relationship, especially when gender roles are being questioned as never before. Financially independent women need to see how old-fashioned her partner is going to be around the house. If it is not going to work out, she needs to be able to end the relationship without involving their respective families.

However, despite the dramatic increase in the number of university-educated women and the number of women in the workforce, the older generation is reluctant to change its attitude, and their intransigence is having an impact on modern childbearing. It is easy to characterize this as a problem of domineering older men on one side, and a new generation of independent women on the other, but in fact the oppressors tend to be older women, who have fixed ideas about a woman's place in the home. Their determination to cling on to the post-war ideal of family life is inadvertently contributing to the low birth rate.

One obvious way to raise Japan's fertility rate would be to make it easier for people to have children without getting married.[23] Children born to unmarried parents make up more than half of live births in the UK, France, Sweden, the Netherlands and Portugal. In the United States, about 40 per cent of children are born to unmarried mothers. American women rarely see getting pregnant as a good reason to get married, and less than 10 per cent of unmarried mothers agree to a 'shotgun' wedding. They see having a child, whether inside or outside wedlock, as a sign of maturity and far preferable to rushing into marriage or having an abortion.[24]

This is quite a contrast to the situation in Japan, where only 2 per cent of children are born to unmarried parents.[25] Most unmarried Japanese women regard having a child outside wedlock as the worst possible response to a pregnancy. They would rather get married, even to a less-than-ideal man. Perhaps Japanese women have a more clear-eyed view of married life than American women. They tend to regard marriage as primarily a practical arrangement for rearing children and tend not to be as concerned by all the things that can potentially go wrong in a marriage as their American counterparts.[26]

*

Looking around the crowded beer hall with Akiko, I couldn't help noticing how gender-segregated the place was. Most of the tables were occupied by groups of office workers in white shirts, but hardly any of them were mixed. Men and women have long lived separate lives in Japan, and gender equality in the workplace, such as it is, doesn't seem to have made much difference. What was novel was the number of women drinking with other women, and the fun they looked to be having. Something told me that they didn't have kids at home, and if they did, it was their own mothers, not their husbands, who were looking after them for the evening.

How can women combine a career with motherhood? Akiko and

58

I talked through the options available. There are three models. The first is to leave it to the free market, which is what prevails in the US, where many working mothers hire nannies to look after their young children. This model is posited on gender equality, meritocracy and the cheap domestic labour of mainly immigrant women.

The second is the social democratic model that prevails in Scandinavia, where working mothers can drop their kids off at subsidized nurseries. In Sweden, the gender pay gap is much smaller because men take paternity leave to look after their young children when their partners go back to work. Sweden seems to have cracked the nut: it has the highest female labour participation rate in the EU and, at the same time, a relatively high fertility rate (1.84).[27]

The third is the traditional breadwinner model, which holds that men should go out to work, while women stay at home to look after the children. This is the model that prevails in Japan, at least in the minds of the old men who run the country. In reality, these days, women go out to work too, which means that when they do have children, they either have to quit their jobs or find someone else (a relative or a nursery) to look after them.

This is far from easy, as the cost of childcare is often prohibitively expensive. Some working mothers, like nurses, can get 24-hour access to nurseries for their children, but most cannot. Even today, there is some social stigma to leaving your child in a kindergarten. The old belief that a good mother should have her child with her all day is still strong. 'In Japan, there is a popular traditional myth that the mother should be with her kid until it turns three, otherwise it will have mental problems,' Akiko told me. 'My dad certainly thinks so. After I had my first daughter, he said, "Your husband is working, so you don't have to go back to work."'

The Japanese government would certainly like to see more two-kid, dual-income households, because it sees them as key to addressing chronic labour shortages and the low birth rate. But it wants to have its cake and eat it. If it is serious about getting more women into the workforce, it should provide the kind of childcare services that allow them to combine motherhood with a career.

Unfortunately, it seems this is just too radical a step for the stodgy old men who fill the ranks of the LDP and the boardrooms of Japan's biggest companies.

As Akiko described her situation to me, I was amazed by just how unsustainable the whole system seemed to be.

> You have to work really hard to have a nice life in Tokyo, and you have to earn double once you have kids. Giving them a good education is really expensive. After school, most kids go to *gakudo* ['study room'] until their mum or dad picks them up, and then to *juku*. It's really competitive, and if you drop out, you end up poor. If your parents are poor, you don't stand a chance, even if you are clever.

In theory, employment is good for Japanese women because it allows them to become financially independent of men. In practice, they get the worst of both worlds: not just a thick glass ceiling that keeps them out of positions of authority, but also the opprobrium of traditionalist men, who resent their growing independence and accuse them of shirking their responsibility to run households and rear children. This makes Japan an unattractive place for a woman to build a career, and a terrible place for a working woman to have children.

The novelist Sayaka Murata has spoken about life on the fault line of these dramatic changes in gender roles. In 2016, she won the Akutagawa Prize, Japan's most prestigious literary award, for her novel *Konbini Ningen* (*Convenience Store Woman*), which went on to sell 1.5 million copies in Japan alone. It is the story of 36-year-old Keiko, a *freeta* who models her behaviour, dress sense and even her speech patterns on those of her co-workers. She has few friends apart from her sister, who can't understand why she is still single and working in a convenience store. It is a scathing critique of conformity and what it does to the human psyche.

'I was shocked when I was in university and people told me I had to search for a rich marriage partner and think about having children,' Murata told the *Guardian* in 2020. 'If that's all that university was for, what was the point of getting qualifications? . . . I thought when I was this age, women and men would be equal, but that's not how it has worked out.'[28]

The resentment that many Japanese women feel at having to sacrifice their careers to raise children runs through another of Murata's novels, the dystopian *Satsujin Shussan* (*The Birth Murder*), which came out in 2014. The premise of the story is that bureaucrats have solved the problem of Japan's declining birth rate by giving men artificial uteruses and allowing both sexes to kill one person if they successfully reproduce ten. It is a pithy play on the murderous urges welling up under the harmonious veneer of Japanese society.

*

Between us, Akiko and I had by now ploughed through several litres of lager and wolfed down ten skewers of salty pork, chicken's gizzards, green peppers and onion. Before we went our separate ways, I asked her how Japanese people feel about the ageing and shrinking process afflicting their country. This elicited a deep sigh, as it did whenever I raised the subject with my students. 'It depends which generation you belong to,' she said. 'People in their 50s and 60s remember the late 1980s, when Japan was *nanbāwan*. They are more worried than the younger generations, who never experienced being on top. The younger generations are more relaxed about the birth rate falling.'

How did she explain that?

They're comfortable. The number of kids is going down, so their parents can look after them until they are in their 30s. They are not very old, and not very mature, and they don't think about the future. These days, parents don't put pressure on their kids like my dad put pressure on me. My mum and dad both had six brothers and sisters, so their parents didn't care about them so much.

On the page, Akiko's words might read as if she resented young people for their apathy, but I don't think she did. She sounded more disappointed, and possibly worried, than anything else. Or maybe she was just wistful, looking back on how ambitious her generation had been.

> Everyone is quite relaxed. The changes are happening gradually, and the majority of people don't even realize what is happening. I think the government should say it loud: 'We are in a dangerous situation, and we have to change something. So we are going to give you a level of support that you don't have to worry about having kids.'

I asked her if she and her female friends felt any anger towards the old men running the country. 'Not really. We have just given up. The majority of LDP supporters are older men, and as long as the LDP depends on them for its power, it's really hard to change things.'

★

Is the rising number of single, childless people down to more women entering the workforce? Certainly, it has a lot to do with gender inequality – discrimination at work makes it hard for ambitious women to keep their jobs once they have children, and this may well put them off the idea of getting married. But it's not just down to that. There is also a pervasive gloom surrounding the Japanese economy, and people are too worried about their future earnings to make long-term plans.

This is nothing new; whenever the economy is in trouble, the fertility rate dips. News that the fertility rate had dropped below replacement level for the first time coincided with the oil shock of 1973. Prices shot up, everyone started worrying about their finances, and nine months later there was a sudden drop in the number of newborns. In 1974, only one in twenty Japanese women was childless, but by 1977 this had risen to one in four. The same pattern can be seen in South Korea, where there was a big drop in the fertility rate after the collapse of Lehman Brothers and the credit crunch of 2007–08. Before the crash, one in seven South Korean women was childless, but this rose to one in three in the years that followed.[29]

Changing gender roles, the rise of the dual-income household and stagnating incomes have thrown up lots of obstacles to anyone considering having children. But these are not the only things holding people back from reproducing. Over the last 25 years, Japan has also been suffused with a sense of instability that has undermined confidence in the future. It is not easy to prove an empirical connection between anxiety and the declining birth rate, but according to a Cabinet Office survey conducted in 2007, 69 per cent of respondents said they were anxious about life, a record high.[30]

It may be hard for Westerners to imagine why: Japan always seems so orderly and peaceful. But in the years I was away, the country suffered a series of disasters that shook the public's faith in the authorities, the state and, indeed, the future. The first was the Kobe earthquake of 1995, which proved to be a technical as well as a natural disaster. Only months before it struck, Japanese engineers had gone to Los Angeles to investigate a recent earthquake and returned confident that their superior building techniques meant such a catastrophe could never befall a Japanese city. In fact, the destruction in Kobe was much worse. The reclaimed land on which parts of the city were built turned to mud, and buildings and highways that engineers had confidently proclaimed to be earthquake-proof 'collapsed like cards'.[31]

The failure was administrative as well as technical. First on the scene with blankets and food were not the public authorities, but the *yakuza*, the Japanese Mafia. While the government dithered, tens of thousands of volunteers went to Kobe to help the survivors. The government's cack-handed response came as a shock to a society accustomed to a strong, even overbearing state. It also gave Japan's civil society organisations a much needed shot in the arm. In 1995, in belated recognition of the outsized role they had played in the aftermath of the earthquake, the National Diet, Japan's state legislature, passed the Disaster Basic Act, which supported civil society's involvement in crisis management and disaster relief.

If the Kobe earthquake rattled people's faith in Japan's construction companies, politicians and bureaucrats, the gas attack on the

Tokyo metro two months later rattled their faith in society itself. Thirteen people died and at least 5,800 were injured when followers of a new religion called Aum Shinrikyo released sarin gas on three train lines.

More than a religion, Aum was akin to an opposition party. Until the day of the gas attack, many commentators had admired it for its sweeping condemnation of the materialism and corruption of the post-war order. The novelists Haruki Murakami and Kenzaburo Oe had both written with something like sympathy for Aum's original, pre-criminal intent. 'They wanted to show the Japanese people how we have reached a dead end in our mental situation, a dead end in our soul,' said Oe.[32]

Almost as shocking as the organization's murderous intent were the privileged backgrounds of many of its members, among them many young graduates of Tokyo University, the best in the country. In the aftermath of the gas attack, people had to face up to the possibility that many critics of the post-war order were themselves deranged, not to say criminally insane. 'The structure of society is very unstable,' Murakami told journalist David Pilling.

> We have come to think that there is something wrong with our system. It is a time of great change in our way of thinking . . . Most Japanese don't have any sense of direction. We are lost and we don't know which way we should go. But this is a very natural thing, a very healthy thing. It is time for us to think. We can take our time.[33]

After Kobe and Aum, the third crisis to rattle the public's trust in the authorities was the earthquake and tsunami that devastated the north-east of the country on 11 March 2011. Following the meltdown of the nuclear reactor at Fukushima, government ministers and representatives of Tepco (Tokyo Electric Power Company) and the Nuclear and Industrial Safety Agency briefed one press conference after another, doing their level best to duck responsibility for the disaster. But nobody believed them, and the public came to regard the country's newspapers and TV broadcasters as complicit in the official failure to come clean about what had happened. Thereafter, many people stopped following official media channels and turned instead to social media for information.

As well as spurring on the decentralization of news-gathering and general scepticism towards officialdom, the tsunami had a significant impact on people's attitudes to the mass consumerism of the 1980s. Takashi Tsujii, also known as Seiji Tsutsumi, is the man who established the pared-down retailer Muji.

> An earthquake sends a tsunami washing ashore, and cars are sent tumbling over and over like toys. You see that, and suddenly you stop wanting to own a car after all. Just from [watching those scenes of the disaster on TV], I think there is a feeling spreading among a lot of people that we can get by without owning all those things we used to think we couldn't live without.[34]

Together, these three disasters convinced many people that the root causes of Japan's Lost Decades were not just economic. The American-inspired society that had emerged from the devastation of World War Two had had strictly material goals: to rebuild and become prosperous. Japan did this handsomely, but as satisfaction turned to satiety, the complacency of the post-war leadership was challenged by spasms of collective self-doubt that shook Japan's national self-image to its core. Only now is it becoming clear that among the institutions that have shown themselves to be too fragile to survive is the nuclear family.

4.

A Wedding and Four Funerals:
On Being Single in Matsudo

After my meeting with Akiko, I made my way from Otemachi to Ueno, where I caught an express train back out to Matsudo. Walking back to the share house from Matsudo station, I passed a party of workmates in an *izakaya* who were toasting a man who looked to be their boss. They were a rare example of suburban sociability; all the diners in the cheap chain restaurants I passed were alone, hunched over bowls of donburi, udon and ramen. I couldn't help thinking that there had to be a connection between the cloistered daily behaviour of the people around me, and the country's demographic plight.

There was no better emblem of mass solitude than the glittering pachinko parlour I passed every day on my way back from work. It was full of solitary players transfixed by the passage of a shiny silver ball down a brightly lit screen. Unlike pinball, to which it is sometimes compared, pachinko is all about the first drop of the ball. Thereafter, the player can only watch as it ricochets from pin to pin, its trajectory at once predetermined and unknowable. If it falls into the right hole, he wins more balls; if it doesn't, he wins nothing.

Personally, I couldn't see the appeal, but to its aficionados pachinko is said to offer a lesson in the power of fate. The French philosopher Roland Barthes, who first visited Japan in 1966, describes visiting a pachinko parlour where he watched a man 'inserting, propelling, and receiving his marbles, with three gestures whose very coordination is a design'. Barthes saw pachinko players as engaged in 'deliberate, absorbing labour; never an idle or casual or playful attitude, none of that theatrical unconcern of our Western players lounging in leisurely groups around a pinball machine and quite conscious of producing for the other patrons of the café the image of an expert and disillusioned god.'[1]

Rituals, processions, precision and endless work . . . yes, Barthes was certainly onto something. I rounded the corner with a sigh and turned down the empty street that led to the share house. While the older generation took refuge in the pachinko parlour, the youngsters would be at home gaming. Considering the oppressive quiet and anonymity of Matsudo, I could see why so many of them opted to spend their downtime online, fantasizing about righteous vengeance and building better worlds. But by holing up in their bedrooms, they made the city's public spaces feel even more bereft.

My share house reminded me of a student hall of residence, with 200 or so little rooms spread over four floors. Two of the floors were unisex, one was only for men, and another only for women. A few of the residents were foreign exchange students, but most of them were Japanese, some students, but most *freeta* or regular office workers. They would give me a short, wordless bow of the head when I passed them in the long, shiny corridors, before scurrying back to their rooms. Saying 'good morning' or 'good evening' to a stranger was not the done thing, and on the few occasions I tried it, I got only blank looks in return.

The unfriendliness of the place wasn't helped by its anonymity. Walking back from the shared washroom, I often mistook the room next door for my own. Opening the door, I would walk into a room the same as mine but different, and see someone else's possessions where mine should have been, as if someone called Tom had packed up and moved out while I was brushing my teeth. I would come to as if waking from a bad dream, and dash back to my own little cubbyhole as quickly as I could, hoping no one had seen me.

One morning, I passed not one, but two recently vacated rooms. There was no sign of whoever had lived there, as everything had already been cleared out. Now they were vacant, the rooms looked identical, and I had no recollection of what the previous occupants had looked like. I imagined washed-out versions of them floating through cyberspace. If anime fantasies like *Ghost in the Shell* and *Zombie Revolution* are anything to go by, many young Japanese live with the fear, not just that not they are going to spend the rest of their lives alone, but that in the process they will be hollowed out by loneliness and eventually disappear.

I was aware that I was going through one of the early stages of acclimatization. By this time, I had been back in Tokyo for a year. Eventually, I would become acculturated, and learn to accept Japan on its own terms. For the time being, though, I was stuck in 'resistance' mode, which is to say, I still baulked at the indifference to strangers that passed for normality, and the highly mannered etiquette that passed for hospitality.

One evening, a fellow resident joined me in the smokers' room with a can of beer in her hand. 'Why did you come to Japan?' Sachiko asked me, as if surprised. She had lived in London for seven years but had had to leave. 'Visa problem,' she said, by way of explanation. 'To tell the truth, I did not want to come back to Japan.' Like me, Sachiko was 50 and unmarried. Although the number of Japanese people getting married is falling and more people are postponing getting hitched until later in life, most women still expect to marry sooner or later. Some of them are lucky enough to marry a man who makes it possible for them to combine a career with motherhood. Sachiko was one of the foolhardy few who had rejected both marriage and a career to pursue the dream of living abroad, and she had come home only reluctantly.

Enterprising women often inspire fear in conformist men, and Sachiko was paying the price for defying convention by eking out a living as a *freeta*. She worked part-time at an anonymous office job. 'It meant taking a pay cut, but it was the only way I could avoid the long working hours. Having to work overtime every day and go for tedious drinking sessions with colleagues isn't my idea of fun.'

★

As singledom becomes more common in Japan, so does living alone. In 2010, the number of one-person households surpassed the number of nuclear family households for the first time and by 2020, they had become the most common type, accounting for 38 per cent of households.[2] Forecasts suggest that by 2035 half the Japanese population will be living alone.[3]

With living alone becoming the new norm, an emerging genre of 'solitude literature' is shifting popular understanding of the word *kodoku* ('solitude') from a pitiable state into something more akin to liberation. These books, among them titles like *Kirawareru yūki* ('the courage to be disliked') and *Gokujō no Kodoku* ('supreme solitude'), encourage Japan's burgeoning population of single people to enjoy living alone.[4] Several of the best-known examples of solitude literature warn readers of 'the exhaustion caused by trying to be liked,' and rail against the constraints of family life. Some have spent months in the bestseller charts, with *Kodoku no Susume* ('advice for the lonely') proving especially popular. 'The reason I feel fulfilled,' author Hiroyuki Itsuki declares, 'is because I am not afraid of loneliness.'

The novelty of Itsuki's book lies in his ambivalence towards the age-old ideal that we should all have a romantic partner. It used to be that the security of a relationship was what set you free from loneliness, but these days, for some people at least, being in a relationship has become more trouble than it's worth. Is loneliness really the price we have to pay to escape the vice that so many intimate relationships appear to have become?

Certainly, living alone is good for those who have grown tired of other people, but not everyone who lives alone falls into that camp. Running counter to the 'single and proud' trend is the traditional approach, which sees solitude as a potentially harmful state, to be avoided whenever possible. In *Sekai Ichi Kodoku na Nihon no Ojiisan* ('Japan's old men are the world's loneliest'), Junko Okamoto decries Japan as a 'loneliness superpower'. 'Society is not doing enough to address loneliness and people don't want to admit how unhappy they are', she said in an interview with the *Financial Times*. 'They use these pro-loneliness books to comfort themselves. They want to feel that what they are doing is right.'[5]

Living alone is a rapidly growing trend in other countries too. Countries in which more than 30 per cent of households have only one occupant include the Netherlands, Switzerland, Austria, France, Latvia, Belgium, Bulgaria, Hungary and Italy. The highest rates of solo living are to be found in Scandinavia, where over 42 per cent of households have only one occupant.[6]

Do these people actually want to live alone? After all, in the past, living alone and feeling lonely were practically synonymous, and nobody enjoys feeling lonely. American sociologist Eric Klinenberg, author of *Going Solo: The Extraordinary Rise and Surprising Appeal of Living Alone*, cites a study that found 85 per cent of Americans believe that anyone who actually enjoys living alone must be either sick, neurotic or immoral.[7] But that is an outdated belief from an age when practically all Americans got married and had children. In 1943, the year Edward Hopper painted his famous *Nighthawks*, with its pair of lonely customers sitting at the counter of a late-night diner, 22 per cent of adult Americans were single and only 9 per cent of households had only one occupant. Back then, most single-tons were migrant workers living in states where they had no social networks. Fast-forward to 2023, and just under half of Americans are unmarried and nearly 30 per cent of American households have only one occupant, both record highs.[8]

Klinenberg found that most Americans who live alone actively choose to do so, with many of them saying that they enjoy the freedom and sense of control over their lives that it gives them. Over the past half-century, growing numbers of people have embraced the values of independence, honesty and self-expression. They equate solitude with self-realization, discovering who they are and what they really want from life, even if that sets them apart from more conventional life paths, such as getting married and having children.

In Japan, the emotional landscape is somewhat different. When sociologist Kazuhisa Arakawa asked middle-aged men why they lived alone, many of them said it was because they couldn't afford to get married or have children. For others, it was an active choice, inspired by a desire to be free of the domestic responsibilities that come with living with someone else. Many of this second group were trepidatious about getting married: having grown up in the high-growth era, they had largely been raised by their mothers and rarely saw their workaholic fathers. When their fathers retired, their mothers found themselves living with a stranger, and many promptly filed for divorce. They did not want to fall into the same trap.

When Arakawa asked middle-aged women why they lived alone, the main reason they gave was freedom. Only having to look after themselves meant they had more free time, and this allowed them to have a wider range of friendships than they would have had if they had been married.[9] Traditionalists might call these committed singletons selfish, but for many Japanese women choosing to live alone is a response to male selfishness. They want to escape the stress and drudgery of holding down a job while looking after a household in which their partner doesn't pull his weight.

Conservative commentators often say that, notwithstanding the many unhappy marriages in the world, the institution remains a building block of society. But is it? Certainly, a few generations ago, coupledom allowed men and women to expand their social connections into their extended families and the wider community. But families and communities are not what they used to be, and these days couples are more likely to view themselves as a self-sufficient, autonomous unit.

Many Japanese commentators interpret the growing number of single-occupant households as a sign of young people's estrangement from wider society, but it is not as simple as that. The rise of solo living has gone hand in hand with improved communications: the telephone, the radio, the TV and now the internet. With each advance, it has become easier to spend time alone without feeling isolated or disconnected from other people. Indeed, in the age of the 24-hour news cycle and information overload, plenty of us equate other people with confusion, and solitude with peace. The madding crowd may be the root cause of our desire for more time alone, but it is only our advanced state of interdependence that makes this new wave of independent living possible.

The internet, for example, has allowed us to widen our social circles, but also to handle friends and acquaintances at some remove. This relates to what American sociologist Mark Granovetter calls 'the strength of weak ties'. He argues that weak ties with acquaintances have become more important than the strong ties we used to enjoy with close friends, family and workmates. This is partly because we change workplaces and occupations more often than we used to, but also because strong ties can be stifling. In the words of Zygmunt Bauman, we are living through 'liquid modern' times. We don't value the social bonds that connect us as much as we used to, and that includes family ties. Instead, we set store by freedom and self-realization, and we are shrinking our families and expanding our social circles to fit around these new values.[10]

Eric Klinenberg believes it is oversimplistic to decry the popularity of living alone or put it down to estrangement from society or narcissism. In the United States, at least, people who live alone don't necessarily want to be alone all the time. Indeed, many of them spend much of their emotional energy outdoors, unlike married couples, who tend to invest it at home in their partners and children. His research shows that, contrary to what you might expect, public life blooms brightest in those American cities that have the highest number of single households.

That's because single people who live alone are more likely to spend time with friends and frequent bars and restaurants than married couples. They are also more likely to be politically engaged, volunteer for good causes and look after their parents, siblings and neighbours. The impact of these 'solo livers' has been huge, says Klinenberg. By spurning the introspection of the nuclear family, they have turned the city into their kitchen, dining room and living room, returning home only to bathe and sleep. Indeed, the revitalization of America's inner cities that has taken place since the 1990s could not have happened without them.

★

The following morning, buoyed by an unexpected feeling of optimism, I took a stroll from my share house to the nearest convenience store. On the way, I stopped for a smoke on a bridge over a canal and looked up the length of the water towards the River Edogawa. It was a typically clear winter's day, cold but almost balmy when the sun was on my face. In the shadow cast by the bridge, some big, dark-grey carp were swimming languidly in the murky green water. One of them had a white splodge on his head and I found myself watching the others for signs that they were marginalizing the odd fish out.

A little boy came along and started pointing at '*Koi-san*' ('Mr Koi Carp'), so his mum got down on one knee and let him stand on her bent leg so he could get a better look. Since returning to Japan, I had spent a lot of time dwelling on points of difference, but watching the little boy and his mum, I was overcome by a welcome feeling of familiarity. I'd felt something similar the day before, when I'd heard the sound of a group of children passing under my window on their way to school. Their carefree jostling and babbling, oblivious to the outside world, was reassuringly normal and quite unlike the restrained, watchful adults that society expected them to become.

Yusuke Morimura had waved away my question when I put it to him, but children *are* becoming less visible in Japan. They account for just 11.9 per cent of the population, the lowest proportion of any country in the world.[11] This is not slow or incremental change: between 2010 and 2020 alone, the number of schoolchildren fell by around a million to 9.56 million.[12] Two-thirds of households are without children, and growing numbers of people, me included, simply don't have any contact with them.

I left the canal, and soon reached the convenience store. After the monastic quiet of the share house, I found the J-pop tinkling over the instore stereo a welcome relief. I bought myself a steamed *char siu* bun, a *yakisoba* sandwich and a *sakura*-flavoured soft-serve ice cream, and took a seat in the window to eat.

In most of the world's big cities, people struggle to reconcile their working lives with their desire for home cooking. They want to cook for themselves (or want their partners to cook for them) because home cooking is generally tastier, better for your health and cheaper than eating out. That is why city dwellers the world over rush home at five o'clock, snarling up the roads with their cars and turning commuter trains into sardine tins on wheels. The people of Tokyo, however, don't have to wrestle with this conundrum. Their city might be huge, but it is supremely well-organized, and rarely congested. It is also full of convenience stores, where they can buy fresh, nutritious, ready-made meals 24 hours a day.

Tokyo residents depend on convenience stores for sustenance to a degree unimaginable anywhere else. There are almost 7,000 *konbini* in the city, which works out at one for every 1,860 residents. Three-quarters of the revenues of *konbini* come from food products, and half of these are fresh baked goods, side dishes or fast food, which are delivered to stores three times a day.[13] In other advanced economies, the convenience of such stores comes at a high price. The food they sell tends to be highly processed, tasteless and usually stale. Not so in Tokyo, where a demanding public and an obsession with efficiency have combined to create a wonder of modern big-city living.

Every day, roughly 40 million Japanese people – a third of the population – buys something from a convenience store.[14] Though ever-changing and always up to date, these stores are paragons of dependability, for they are all basically the same. Everything they sell, including the ready-made food, is produced on a vast scale, according to the diktats of central planners. Everything is uniform, nothing is local and everything is delivered by road.

The rise of the convenience store is inextricably bound up with the breakdown of the nuclear family. As the family home has splintered into a million single-occupant apartments, the contemporary Japanese kitchen has been reduced to a fridge and a microwave. As kitchens shrink, the neighbourhood convenience store has expanded to become a multipurpose larder, bookshop, playroom and office. The *konbini* has evolved to become a handy one-stop shop for every imaginable chore, from paying utility bills to picking up Amazon deliveries and withdrawing money. *Konbini* sell iPhone cables and underpants, hair dye and whiskey, newspapers, manga and soft porn.

Whenever I asked my students why they liked living in the capital, the word they most often used in reply was 'convenient'. But what does convenient mean, if not being able to focus on work or leisure, without having to worry about any of the mundane in-between things, like housework, preparing food, and doing chores? In Tokyo, machines clean people's homes, food comes ready prepared, and you do all your paperwork in the nearest convenience store. As life becomes more convenient, it requires less teamwork, and this allows us to indulge our yearning for autonomy.

Perhaps this is one of the causes of the slow collapse of the nuclear family that is taking place in Japan. Just as the expansion of higher education and the creation of a female workforce has allowed women to live alone without being financially dependent on men, the rise of the convenience store allows men to live alone without depending on women to prepare their food.

*

Extrapolating from a survey, 25 million Britons say they 'occasionally, sometimes or often' feel lonely.[15] However, while the popularity of books like *Bowling Alone*, *Alone Together* and *The Lonely Crowd* might suggest that we are living through an era of unprecedented loneliness, there is no evidence to suggest that this is because more of us than ever are living alone. Loneliness and isolation are often used interchangeably, but they're not the same. Isolation is the objective state of being physically apart from other people, whereas loneliness is the subjective experience of disconnection from other people. Loneliness may be a result of being physically isolated, but that is not a precondition. Lighthouse keepers, for example, are isolated, but that is not to say they are lonely. Moreover, plenty of people are surrounded by others all the time, yet still feel lonely.

Why might that be? According to Kasley Killam, a social scientist and expert in social health, connection and loneliness, 'loneliness can arise from not feeling seen, understood, or validated. It can come from spending time with people who don't share your values or interests. It can also come from too many superficial interactions and not enough deeper connections.'[16] This certainly tallied with what I had seen in Tokyo: thanks to a longstanding dedication to work, self-negation and an insistence on good manners, millions of Japanese people were suffering the effects of 'too many superficial interactions and not enough deeper connections'.

Social isolation is a growing phenomenon in Japan. The country's health ministry defines a *hikikomori* as someone who 'has remained isolated at home for at least six months, avoids school or work, and rarely interacts with anyone outside their immediate family'. In 2014, a government report found that there were 500,000 *hikikomori* in Japan. Back then, the term was usually used to describe socially awkward young men confined to their bedrooms and hooked on video games, manga and anime. However, their ranks swelled during the coronavirus pandemic, as those inclined to shun interaction with other people realized how effective teleworking, remote learning and home delivery services could be.[17] Even after the lockdown was lifted, many of them chose to remain in isolation and, as of 2023, almost 1.5 million people of working age – one in fifty – are described as *hikikomori*.[18]

It is well known that the Japanese are having less sex and fewer relationships than other nationalities, but the sheer number of *hikikomori* suggests that they are also becoming more isolated and lonelier than ever before. In her 2013 book *Precarious Japan*, sociologist Anne Allison argues that Japan is becoming an increasingly impoverished country. 'This doesn't just mean financial poverty,' she writes in a 2009 paper. 'Rather, it is a state of solitude and desperation that carries people precipitously close to death. The reserves that Japanese people were once able to count on – whether savings in the bank, families one can turn to in time of need, or educational credentials – are drying up.'[19]

This state of solitude and desperation disproportionately affects the young. There are thought to be between 650,000 and 850,000

NEETs (Not in Employment, Education or Training) in Japan, and many of them are *hikikomori*. Quite apart from their inability to find work or a partner, most *hikikomori* can't even subsist on their own. The typical pattern is for a parent or sibling to prepare their food and leave it outside their room, thereby avoiding physical contact – as requested by the *hikikomori*.

However, not all *hikikomori* are young, and they don't all live with their parents. Plenty of them live alone, and while online deliveries mean that they never have to leave the house, some of them do go out from time to time, if only to the neighbourhood *konbini*.

After I put the word out that I was writing a book about the rising number of single, solitary people in Japan, people began to get in touch with their stories. One was Mario, a half-British, half-Japanese guy who had left Japan for the UK when he was 12, been through the British education system and then returned to Japan to work. He wanted to introduce me to his friend Sōichiro. 'He is a *hikikomori*. He lives on social care, which is not great in Japan,' he texted me. They hadn't seen one another for a year but had recently arranged to go to the local *sento* for a catch-up. Mario suggested we meet at a Korean *yakiniku* place around the corner afterwards.

Sōichiro lived in Saginomiya, about 20 minutes west of Shinjuku. It was only a mile or so from Ogikubo, which I had always thought of as quite a salubrious part of town, but when I got there, I found it to be a typical, quiet neighbourhood of flimsy, frayed-at-the-edges houses crouching in the shadow of the Chūō line. The telegraph poles lurched, the fluorescent sign above the neighbourhood *konbini* flickered and there was not much greenery.

Mario and Sōichiro were the only customers in the restaurant. Mario was billowing huge clouds of smoke from his vape, while Sōichiro sat there quietly frying thin slices of beef on the tabletop barbecue. The TV was bubbling away in the background.

'This rain is no good,' Sōichiro rasped, glancing over my shoulder at the drizzle as I sat down. 'It turns the fag butts to mush.'

Mario smiled. 'He smokes dogends he finds on the street.'

Fortunately for Sōichiro, Mario had bought him a fresh pack of Seven Stars.

'Are you from Tokyo?' I asked him.

'Yes. And I hate it,' he said matter-of-factly.

'Do you have brothers and sisters?'

'No. I'm an only child.'

'What are your parents like?'

'My dad is a violent person. My mum is a big spender.'

'When was the last time you saw them?'

'Two years ago, when I went into hospital.'

Sōichiro hadn't been well recently. He had lost his voice, so Mario did most of the talking for him. 'At high school he was quite big, and he was bullied. It was quite bad. I recall him saying that he got his face shoved down the toilet.' This chimed with what I had read about *hikikomori* online. Among the reasons they gave for their retreat from the world was the experience of being bullied by classmates or work colleagues. Others cited the terrible pressure to succeed, first at school and then at cram school, which left them with little time to make friends. Many of them had grown up in lonely households, with parents who were out at work all day (and sometimes late into the night as well).

'Sōichiro's parents were not supportive,' Mario went on. 'They blamed him for becoming the victim of the bullying. He couldn't sleep, so the doctor put him on Xanax – which are strong and very addictive sleeping pills. At university, he basically starved himself and became very thin. Then he started DJing and became quite a popular kid.'

'We first met at a private party in the Prada building,' piped up Sōichiro with a grin. 'Yes,' said Mario, smiling at the memory. 'Sōichiro was the DJ. That must have been about 12 years ago.' This came as some surprise. I had been past the Prada building. It was in Omotesando, on one of the wealthiest shopping streets in the city – a world away from Saginomiya. 'He was also working as a host, so he was making lots of money, but he was spending it all on booze, parties and drugs. They helped him to deal with his insomnia and the side effects of his medication.'

'Everything bad happened in the space of a couple of months. He lost his fiancée; he lost his job and then his parents disowned him.' Shortly afterwards, Sōichiro's mental health took a turn for the worse. He started hallucinating and became unable to look after himself. 'His parents weren't there to deal with him, so he came and lived at my house. But after a month, my dad said, "No more."'

Along with bullying, another experience common among *hikikomori* is the lack of parental support. Japanese society tends to give short shrift to those who do not work, and onlookers often accuse *hikikomori* of being spoiled or lazy. But their rush to judge is often just a mask for their own bewilderment. The *hikikomori* is the exact opposite of the *salariman,* a man so tied to his company that he is hardly ever at home. By contrast, the *hikikomori* is a sedentary homebody who has retreated into himself, acknowledges no duties and exercises no rights (apart from his right to be left alone).

'I tried to get him some medical help,' Mario told me, 'but every time he would sneak out for a drink and then the hospital would kick him out.'

'Once I tried to jump out of an ambulance because I thought the doctors were trying to harm me,' croaked Sōichiro.

'Eventually, I got him into a Cold War-style psychiatric hospital called Hasegawa,' Mario went on, blowing out another cloud of vapour. 'It was basically prison for four months. After he was discharged, he became an outpatient at a mental hospital near Ikebukuro.'

'I have been diagnosed with depression,' said Sōichiro, deftly fishing some pieces of grilled meat off the tabletop barbecue for me.

'Do the meds work?' I asked.

'Oh yes,' he enthused.

'What do you do at the hospital?'

'I go there from ten in the morning until four in the afternoon. I read the newspaper, but sometimes the words don't sink in. I'd like to work and become more independent. That's what everyone else is doing.'

'What kind of work would you like to do?'

'Well, IT. But the hospital says I still can't work.'

'Why won't the hospital let you work?'

'I don't know.'

Mario explained that Sōichiro couldn't apply for a normal job because the only ID he had was his social care card. 'I went into the doctor's room with him, and I told them, "He is addicted to alcohol, and he is addicted to the drugs you are giving him. They are not helping him. He needs someone to talk to." But the doctors weren't listening.'

'What is the hospital expecting?' I asked Sōichiro.

'I don't know,' he said.

'You must feel quite powerless.'

'Something like that, yeah.'

I tried to talk to Sōichiro about his life as a *hikikomori*, but he could only reply in monosyllables. There wasn't a trace of self-pity in his voice. It made me think I didn't know how to recognize sadness in Japan. Japanese people have always tended to be reserved – 'shy' is the word many of them use to describe themselves. It is not hard to see why; in a competitive and highly regimented society, those who cannot find their place will always be burdened by feelings of shame.

'It is sad,' said Mario, who had read my mind. 'Japan is just very conformist. We try to put everything into boxes. Once people are outside the system, no one wants to touch them. Usually, all they need is some good counselling and a place to feel safe and they'll be fine. Instead, they just get put on strong medication and isolated from society.'

From the *yakiniku* place we walked to the nearest *konbini* to buy some more beer and then went back to Sōichiro's place. From the outside, it looked completely inconspicuous, just another tiny, newish apartment of the type occupied by millions of single people across the city. It was only when we stepped inside that I saw what lay behind the facade of normality. The place was absolutely full of rubbish.

Yet, in spite of the squalor, it was remarkably tidy; Sōichiro had piled his empty beer cans in one corner, another corner was stacked high with paper and cardboard, and there was a mountain of plastic bags in another. He sat down where he slept, in a tiny space that he had cleared in the middle of the floor. Mario managed to find a seat on a pile of cardboard, while I sat on top of the beer cans, which must have been a metre deep. Sōichiro put on some music, and we kidded ourselves that we were just three friends having an after-party.

'He's borrowing electricity from his neighbour to power the fridge and the air conditioner, which is scary because if he gets reported to social services, they'll cut him off and he'll have to live as a homeless person,' said Mario.

I asked if his neighbour knew he was stealing his electricity.

'His neighbour is a Nepalese man. He knows about Sōichiro borrowing his electricity and he was kind enough not to report him to the police. He just put up a sign saying, "Please don't steal my electricity."'

Were it not for the rubbish, Sōichiro's apartment would have been practically empty. There was just one room, with a tiny hob and sink in one corner, a separate shower room to the side and a single bunk bed overhead. All he had in the way of possessions were a couple of T-shirts on hangers, a pair of flip-flops and his iPad. It was shocking, but it was also quite familiar. There are two big parks in Tokyo – Yoyogi Park and Ueno Park – and there are lots of homeless people living in both of them. They live under tarpaulin sheets and, seemingly without exception, their encampments are incredibly neat and tidy.

I asked Sōichiro if he had many other friends.

'One from high school,' he replied.

'One of the things that upsets me is that, although we shared quite a wide circle of friends, when Sōichiro had his breakdown, they offered no help,' said Mario. 'People lead such fast-paced lives in Tokyo that the old-fashioned sense of friendship no longer exists.'

I nodded and made a comment about how hard it was to meet women, too.

'Yes, I agree,' said Sōichiro. 'But there are various ways. There are a lot of apps. Tinder and stuff . . . I used to use them but not any more.'

'Back in the day, he was quite a player,' chipped in Mario. 'He even picked up a girl in a *konbini* once.' They had a laugh, remembering.

'What do you do in the evenings?' I asked.

'I sleep.'

'And he watches TV,' put in Mario. 'When he can get wi-fi at the pachinko parlour, he downloads TV shows to his iPad from a Chinese website.'

'Do you like pachinko?' I asked him.

'Not at all,' he said. 'I never gamble.'

I detected a note of resolution in his voice.

'He is very clever,' said Mario. 'He produced music. I think music was his strong point, and that talent just seems so wasted.'

'Do you still like music?' I asked Sōichiro.

'A bit. But I've lost my confidence.'

'It's hard for me to meet him,' said Mario. 'It brings back bad memories.'

I felt that I was interrupting a conversation. They must both have been feeling guilty, and sad. I could see that Mario was angry at the social care system. I still didn't know how Sōichiro felt about it though.

'Long time, no see,' said Mario.

'Yes, long time no see,' said Sōichiro, and he smiled. For the first time, I heard a tone of regret in his voice. He was not hopeless; just lost, unhappy and lonely. Like a lot of *hikikomori*, his life had come unstuck, he had been unable to challenge the sea of disapproving faces and had turned inwards.

*

When I had got off the train, I had taken Saginomiya to be just another run-of-the-mill dormitory town, but walking back to the station, the neighbourhood took on an air of sour pinchedness. I was in shock, not just at meeting a real-life *hikikomori*, but at the veneer of polite discretion that masks the mass dysfunctionality lurking underneath. Sōichiro's story was not unusual. Only a few days before, I had seen a flyer for a cleaning service for single people – presumably men – who were living alone, which offered to go in and clean out all the trash. 'Are you living in a horrible environment? Let us clean up your mess,' ran the blurb. All it takes is a certain amount of chaos in a solitary life, and we can all end up living in our own shit, surrounded by beer cans.

Preoccupied with material pursuits – less with getting ahead than not falling behind – Japanese people are both more affluent and more individualistic than they were a half a century ago. But they are not rugged individualists, and exhibit a higher degree of psychological distress and have fewer social skills than their forebears. The internet has allowed for the creation of virtual worlds, enticing anyone tired of the disciplined selflessness of Japan's schools and offices with the promise of escape. And, as it has elsewhere, it has also created a new breed of antisocial fantasist who wants to have as little as possible to do with other people.

The growing incidence of depression is a worrying characteristic of Japanese society in the twenty-first century. According to an estimate by the Ministry of Health, Labour and Welfare, clinical depression went from being the fourth most prevalent disease in 2000 to the second most in 2020.[20] Between 1998 and 2010, there were over 30,000 suicides a year, one of the highest rates in the world. Contrary to popular perception, Japan is no longer a global suicide hot spot – there are twenty-five countries in which a higher proportion of people die by suicide every year – but suicide remains the leading cause of death among men aged 20–44.[21]

Once I started looking for them, I saw signs of the high suicide rate all around me. While I had been away, barriers had been installed on the platform of every station in the city. Apparently, they weren't there to stop people being pushed onto the tracks during the rush hour after all.

In countries with high crime rates, onlookers often blame the victims of crime for not being more careful. There is no point blaming the criminal, they say, because crime is a fact of life, both rife and irredeemable. In Japan, people employ the same twisted logic to justify their indifference to suicide. Victims of suicide are blamed for not being sufficiently stoical in the face of adversity. There is no point blaming loneliness, they say, because loneliness is a fact of life, both inevitable and on the rise. Life can be tough, but you have to *gaman suru* – 'persevere'.

Suicide is taken seriously in Japan not because it is tragic, but because it causes trouble for other people. It might be the ultimate act of self-effacement, but it is also regarded as supremely selfish. That's why, when someone dies by suicide by jumping in front of a train, their family is liable for a fine equivalent to £46,000. This is supposed to cover the cost of cleaning up the aftermath, as well as the disruption of train services. I have always admired the Japanese for their lack of self-pity, but I find such a lack of pity for those suffering from loneliness, depression and anxiety hard to digest.

Among other things suicide is a tragic symptom of a shrinking population: one of the most common reasons people give for attempting suicide is losing hope in the future. That explains why the suicide rate in the northern prefecture of Akita, where depopulation has become an existential threat, is a third higher than the national average.[22] It is also prevalent among young women in Kabukichō, Tokyo's largest red-light district. A priest who features in the documentary *Saving 10,000: Winning a War on Suicide in Japan* explains that, as the countryside becomes an unsustainable place to live, more young people are leaving for Tokyo. Some of the women end up working as prostitutes or hostesses, some are badly treated by boyfriends or pimps, and some take their own lives.

There is help on offer for people with mental-health problems in Japan. Sōichiro's ward office gave him an allowance, and I came across several examples of lonely, depressed people coming together to help one another. Kowaremono ('broken people'), for example, is a self-help group of young to middle-aged adults who have a mental-health condition of some sort, be it depression, alcoholism, an eating disorder or extreme reclusiveness. They perform at 'talk events' in Tokyo, where they re-enact the travails that they have been through in their lives through spoken word, poetry and music. The performance ends with the players inviting the audience to join their community or to create their own. The founder of Broken People is 43-year-old Kōji Tsukino, who spent several years living as a *hikikomori* and alcoholic before writing a self-help book, *Ie no naka no Houmuresu* ('being homeless at home').[23]

Another organization working to support lonely people is Hanhinkon ('reverse poverty'), which runs a network of self-help groups around the country. It was co-founded by Makoto Yuasa, who is also co-director of an NGO called Moyai that offers free advice to anyone trying to find a job or an apartment or apply for welfare. Reaching out to those caught in the cycle of loneliness, Moyai not only helps people to become truly independent, but functions as a 'life support centre' and all-purpose stand-in for the family home.

As we have seen, NGOs were thin on the ground in Japan until the Kobe earthquake of 1995 and the Fukushima disaster of 2011. The concept of 'civil society', independent of the state and local government, is still in its infancy, but as more people become aware of the growing scarcity of human relationships and the risks inherent in mass isolation, they are reaching out to help one another. In a country where the authorities have long had a monopoly on defining and treating social problems, this amounts to a sea change.

Of course, not every solitary young person browsing manga in his local *konbini* is at risk of dying by suicide, and it is important to acknowledge that not all *hikikomori* are in need of help. Sōji Nito, for example, has lived as a *hikikomori* for the last ten years, but he is also the developer behind *Pull Stay*, a hugely popular game that was released in 2020. Contrary to the stereotypical camera-shy social recluse, he regularly shares glimpses of his daily life on YouTube.

Increasingly, writers who are not exactly *hikikomori* but lead relatively reclusive lives have gained prominence in the Japanese book market. Henri Ohara, for example, is the author of *Seclusion in One's Twenties: How to Live a Comfortable Life with Five Free Days a Week*. Having decided to 'retire', as he puts it, at the age of 25, Ohara has had to learn how to live cheaply. He says that by living on vegetables, tofu and fruit, he is able to spend most of his time 'walking, reading and thinking'. Turning his back on what he calls 'restrictive social norms' has meant defying convention, which is never easy in a conformist society, but it has done wonders for his mental health, he says.[24]

Those inclined to emulate the lifestyle of low maintenance, economy-mode singletons like Henri Ohara should take succour from history. Curiously, this is not the first time that Tokyo has been dominated by single people. Reading up on the history of the capital, I was surprised to find that, in this regard, post-modern Tokyo is remarkably similar to pre-modern Edo, as the city used to be called. In 1721, Edo had a population of 1 million, making it, as it is now, the biggest city in the world.[25] Intriguingly, the proportion of single-occupant households was the same then as it is today – half of the men in the city lived alone, and, though plenty had families back in their home provinces, many of them would have been single.

This was because so many of them led peripatetic existences. The Tokugawa shoguns stipulated that all regional *daimyō* (feudal lords) should maintain a household in Edo, the better to keep an eye on them. As a result, *daimyō* spent one year in their castle towns with their families, and the following year in Edo, surrounded by their fellow samurai. Half of the male population of Edo were townspeople, but most of the other half either belonged to the samurai class or their retinue, and that meant they had to follow their *daimyō*. This led to a disproportionate number of single men living in the capital, at least in alternate years, and a dearth of women. In 1750, men outnumbered women in the capital by two to one.[26]

These single men created mainstays of everyday life that survive to this day.[27] The samurai's lifestyle was the prototype of that of the modern *salariman*: he commuted to his lordship's house in the morning and returned to his own lodgings in the evening. Since most men didn't cook, food deliveries were commonplace. Sushi and tempura both came into vogue in the Edo period (1603–1868) and soon became the fast-foods of their day. *Izakaya* and late-night soba stalls also became mainstays of the city's culinary life.

There are intriguing parallels between the cultural lives of post-modern Tokyo and pre-modern Edo as well. As the cultural centre of gravity shifted from courtly Kyoto to Edo, the samurai and townspeople created an Epicurean literature, based on the maxim 'Let's enjoy the here and now.' In the eighteenth century, *ukiyo-e* (woodblock prints) were the pop-star picture books of their day and *kibyōshi* ('books with yellow covers') were illustrated story-books similar to manga.

I had visited cosplay restaurants in Akihabara where costumed staff treated customers as if they were the masters and mistresses of a private home rather than mere customers. These maid cafés, where the waitresses dress up in old-fashioned maids' outfits, hadn't existed the first time I lived in Tokyo, but they, too, were a throw-back to the Edo period, when young men would queue outside famous teahouses to be served by their favourite waitress. Some of the most celebrated of these young women are depicted in the prints of Harunobu Suzuki, a famous Edo-era woodblock artist.

It is in the conservative temperament to interpret any change as a sign of decline, so it's hardly surprising that the growing number of unmarried men and women in post-growth Japan has set alarm bells ringing. I have to admit, I didn't much enjoy the monastic vibe in my share house, but that's not to say it was representative of the country at large. It may well be that the baby boomers who dominate the Japanese commentariat are exaggerating, and most one-person households are occupied by 'the happy youth of a desperate country', to borrow the title of a book by sociologist Noritoshi Furuichi that made quite a splash when it came out in 2017.[28] Either way, I was heartened to learn that mass singledom has a long history in Japan – as does escapist make-believe.

5.

'I Want to Do It but I Can't Be Bothered'

After a year and a half at the Japanese-language school, I decided to leave. I had passed the Japanese Language Proficiency Test N2 exam, which I had taken but failed shortly before leaving Japan back in 1993. I was confident that I could teach myself from then on, but my decision was also motivated by money – it was time to find more work.

I found a job writing articles for an English-language website aimed at expats and tourists. It was the worst variety of freelance journalism. The budget didn't extend to interviews, so I spent a lot of time finding stories online, poaching other people's work and ripping off press releases. But in a roundabout way, it was a good way of improving my understanding of the language. I became adept at running Japanese-language articles through online translators like Deep L and then rewriting the translation.

More importantly, my editor allowed me to write whatever I liked about Japan. For every five hack pieces I knocked out about the launch of a new rich tea biscuit-flavoured ice cream or the release of the latest Evangelion anime boxset, I would treat myself to writing one piece that appealed to my own interest.

Drilling down into the bedrock of Japanese society, culture and history allowed me to develop a better understanding of the social changes I was seeing around me. I came to appreciate the long road Japan had travelled since Commodore Matthew Perry and his black ships arrived in Tokyo Bay back in 1853, demanding that the shogun open up his country to foreign trade. A hermetically sealed, feudal society had had to adapt to the challenge of the West. I developed a deep respect for the country's capacity for adaptation, organization and mobilization. Along the way,

I took another step towards acclimatization. I accepted Japan for what it was and stopped expecting it to be like my own culture. Indeed, I started to appreciate the things that Japan does better than we do.

*

Clearly, not everyone who lives alone is single: some are in relationships but choose not to live with their partners. Yet it does seem that there is something in the way in Japan; something that is preventing young people from forming close, physical, loving relationships. Wanting to find out more about the connection between their newfound taste for solitude and their attitudes to sex and intimacy, I arranged to meet Alice Pacher, an Austrian-born lecturer in the Department of Clinical Psycho-Social Science at Meiji University. She had written a paper on sexlessness that had caught my attention. It was called '*Shitai kedo mendō kusai*' ('I want to do it, but I can't be bothered') and it conjectured that by 2040, 47 per cent of the adult population is going to be single.

We met at a café in Jigūgaoka, not far from the Tama River on the border between Tokyo and Kawasaki. Being quiet and pleasant, and less than ten minutes by express train from Shibuya, Jigūgaoka is popular with well-paid young couples, though judging by the occupants of the prams I passed on my way to meet Alice, more of them are opting to buy pet dogs than have babies.

I put it to Alice that, considering that the future of the country is at stake, it is amazing how little work is being done to understand the underlying causes of the reluctance to reproduce. 'In Japan, no one talks about sex, and everything is taboo. It's very complicated and very fascinating,' she said.

Being half-Japanese and half-Austrian, Alice had spent many years in both countries, and this had given her the opportunity to observe and compare the love lives of people in each of them. 'In Austria, if you read a lot of books, or watch movies, you always see relationships between real couples. But in Japan, it's always a one-sided relationship – someone falls in love, but the other person rejects them, so they suffer. They love this kind of tragedy. They think it is beautiful.'

Anyone familiar with anime and manga will appreciate that it tends towards the sentimental. The word for 'sentimental' – *kanshōteki* – is telling: its literal meaning is 'feeling the wound'. The shadow of impending tragedy lends all treatment of matters of the heart a hint of mawkishness. In a classic instance of life imitating art, it seems that people are learning how to love from the culture, and it is teaching them that other people are not to be trusted.

'When I talk to my students, I find that many of them have been rejected by lovers in the past. For years and years, they are very traumatized, and they don't want to have sex any more. They are very passive, and they suffer alone – or they write on X, which has become a very important tool in Japan.'

Yet practically all the young people that Alice had interviewed told her that they wanted to get married one day. 'They say, "I would like to have a relationship. I would like to know love." And at first, they say they want to have sex. But when you talk to them about it, you find out that they don't really. They say, "It is not enjoyable. I don't get any pleasure from it."'

A sex therapist might say that they should work out what gives them sexual pleasure by themselves, and if their partner isn't doing it right, tactfully show them how to do it. But that requires verbal communication, which is fraught with risk. 'They never talk about their sexuality. They say, "I don't know how to talk to my partner about this." This is not a culture where you can talk to people directly, so you have to guess what he or she likes.'

When I asked Alice why young people find it so hard to talk about sex, she said, 'Because there is no education.' This seemed to me a rather abstract way of explaining the problem, but as she went on, I saw her point. 'Sex education is on the curriculum, but it is limited to diseases. If schoolkids ask about sex, their teacher says, "Don't ask. That is a taboo." So, of course, they think, "I did something wrong," and stop asking questions.'

It struck me that this is one of the tragedies of being so obedient.

My generation didn't have any sex education either, but our parents' squeamishness only encouraged us to find out for ourselves. But initiative is rarely prized in hierarchical societies, and it doesn't help that women are expected to follow the male lead. 'The younger generation are wary of having sex because they are afraid to get pregnant. They don't have information about contraception and couples don't talk about it. They don't say, "OK, what do we want to use, condoms or the pill?" It is never *we*. The woman always asks the man, "Well, what do *you* want?" '

It is not surprising that men are in charge of contraception in Japan. One of the peculiarities of the nation's sex life is lawmakers' longstanding hostility to the contraceptive pill. I was amazed to learn that it wasn't even legalized until 1999, making Japan the last member of the United Nations to approve its use.[1] There were no medical grounds for their opposition to the pill; rather, they worried that giving women access to contraception would 'disturb the social order'. Such was their hostility to putting contraception in the hands of women, they approved use of Viagra before they allowed women to take the pill. Even today, condoms account for over 80 per cent of contraceptive use in Japan.

However, the ageing of the population, a decline in the number of young people and lower rates of sexual activity have combined to drive sales of condoms into a steep decline, going from 700 million per year in the early 1990s to just 200 million per year in the late 2010s.[2] Surveys confirm what Alice was telling me: young Japanese people are having less sex, and Japanese women, in particular, are going off it altogether. Polls conducted by the Japanese Association for Sex Education show that the percentage of young women who agree that 'sex is enjoyable' has been in decline since 1999. That year, 90 per cent of respondents said that sex was an 'enjoyable' or 'more or less enjoyable' experience; by 2017, this had dropped to 64 per cent.[3]

No less remarkable is the number of people who are not interested in finding a partner. According to a survey conducted by the NIPSSR in 2021, growing numbers of single men and women regard relationships as more trouble than they're worth. One in three singletons said that they were not interested in having a relationship with a member of the opposite sex.[4]

'The problem is that many people have never experienced positive sex,' said Alice. 'Sex is always seen as something dirty or painful, and they would rather focus on happier things. They have internalized the idea that men are bad, and women are always the victims. I think that is why the number of people who want to stay single has increased.'

Progressives might argue that the real passion killer is Japan's man-centric culture and the shame and ignorance it encourages in women. But Alice thought that the strongest driver of the trend towards sexlessness is a broader form of misanthropy. 'My students don't want to share anything with other people. They say that spending time with other people is tiring. Going to a coffee shop or a restaurant alone is much more relaxing, because they don't have to think about other people.'

I wasn't entirely convinced, and Alice admitted that she, too, was often mystified. 'Maybe the idea that sex is dangerous comes from the fear of disease. Because of Covid, more and more people think, "Oh, human skin is dirty, I can get an infection."'

It is tempting to think that the national obsession with cleanliness is down to Shintoism, Japan's native religion, whose ceremonies are almost entirely concerned with purification. As travel writer Alan Booth put it in *The Roads to Sata*, Shintoists hold that 'cleanliness is not merely next to godliness, it is far and away the preferred choice'.[5]

Certainly, cleanliness, happiness and moral virtue are closely entwined in the Japanese imagination. Still, I am not convinced that modern germophobia has anything to do with Shintoism. The effort to avoid contagion by the outside world seems more like a misplaced attempt on the part of solitary, anxious individuals to resist the encroachment of anything that might lead to disorder. Novelty is fine if it just means the latest episode of *One Piece*; but the novelty of taking off your clothes and getting into bed with someone you hardly know is fraught with risk. For many people, the unpredictability of sex is part of its appeal, but in a land of control freakery it has become one more thing to be avoided.

It stands to reason that anyone who feels threatened by the proximity of other people is going to have a lousy sex life. Young people still want to fall in love, possibly even more than they want to have sex, but when reality doesn't oblige, they turn to fantasy. 'When they fall in love, everything is imagined, you know?' Alice told me. 'My students fall in love with celebrities or musicians or manga characters. There are so many stars who look like anime characters, and they feel an emotional bond with these people.'

But for most people, sexuality is bound up with physical intimacy and the touch of a fellow human, isn't it? 'Yes! But they are engaging with sex in a different way. There are so many erotic manga, anime and video games, so everything is technological. Sex is no longer body to body. It is outside the body, and they are satisfied with this. They don't want to have a hug. They don't miss this physical touch.'

One of the most distinctive features of the prevailing feminine ideal in Japan is how *kawaii* ('cute') she is. The cute cartoon character has become emblematic of modern Japan, and the legions of manga and anime fans around the world show that the *kawaii* look is striking a chord in other countries too. It might be said that by idealizing girls, manga and anime producers are ignoring women, but a generation of *otaku* (manga fans) would say that the world of girls offers adults of both genders an opportunity to escape the strictures of the grown-up, all-too-male world.

Seen in this context, the love of all things *kawaii* starts to make sense. Falling for someone who cannot reciprocate might be self-defeating, but it is predictable and safe. 'There are so many Japanese men who are sexually attracted to these *kawaii* girls,' Alice explained. 'They are never angry, so they make men feel very secure. Men who have complexes are very happy with this kind of girl. And women like *kawaii* boys – this kind of asexual man, who is not very masculine.'

Plenty of young women struggle to live up to the *kawaii* ideal and spend their lives speaking in falsetto as a result. Personally,

I found it both infuriating and mystifying, but it seemed to whip the Japanese pony into action. However, the appeal of the hyper-girl has its limits. 'When they get married, men want a different kind of girl. Of course, she still has to be *kawaii*, but she also has to cook and clean.'

Somewhere in the transition from girl to mother, a woman's sex appeal seems to go up in smoke. 'Once they get married, they see their partner not as a wife, but as a mother. So their sex drive declines, until there is no sex drive any more.' In Japan, it is very common for married couples not to have sex. A survey conducted by the Japan Family Planning Association in 2024 found that 48 per cent of married couples were sexless, which is to say they had not had sex for at least a month. This is a considerable rise from 31 per cent when the survey was first conducted in 2004.[6]

Once they have a child, many married couples either sleep in separate beds or share the marital bed with their child. The custom is common enough for there to be an expression for it: *kawa-no-ji,* or 'the character for river', so called because, with the child sleeping between the couple, the three of them look like the *kanji* for a river: 川.

Tellingly, when a survey asked men why they had stopped having sex with their wives, 12 per cent of them said they were less interested in sex after the birth of their child, and another 12 per cent said it was because they saw their spouse as an immediate family member rather than a romantic partner. However, far and away the most common reason, cited by 35 per cent of married men, was that they were 'too tired from work'.

Married women gave slightly different reasons for not having sex with their partners. Twenty per cent of them said they had lost interest in sex after giving birth, and 17 per cent blamed overwork, but the most common reason, cited by 22 per cent of respondents, was that sex was 'too much hassle'.[7] As Alice's paper intimated, *shitai kedo mendō kusai* ('I want to do it, but I can't be bothered').

This may be because once a couple is married, their expectations of love change. 'They think, "OK, my partner is 'mother' or 'father'" and they don't feel this sexual excitement,' Alice told me. 'They don't want to have a fight, or a difficult discussion. They want to be able to sit together without talking, and they would rather be silent than feel awkward.'

'So, they just want company, and someone to help around the house?' I asked.

> Yes. It's not about communication, having fun together or having sex. They want a peaceful relationship, and this is what they call 'love'. In the days of the arranged marriage, a woman had to have sex with her husband because it was considered her duty. Now she can say, 'No, I don't want to.' The problem is that women have never learned how to say 'Yes' to their sexuality. Even if she gets pleasure from sex, a woman cannot say so, because people will think that she is a slut. So she tries to suppress her sexual desires.

I wondered how much this had to do with Japanese child-rearing techniques. Though invariably attentive, caring and often extremely indulgent, I had rarely seen a mother hug or kiss her child. 'Yes, and from a Japanese point of view, it is mystifying why Europeans enjoy hugs and physical touch so much. They don't understand why Europeans want to talk about sex, relationships and love all the time either.'[8]

*

As far as the Western press is concerned, Japan has become a case study in the dangers of sexlessness. The new taxonomy of Japanese asexuality that I had learned included the terms 'parasite singles' and *hikikomori*, as well as *otaku* (obsessive fans of anime and manga) – all of whom were contributing to Japan's *sekkusu shinai shōkōgun* ('celibacy syndrome').

The new lingo is backed up by research. According to a survey conducted by Japan's NIPSSR and quoted in the *Guardian* in 2013, 61 per cent of unmarried men and 49 per cent of women aged eighteen to thirty four were not in any kind of romantic relation-ship.[9] The *Guardian* article attracted a lot of attention in Japan, where critics accused its author of manipulating the facts. They argued that, while scrutinizing Japanese people's sex lives might tit-illate salacious Westerners, there are not as many virgins in Japan as the article suggested. Half of the population loses their virginity by their early 20s, and only one in ten is still a virgin by the age of 30.[10]

It is certainly true that 'weird and wacky' Japan has been an endur-ing source of entertainment for Westerners, and the idea that the Japanese are alone in suffering a blight of celibacy has only added to the supposed mystique of their country. There is often a degree of gloating to these stories, as if 'their' sexlessness is somehow good news for 'us'; as if a country's competitiveness can be measured by the vigour of its menfolk's sperm, with every fertilized egg giving a boost to its sexual GDP. It is part of the unquestioned narrative that growth, whether economic or demographic, is inherently good, while stagnation or decline is akin to impotency.

What drives the Anglo-American press's prurient interest in Japanese sex lives? Talking to Alice, it occurred to me that perhaps Westerners are just more interested in sex than people from other cultural backgrounds. That is not to say that they have more sex, but rather that they value it more than other people do. Having been schooled in Freudian thinking, and living in the wake of the sexual liberation of the 1960s, we are brought up to believe that having sex frequently and achieving sexual satisfaction are essential parts of a healthy relationship. By this reckoning, having no sex can only be bad news.

However, even if your interest in the sex lives of the Japanese is purely demographic, the process of mass uncoupling taking place should be cause for concern. According to a survey conducted in thirty-one countries by marketing research firm Ipsos, Japan is the least satisfied nation when it comes to romantic and sexual rela-tionships. Worse still, those aged eighteen to twenty-eight had the lowest satisfaction rates: only 25 per cent were satisfied with their romantic and sexual relationships, and only 52 per cent expressed satisfaction with their relationships with partners or spouses. In both cases, their satisfaction was 10 percentage points lower than that of other generations.[11] In this sense, the Anglosphere can flatter itself that it is in better psychosexual health than Japan.

But if sexuality is a matter of personal choice, what is wrong with having less sex, or no sex at all? It might be argued that sex has always been a relatively low priority in Japan, where chastity is regarded as a virtue, and the sex act is considered base. Indeed, it could be said that sex is a relatively low priority everywhere outside the hypersexualized West, where self-esteem is closely tied to physical attractiveness, and personal worth is measured in terms of one's ability to sexually arouse other people.

For most Westerners, sex is about gratification, for oneself and one's partner. Could it be that Japanese society just doesn't value personal gratification, sexual or otherwise, as much as we do? Many Japanese would argue that Westerners are obsessed with their personal feelings, need constant reassurance and place no value on self-containment. Westerners also wilfully confuse sex with love, which makes for millions of disappointed and sexually frustrated middle-aged men and women.

Whatever the truth – and the subject is by its nature hard to research let alone measure – it's worth remembering that an active sex life has little bearing on fertility rates. Just as a couple might have sex hourly and never have children, they might have sex only three times in their entire lives and still produce three offspring. In most countries, the average adult has sex between eighty and 120 times a year. The most sexually active country in the world (if you trust people to report their sex lives truthfully) is Greece, where respondents to a survey claimed to have sex an average of 140 times a year. The country where respondents claimed to have sex least often – forty-two times a year – is Japan. Yet the fertility rates in Greece and Japan are practically the same.[12]

Besides, the declining frequency of sex can be observed in many other countries as well. In 2019, the *British Medical Journal*, surveying data from around 34,000 Britons, found that a third of men and women had not had sex in the past month.[13] The average Briton under the age of 45 went from having sex six times a month in 2001 to five times a month in 2012, and similar declines have been observed in Australia, France, Spain, the Netherlands and the United States. Data from the General Social Survey shows that, in 1990, the average American adult had sex sixty-two times a year; by 2014, this had dropped to fifty-four times.

Interestingly, the same trend has been observed among younger Americans. Over the last 30 years, the proportion of high school students who have had sex has dropped from 54 per cent to 40 per cent. In the space of a generation, sex has gone from being something most high school students have experienced to something most of them have not.[14] Less sex has gone hand in hand with a decline in coupledom. About 60 per cent of adults under the age of 35 now live without a spouse or partner and 30 per cent of them still live with their parents.

One reason for the rising number of single people in the United States is that men have become warier of approaching women. Hitting on someone in person has gone from normal behaviour to borderline creepy. In 2017, an Economist/YouGov poll found that 17 per cent of Americans aged 18 to 29 believe that a man asking a woman out for a drink 'always' or 'usually' constitutes sexual harassment.[15]

The popular perception is that the search for a partner has simply moved online, but the data suggests that online dating is not an effective way of finding someone to have sex with, let alone a lasting relationship. According to Tinder, the average user logs into their account eleven times a day and spends a total of about an hour and a half a day using the app. What do they get in return? Tinder says it logs 1.6 billion swipes a day, but only 26 million matches – and most matches don't lead to a two-way text exchange, much less a date.[16]

Once you start comparing Japan with other countries in the rich world, it becomes clear that the declining frequency of sex and the rising number of singletons are symptoms of a broader withdrawal from all forms of in-person socializing. As in Japan, not only has the percentage of teens who report going on dates gone down, but so too has the percentage who report taking part in other activities associated with crossing the threshold between childhood and adulthood.

This certainly chimes with my own experience. When I was a teenager, anyone who didn't have a driver's licence and a badly paid job by the time they were 18 was considered to still be a kid. If you hadn't drunk yourself into a stupor and lost your virginity by then, you were derided as 'square'. These days, being a nerd has become cool and no one even uses the word 'square'.

The rise of the nerd may be down to parents' increased anxiety about their children's educational and economic prospects. Rates of anxiety and depression among Americans have been rising for decades and in recent years they have risen sharply among people in their teens and 20s as well.[17] Many of them have absorbed the idea that fun, play, sex and love are secondary to academic and professional success, or, at any rate, best delayed until they have been secured.

Whether this is a cause or a consequence of the great uncoupling underway is a moot point, but it points to one of the fundamental contradictions of our time. We live in an age of unprecedented physical safety, with crime rates down across the board in rich countries, yet for growing numbers of people, something about twenty-first-century life is triggering autonomic responses associated with danger: anxiety, constant scanning of our surroundings and fitful sleep. Whatever the root cause of this collective restlessness, we are learning that the human sex drive is more fragile and more easily stalled than we once thought.

*

After my meeting with Alice, I took a train from Jiyūgaoka back to Shibuya and waited for the next Yamanote line train to Ueno. Up on the platform, the massed ranks of commuters were standing in line, their faces expressive of stoicism and sometimes quiet fretfulness. The train came barrelling down the long, straight track, right on time.

The Yamanote line is Tokyo's version of London Underground's Circle line, and we travelled in an arc through the north of the city. It was the late afternoon of another beautifully clear, still day, and golden winter light was streaming through the windows of the carriage. Looking out of the window, the tightly packed neighbourhoods reminded me of toytown. All the buildings were of roughly the same age and made of the same concrete, steel and glass. Although they were not old or badly made, they looked insubstantial, as though they could all be taken down overnight if the people who lived in them ever had to leave in a hurry. Racing through the vastness of the city, with its towers and apartment blocks, Mount Fuji is a rare sight, but on that day I could see the sacred mountain, covered in snow, far off to the south-west of the city.

The train pulled into Sugamo, a neighbourhood renowned for its elderly population. The streets were spotless, and some of them were cobbled, like in a pastiche of a Californian town that is pretending to be Mediterranean. From a distance, the pedestrians looked like the little people that architects put on their models to help you imagine what it would look like in real life, the old women with their bandy legs and funny granny smocks, and the younger ones in the shapeless tunics they wear to hide the shape of their bodies. Walking the city's streets, I had often found them to be eerily quiet, even when they were crowded. Perhaps that was because so many people walked alone.

We headed east and then south to Ueno and passed Yanaka cemetery. I wondered how many of the apartment blocks we were racing past were home to *hikikomori* like Sōichiro. Judging by their size, they could only have been built for one occupant. They looked deserted. They weren't, of course, but the windows were invariably frosted and had lace curtains behind them, so it was impossible to see what was going on inside. I thought about the many lives we were passing by. Living alone is expensive. In the UK, the Good Housekeeping Institute published a study that found living alone typically costs £2,000 a year more per head than living with someone else.[18]

Naturally, this makes people who live alone less able to save, which only heightens their vulnerability later in life.

Environmentalists should also be concerned by the growing number of people choosing to live alone. It's not just a question of stocking a fridge for one and throwing half of it in the bin at the end of the week. More solo households means more apartments, and that means more fridges, boilers, cookers, small appliances, flatpack furniture, foldable goods and all the other products a household requires.

That might be good news for manufacturers, retailers and service providers, but it is incredibly wasteful, for, like the buildings, their contents are not made to last. Modern Japan is furnished in beige and white chipboard, hardboard and laminated plastic by the retail giant Nitori. Entire cities are furnished with its interiors, shipped over from China. They are used for a couple of years, before being put out for the binmen and incinerated at high temperatures.

This mass wastefulness is not entirely thoughtless, though: once Tokyo's rubbish has been reduced to ashes, they are raked out of the incinerator and compressed to make setts for the city's streets. It was strange to think that those Californian-Mediterranean cobbles may well have been someone's bed not so long ago.

I shook these thoughts away. It was a very pleasant atmosphere on the train. The carriage was wonderfully clean and peaceful, and although it was crowded, no one seemed to mind. When I lived in Tokyo in the early 1990s, the commuters I saw on the Yamanote line were usually asleep. Now they spent the journey playing solitaire, Candy Crush or Sudoku on their phones. As we neared Ueno, the carriage grew more crowded and I found myself peering over the shoulder of a woman who was frantically scrolling through the pages of an online shopping catalogue.

As well as being astonishingly clean, Tokyo's trains are remarkable for the preponderance of adverts. They were everywhere: above the carriage doors, on the doors themselves, just above eye level over the windows, even hanging mid carriage, like the *noren* curtain that hangs over the entrance to a restaurant. In a typical

Japanese advert, the face is dominant and much less importance is attached to the text. It was unnerving to be surrounded by so many inscrutable passengers, who never looked at one another, and all the young, female faces in the ads, commanding you to stare.

Some affected the bored, pretty look you get accustomed to seeing in the West, but most were going for something altogether more wholesome. Many of the adverts' images and text related to the fulfilment of dreams, wishes and hopes. Among them were a lot of ads for salons offering the removal of women's pubic hair, which put me in mind of what Alice had told me about the obsession with presenting a hairless, supposedly 'clean', but somehow not-quite-human body.

I did not see anyone doing what I was doing: looking around the carriage, wondering about my fellow passengers. Wondering – isn't that part and parcel of eroticism? But there was nothing erotic about the atmosphere on the Yamanote line train. No one made a hobby of catching the eye of a good-looking stranger, and few of them flaunted their physical charms. I was put in mind of what the Hungarian-born writer and humourist George Mikes wrote of the English in 1946: 'Continental people have sex lives; the English have hot-water bottles.'[19]

Being sexy has always been a risk for Japanese women. I remembered sitting opposite a good-looking young woman in a mini skirt on a Yamanote line train back in the 1990s (this was before the girl-ish *kawaii* aesthetic conquered the popular imagination). Anywhere else, she would have been the object of desire, envy or admiration from the other passengers. In Tokyo, she was an object of scorn: the young men, the older *salarimen* and the middle-aged housewives all looked at her as if she were a prostitute. I could see why so many women went around in loose-fitting dresses that reached from their necklines to their ankles.

6.

Super Dry: The Sex Lives of Solitary Singletons

Although my precarious finances dictated that I should live in Matsudo, Ueno had been my stomping ground when I lived in Yanaka in the early 1990s and it was still my favourite part of the city. From the station, I walked to Shinobazu Pond, which would be covered in lotuses come the summer, and then up the gentle hill that rises through the trees of Ueno Park to the museums. From there, I crossed the park to its eastern edge, where it meets the tracks of the Yamanote line and followed them north to Yanaka cemetery.

I remembered that on hot summer nights I would often watch the trains screeching and scraping their way along the tracks on their way to and from Ueno station. The summer heat was always quite oppressive, trapping people in their homes. All living things suffered in the heat: the city's dogs and cats no less than its people. I remembered how the sound of the first cicadas of the year would come whirring from the trees overhead. The racket they made was always impressive, but it was only on the rare occasions that I found myself in the open green space of a park that I was able to hear them *en masse*. Their buzzing put me in mind of thousands of spinning metallic discs, picking up speed until the noise filled the air, before gradually slowing down again. It reminded me that, despite the city planners' best efforts to extinguish all traces of its natural state, Tokyo was once a jungle.

Perhaps because Ueno is one of the city's biggest termini and serves Tōhoku, the poorer north-eastern part of the country, the neighbourhood south of the park is not very flashy. After the war, a black market sprang up under the tracks. It was called Ameyokochō – 'America street' – because the goods were all from the US. Although the contraband is long gone and the *yakuza* are harder to spot than ever, a lot of American clothes are still sold in Ueno, and there is still an illicit air about the place.

There were foreigners about – not the embassy and corporate types of Roppongi or the tourists of Shibuya and Shinjuku, but other Asians: Chinese, Filipinos, Koreans and Thai. Like me, they came to Ameyokochō to do their shopping, for the narrow streets on either side of the elevated railway lines were crowded with shops selling imported food and drink. Scanning the faces, I got a glimpse of the embryonic multicultural society taking shape in post-growth Japan.

I ducked under the *noren* curtain of a *tonkatsu* restaurant on the main road heading north towards Senju. In the early days of my time in Tokyo, I would often go there before attending a Meetup at the British pub. It was a quiet place, run by a kindly old waitress and an old chef, who hardly said a word and would look at me with quiet alarm whenever I came in.

While he cooked my breaded pork cutlet, I picked up a copy of a free monthly magazine called *Shokuba no kyōyō* ('Workplace Culture') from the counter. It was like a parish newsletter, with a moralizing anecdote for every day of the month ahead, and was full of lyrical portraits of selfless workmates, tips on the importance of teamwork and cautionary tales about cocky young office workers who didn't listen to their superiors' advice. I read it for want of anything more interesting, but it was good reading practice.

After my *tonkatsu*, I walked back towards the railway tracks, and was soon in Uguisudani, a warren of dog-legged alleyways just north of Ueno. The name means 'nightingale valley', not that there was a blade of grass, much less a bird, to be seen. It had the same down-at-heel flavour of the post-war years as Ameyokochō and was known for its love hotels.

Love hotels rent rooms by the hour, but they are not brothels. Rather, they appeal to couples with nowhere else to go to have sex. The original Hotel Love opened in Osaka in 1968. For the post-war generation, they were a godsend, as most of the houses built after the war were so small that married couples used their bedroom as a living room during the daytime and shared it with their children at night. With privacy so hard to come by, they took to frequenting love hotels, and their kids, when they came of age, used them for their dalliances as well.

I had used them a few times myself back in the 1990s, and had always marvelled at how discreet they were. The entrance was usually hidden behind a wall, and the receptionist would hand me my room key from behind a frosted glass screen. I remembered passing the car park of a love hotel in Uguisudani and seeing a uniformed member of staff unobtrusively hang a small velvet curtain over the number plate of a car, so that its owner could not be identified. This kind of pragmatic, non-judgemental attitude to other people's love lives was particularly refreshing after the finger-wagging prudery that characterized life in Margaret Thatcher's Britain.

Until recently, the annual revenue generated by Japan's love hotels was staggering. As late as 2004, they were raking in an estimated $40 billion a year, accounting for nearly 1 per cent of Japan's entire GDP.[1] One journalist calculated that of the 1.26 billion acts of sexual intercourse that took place in Japan each year, half took place in love hotels.[2] Such a bacchanal contrasts markedly with the mass abstinence of today. Partly because the number of Japanese people in their 20s has fallen by more than a third over the last twenty years, and partly because fewer of them than ever are having sex, the number of love hotels in Japan has fallen from 38,000 in 2013 to just 7,000 in 2023.[3]

Faced with this unprecedented drop in demand, many love hotels have rebranded themselves as boutique hotels, hoping to capitalize on the boom in foreign visitors to Japan. They have introduced English-speaking staff and connected their reservation systems to online travel sites like booking.com. To cater to the altogether more wholesome tastes of tourists, the revolving beds and mirrored ceilings have gone out of the window, and hotels that only a few years ago were selling sex toys in vending machines now offer hot-stone spas, craft beer and curry rice.

★

The notion that the West has had a hand in reshaping Japan's love life doesn't just come from the disappearance of love hotels. Every Valentine's Day for the last ten years, the Revolutionary League of Unwanted Men has been demonstrating in Shibuya in protest at what it calls *renai shihonshugi* ('love capitalism'). Like most holidays imported from the West, Valentine's Day started out as an attempt to get consumers to part with their cash. Department stores encouraged shoppers to buy chocolate for their partners on Valentine's Day, and the holiday gradually became more popular until today it accounts for half of Japanese confectionery companies' annual sales.[4]

The Revolutionary League of Unwanted Men hates Valentine's Day. It says that, by commercializing love, the press and the department stores encourage young women to only value men who spend money on them. In the process, they have turned romance into a luxury that only those in regular, full-time work can afford.

As I'd learned from conversations with my students in Otemachi, many Japanese women have old-fashioned expectations when it comes to men, principally that they be high earners with good prospects. Unfortunately, with so many young men doing part-time work for low pay, few of them measure up, and the consequences of this mismatch are now starting to show. Among men aged 25–39, those on the lowest incomes are ten to twenty times more likely to be virgins than those on the highest incomes.[5] So, while the young men of suburbs like Matsudo might be into gaming, that's not because they like games more than they like women. It's because they can't find a girlfriend.

And yet the League's critique of modern love seems to have contradictory impulses. On the one hand, its members feel disappointed that having a job is no longer enough to get them girlfriends; on the other, they resent women for treating their partners as cash cows. Who is to blame – women, or the corporations that run the consumer economy? Either way, the League says, *'kekkon shitara makeru'* ('if you get married, you're bound to lose out').

The Revolutionary League of Unwanted Men is not alone in

taking aim at modern love. Feminist sociologist Chizuko Ueno has described the Western ideal of romantic love as being akin to an invasive species, intent on wiping out the native variants of love.[6] After the war, the Western way of romance was promoted as a key part of a sophisticated, modern family life. Ueno argues that it was only able to take root in Japan amid the consumerist fantasies that flourished when the economy was growing. It might have been cast as a hip, new-fangled alternative to the emotional ties that bound the traditional extended family, but it only became so highly esteemed in the absence of other connections. Romance was effectively a luxury good for an age of rampant individualism and a fetish for the domestically and economically self-sufficient. Worse, it had corroded the nobler emotional bonds – filial piety, class solidarity and regional identity – that had held Japanese society together for millennia.

Stories in the Japanese press often blame the dwindling frisson between young men and women on a new generation of so-called *sōshoku danshi* ('herbivorous men'). The term was coined by marketing researcher Megumi Ushikubo to describe young men who are more interested in fashion and home life than securing promotion at work or bagging a trophy wife. By her reckoning, this younger generation of 'grass-eating' men is not just more passive and domesticated, but more feminine. They enjoy spending close and intimate time with female friends but show no sign of the assertiveness towards women that she considers 'normal' for 'carnivorous' men.

Sociologist Masahiro Morioka is more sympathetic. He is the author of *Sōshoku-kei danshi no ren'ai-gaku* ('love-ology for the herbivorous man'), a self-help book for passive, socially withdrawn and romantically hapless men. 'In male culture prior to the present, there was a concept that the manly way to do things was precisely to doggedly advance on women, even if they resisted a bit,' he writes. 'The idea was that women might dislike it at first, but that was just a pose; eventually, they would accept the man.'[7] Morioka argues that while the herbivorous man rejects the idea of sex as conquest, his distinguishing feature is not his femininity but his tenderness, which compels him to seek communication and intimacy before he has sex with a woman.

★

If growing numbers of young men can't afford to invite a woman out on a date, believe that romance is a con or are too shy to find a partner, what are they doing for sexual pleasure? I found clues on my walks around Ueno. Unlike the first time I lived in Tokyo, the city was now full of 100-yen shops. One of the most widespread of these cheap new emporiums is Don Quijote, the Japanese version of Poundland. Known to its fans as *donki*, it sells practically everything, including an awful lot of *otona no omocha* ('adult toys').

As sales of condoms have fallen, those of sex toys, which include plenty of male masturbation devices, have risen. It may well be that, in the future, consumer tech companies come up with devices that offer immersive sexual experiences that no woman could ever offer. For now, however, the most enticing toy on offer in Don Quijote was the 'single-use silicon egg' that men were invited to 'fill with lubricant and masturbate inside'.

Part of the explanation for the decoupling of sexual pleasure from other people must lie in the rise of online pornography, which has made solitary sexual gratification easier and more immediate for anyone with an internet connection. Pornhub, the most popular porn site in the world, received an average of 10.8 billion visits per month in 2024.[8]

There is nothing new about masturbating, of course. Even in 1953, almost two-thirds of women admitted to masturbating. However, the internet has made fantasising about sex a lot easier. In a survey conducted in 2008, nine out of ten female respondents admitted to masturbating, and two-thirds of them said they did it 'up to three times a week'.[9] Of course, the rise may be down to masturbating no longer being a taboo, and more women being willing to admit to doing it.

In 2017, Simon Louis Lajeunesse, a professor at Montreal University, tried to make a study of American men in their 20s who had never used pornography. He had to give up because, he said, 'We couldn't find any.' Is the ubiquity of online porn having a detrimental impact on men's sex lives? Professor Lajeunesse, for one, doesn't think so. 'All of our test subjects said they supported gender equality and that they felt victimized by rhetoric demonizing pornography,' he told the *Daily Mail*. 'Pornography hasn't changed their perception of women or their relationships, which they all want to be as harmonious and fulfilling as possible.'[10]

Be that as it may, people are susceptible to the norms that online porn perpetuates. Most of the videos on mainstream porn sites suggest that the only way to give a woman sexual pleasure is by penetrating her; that a man should lead and a woman should follow; and that, when push comes to shove, women like being shoved. Once sex becomes pornographic, partners become performers, and this can be distracting. After acting in one too many bad films, plenty of performers turn their back on the profession altogether.

The fear that online porn is having a negative impact on people's sex lives is the inspiration for the American far-right group the Proud Boys' 'no wanks' policy, which prohibits its members from masturbating more than once a month. The group's founder, Gavin McInnes, who also co-founded Vice Media, has said that masturbating to online pornography is making millennials 'not even want to pursue relationships'.[11]

Surveying the shelves of adult toys in Don Quijote, I wondered: has ready access to online porn really made people less inclined to go out and find real-life partners? If so, perhaps the real problem is not the ubiquity of porn, but the growing number of people who equate having a partner with sexual relief. If that is all you're looking for, masturbating to online porn may well be a better bet than trying to build an intimate relationship with another human. People have always wanted personal validation from their relationships, but in an individualistic age in which narcissism has gone mainstream, the only relationship likely to deliver lasting satisfaction is the one you have with your butler. In the absence of willing servants, many narcissists see relationships as more trouble than they are worth.

Leaving Don Quijote and wandering the backstreets of Ueno, I soon stumbled across another clue to Japan's post-human sex life: the Orient Industries sex doll showroom. The salesman was delighted to see me. A short, stocky man with twinkling eyes, he ushered me in and proceeded to give me a guided tour of the place. 'Love dolls tend to be shorter than a real-life woman,' he said, gesturing towards a row of headless torsos hanging from the ceiling. 'And they are certainly lighter. This one weighs about 35 kilograms,' he said, sliding his arm around the waist of one of the dolls. 'Her joints are made of metal and can be moved to the desired position,' he said, respectfully twisting the doll's arm in a 180-degree arc.

'And since the head is detachable, you can change her face whenever you like.' I followed him to a floor-to-ceiling shelving unit stacked with rows of incredibly lifelike heads. Peering into their eyes was an uncomfortable experience, but perhaps it shouldn't have been. After all, sex dolls are hardly a recent invention, and if I had been looking at these dolls' foremothers in a museum, I may well have found them quaint. In the sixteenth century, French and Spanish sailors would fashion a large cloth doll and stuff it with old clothes to help ease the loneliness they felt on long voyages. During the Rangaku period, the Dutch sold some of these *dames de voyage* or *damas de viaje* to men in Nagasaki, and older Japanese still use the term 'Dutch wife' to refer to a sex doll.[12]

Their contemporary incarnations are much more advanced. The salesman invited me to touch the skin of one of the dolls. It was made of silicon and felt unnervingly cold. 'Chinese manufacturers have been developing thermoplastic elastomer dolls,' he intoned gravely. 'It's a new material that has become popular over the last ten years. They say it feels more like a woman's skin, but it has the drawback of being easily ripped.'

'We also stock the CybOrgasMatrix,' he went on, 'which comes equipped with a pelvic thruster motor, audio capability and a heated orifice.' I had to admire his sales patter; there was nothing lewd or suggestive about it, no acknowledgement of the loneliness or desperation driving his customers through the door. 'Sex dolls are expected to stand in for the missing humans, but there are limits to what they can do for you.' Fellatio is difficult, I was told, because designers have struggled to create a mouth that will open wide and then return to its original position.

A realistic sex doll costs ¥500,000–600,000 (£2,512–3,015). 'We see a lot of demand for second-hand dolls among those unwilling to shell out for a new one,' said the salesman, 'which is why we made the vagina detachable.' He showed me a cabinet stocked with rows of replacement vaginas. Since coming back to Japan, I had noticed that there was now a market for second-hand goods, which I took to be a sign of the straitened times. I would have thought that, like used underwear, there would be no demand for second-hand sex dolls. Apparently, there was. Next to the replacement vaginas was a display of pubic hair – customers could choose long hair or short, depending on their preference – and there were also three varieties of nipple to choose from.

It's easy to write off men who use sex dolls as misogynists, but a clinical case study indicates that not all of them regard their dolls solely as a means of sexual gratification. Some see them as good company, others as objects to cuddle and take photos with; some men even refer to them as their partners. One man told a researcher that his doll had helped him to 'overcome the trauma I suffered after my divorce and get ready to approach a real woman again'.[13]

A review from a satisfied customer on Orient Industry's Amazon page reads:

Feeling loneliness, and a sense of despair about life, I bought this love doll when I was about to die. I will never forget the excitement I felt when I visited the showroom for the first time. Very kind and angelic dolls were lined up. I thought, 'Is this heaven?' That day, a very cute doll with a gentle expression came to my house. Since then, my mental health has recovered little by little, and now I am happy every day!

The salesman said that a lot of his younger customers asked about recycling facilities. Were sex dolls difficult to recycle? I asked him. 'Oh yes. We've had several cases of passers-by mistaking a discarded sex doll for a corpse,' he said. 'We've also had complaints from customers about the time and effort it took them to cut a sex doll into pieces small enough to fit into a household wastebin.'

'So we introduced a service whereby, for a fee, we will come and collect unwanted love dolls.' He led me into the last part of the salesroom, an exhibition of photographs of Shinto priests leading 'separation prayers' for sex dolls at the local shrine. Perhaps I shouldn't have been surprised; after all, Shintoism does not regard human souls as superior to those of any other being, whether animate or inanimate. Shinto priests have been invited to bless industrial robots before they go into service, and at Sensō-ji temple in Asakusa funeral ceremonies have even been conducted for leather workers' needles. When they become blunt and can no longer be used, they are placed in a giant block of tofu in the belief that its softness will please them at the end of working lives spent piercing animal hides.

★

Most sex-doll users are lonely old men, who tend to be burdened with feelings of shame. However, a new generation of single men are wearing their loneliness as a badge of courage, and coming out of the closet with their love of their humanoid sex partners. David Levy, a leading figure in artificial intelligence, is on the Holy Grail to create a robot that is able to 'do things to its user, as well as have things done to it'. The 'sexbot' he is working on is said to be a realistic robot sex partner, made of metal, rubber and resin.

At the International Conference on Love and Sex with Robots held at Goldsmiths College, University of London in 2016, Levy predicted that, 'In the next 10 years, it is perfectly achievable in software to create a robot companion that is everything that people might want in a spouse – patient, kind, loving, trusting, respectful and uncomplaining.'[14] Levy said that he was looking forward to the day when he would be able to marry his sexbot, speculating that this would come some time around 2050.

Human beings are suggestible enough to be able to replicate the sexual experience, and a sex robot is not a million miles away from staring at a pin-up. What marks out developments in Japan is that technology is being dragooned into simulating not just sex, but human intimacy. In 2010, the virtual girlfriend became a reality of sorts when games maker Konami released the second generation of its popular *Love Plus* dating game for the Nintendo DS gaming system. The game's facial recognition technology allows its user exclusive access to their own personalized imaginary girlfriend, at least on their own device.

The following year, Konami arranged a weekend of romantic bliss for *Love Plus* gamers and their virtual girlfriends in Atami, a beach-resort town an hour south of Tokyo. The event was a great success, with local business owners reporting their best weekend's profits in decades. When a journalist asked one gamer to explain why so many young men were opting for virtual girlfriends, the gamer speculated that, 'Maybe we're just advanced human beings who have learned how to service ourselves.'[15] Ironically, in the days when most young men dated young women, Atami was a popular spot for a weekend getaway. But it seems that, in solitary post-growth Japan, an intimate relationship with another person has become just another obstacle standing in the way of complete personal autonomy.

Another singleton blazing a trail where more timid souls fear to tread is Akihiro Kondo, a local government employee living in suburban Tokyo. In 2018, he made headlines when he married the Gatebox version of a popular anime character called Hatsune Miku. Gatebox is a device you install in your home that generates a little hologram of your favourite animated character.

Kondo turned to AI as an escape from depression and loneliness. He used to work as a clerk at public elementary and junior high schools, but after four years on the job he began to be bullied. Two female colleagues would call him 'gross' when he spoke to them, and would not have anything to do with him. This left him depressed, and he became unable to eat. After a doctor diagnosed him with an adjustment disorder, he was forced to take time off work. 'I stayed in my room for 24 hours a day, and watched videos of Miku the whole time,' he recalled.

Discovering Hatsune Miku has helped him to recover his mojo. When he wakes up, the hologram tells him the weather forecast, and if it's going to rain, she reminds him to take an umbrella. While he's at work, Hatsune Miku sends him text messages telling him how much she misses him, and if he texts her before he leaves the office, she will make sure the lights are on and the flat is nice and warm by the time he gets home.[16]

Kondo says that he talks to his new 'wife' as if she were a real person. While he acknowledges that he can't touch her, he calls this 'a technical issue that I hope will be resolved at some point in the future'. In the meantime, he has to make do with a cuddly-toy version of Miku that he keeps as a mute twin to the rather chattier virtual version. It was not a legally recognized wedding, but the manufacturers were happy to issue him with a wedding certificate (indeed, they had already issued 3,700 such certificates to other Gatebox users).

'There are two reasons why I had a wedding publicly,' Kondo told reporters. 'The first is to prove my love to Miku. The second is there are many young *otaku* people like me falling in love with anime characters and I want to show the world that I support them.' To those worried about AI luring people into a fantasy world he says, 'It's not that people can't live in society because they're engrossed in a two-dimensional world. Rather, there are cases where people become captivated as they search for a place for themselves in video games and anime, because reality is too painful for them. I was one of those people.'[17]

Kondo says he cannot imagine having a relationship with a real-life woman and considers himself part of 'a sexual minority'. His message to young singletons is that virtual sex is destined to become the new frontier in the struggle for liberation from outdated social norms like monogamy, marriage and childbearing. Being expected to conform to them was fine in the days when they were within reach, but for more people than ever, they have become neither realistic nor desirable.

Kondo's defiant stance is invested with all the righteousness of one who believes he is at the vanguard of progressive social change. People are taking their lead from campaigns for gay and transgender rights and demanding the right to express their desires without shame. If they believe those desires are better serviced by an avatar, which can be turned on and off with the flick of a switch, than by a real-life human being, who has the right to tell them otherwise?

★

Gentle winter rain trickled down the window. I had been distracted by the rain through several seasons now, and had weathered my fair share of boring days largely spent staring out of the window. But what one person feels imprisoned by, another learns to cherish. Appreciation of fleeting beauty – *mono no aware* – is the most highly valued variety of aesthetic pleasure in Japan. The Japanese know better than to go chasing after the last petals of the season's *sakura* blossom. Once they're gone, they're gone – at least until another season has had its way with our ever-changing, all-too-human moods.

Such was the life I settled into. I kept up my job teaching English to office workers in the windowless basement in Otemachi, and spent two weeks of every month researching and writing articles for the online news magazine. After several seasons struggling to acclimatise to life in Japan, I'd come to the conclusion that Matsudo was remarkably similar to my own country and much of the time I was bored by the life I had fallen into. But even sitting in a convenience store in an anonymous suburb of drab-looking new-builds, there was enough that was new and strange to keep me guessing.

When it all got too much, I had a long soak in the baths at the nearest *sento*. One of my students told me that there were three things that all Japanese people liked: Mount Fuji, the springtime ritual of picnicking under the cherry blossom and *onsen*. The simple pleasure of sitting in hot water is one that Japanese people have enjoyed for millennia. When the country urbanized, its natural hot springs were recreated in its towns and cities by artificially heating water to create *sento*. Public bathhouses remain at the heart of many of Tokyo's older neighbourhoods; indeed, they are one of the few material remnants of old Tokyo to have survived into the modern era.

Sitting in the bath had been one of my favourite things to do when I lived in Yanaka. The blood rushes to the surface of the skin in hot water and retreats in cold water, and after taking alternate soaks in the hot and cold baths, I would feel a strange mix of dissolution and fortification, as if my internal heating system had been recalibrated. Even when it was snowing outside, I would walk home from the *sento* in my dressing gown, one lone straggler among many, glowing from the inside out.

Since the bathhouse I used to frequent had been knocked down to make way for flats, I became a wandering bather, cycling around the city in search of the ideal soaking spot. There I would sit in silence in a huge hot bath with the men of the neighbourhood, listening to the conversation of the women on the other side of the partition wall. There was no talking in the men's *sento*, just communal enjoyment of the calm that comes with a long soak. It was nice to be in the company of strangers without feeling the need to talk to one another. It was the closest I came to Zen Buddhism, with its disdain for spoken communication and its love of silence.

It was in those moments of bathhouse stillness that I liked Japan best. Relaxing in the hot water, it struck me that, since arriving, I had not seen anyone shrug, roll their eyes skyward or curl their lip. They just didn't do the casual disdain or long-suffering exasperation that many British people consider normal. Since coming back, I had found the pace of life in Tokyo surprisingly relaxed, and certainly less frenetic than London. Not understanding the language well enough to know what was on TV or what the people around me were talking about, I was blind to current affairs. I would read about Trump, terrorism and immigration in the online news every morning, knowing that I would encounter nothing to remind me of what was going on outside Japan for the rest of the day.

Listening to the women talking on the other side of the partition wall, I often wondered about the mixed bath houses that had prevailed in the Edo period. Shortly after my meeting with Alice Pacher, she had put me in touch with Maki Hirayama, a sociology professor at Meiji University who has written about the history of sex and the family in Japan. I remembered something that Maki had said about attitudes to nakedness. 'The first Westerners to visit Japan thought the Japanese people were very unusual, or like barbarians.' Schooled in Christian distaste for the human body, they were shocked to see ordinary people going almost naked on the street, and men and women bathing together. 'The Meiji government was afraid, so they quickly banned habits that foreigners found distasteful,' she said.

One of those habits was dressing in loincloths. An ordinance admitted that while 'this is the general custom, and is not to be despised among ourselves, in foreign countries it is looked on with great contempt. You should therefore consider it a great shame.'[18] Japan's leaders had shifted their own discomfort at being looked down on by 'civilized' foreigners onto their own people.

Many of the reforms the Meiji government introduced thereafter were inspired by the prurience of Western missionaries. Another habit that had foreigners aghast was mixed bathing. It certainly sounds oddly bacchanalian for a society as obsessed with orderliness as Edo. 'I suppose the men got used to bathing with naked women, so the sight of naked women didn't stimulate them so much,' Maki said by way of explanation. 'Think about sumo wrestlers. No one feels that they are sexual, even though they only wear loincloths.' I was confused. Attitudes to public nudity in modern Japan seemed less liberal than in the West, yet whenever I had asked why, I was told that it was because of the impact of Western prudery. It seemed contradictory. This elicited a peal of shrill laughter from Maki. 'It is quite complicated,' she admitted.

*

Coming back to the share house from the *sento* one day, I saw three plump pigeons sitting on the fence that divided our building from the neighbouring one. I had often seen them squabbling in the branches of the trees that ran down one side of the block, where they had their nests. Like me, they were wondering where all the trees had gone. A crew of tree surgeons had come by the previous morning; I'd assumed they were only going to prune the trees, but they had clearly cut them down.

The vandals must all have been over 65. One of them had had bandy legs, a sign of calcium deficiency as a child perhaps, and walked with a pronounced limp. I had pictured him limping into the modern world from the post-war years, when a whole generation of Japanese children had grown up undernourished. 'Cold this morning, isn't it?' he'd said with a mild, good-natured smile. His face had a blameless look, and there was something incongruous about watching this crew of kindly Buddhist-cum-Shintoists take up their chainsaws.

I couldn't imagine why the management had decided to do it. As well as making it easier to forget the bland functionality of suburbs like Matsudo, the trees had given the yard some privacy. Now they were gone, it was certainly a lot lighter, not only during the day, but at night as well, because the glare of the security lights on the stairwells of the neighbouring building were no longer blocked out by foliage. Instead, we had an unobstructed view of our nondescript neighbour, with its pristine painted concrete, metal fencing and plastic fascia boards.

That evening, I ran into one of my housemates. Tadi was keen to talk about what the tree surgeons had done. 'Without trees, there is nowhere to rest,' he said. He pointed out that the kanji for 'rest' – 休 – is a combination of the character for human – 人 – and the character for tree – 木. 'The same connection can be seen in the English word "forest" – "for rest",' he conjectured earnestly. It was such a pretty misunderstanding that I didn't have the heart to put him right.

Tadi was one of the few people in the building I'd got to know. Like Sachiko, he was middle-aged and unmarried. He had a thin, nervous voice and in his bearing he was even more modest than most. But he had none of the introverted shyness of the other residents in the building and, given half a chance, he would talk until the cows came home. Over dinner and drinks at a ramen place near Matsudo station, he told me that he was so disgusted by our landlord's wanton vandalism that he had decided to move out.

Not for the first time, Tadi was between jobs. Quitting his last job as a *yakitori* chef had been his declaration of independence, he told me. Apart from the odd weekend spent fishing in Chiba, and a night practising his swing at the local driving range, he seemed to have spent the past month in front of the TV. Now, a former employer was offering him work in his factory making car parts. The conditions were good, he said – no obligatory overtime – and, best of all, the factory was surrounded by trees.

We switched from beer to sake, and Tadi started ranting about the communists and the corruption of the LDP. 'Better we revert to the old days when people and power were bound by trust, and the emperor ruled without recourse to the politicians,' he said grandly. 'Corruption is an inherent part of democracy.' A hotchpotch of conspiracy theories was swilling around his fevered mind, with Koreans a recurring theme: how many of them had come to Japan after World War Two; their malicious influence; and how the emperor protected them, because he too was of distant Korean ancestry.

In search of solid ground, I asked Tadi about his family. It transpired that they had once had a business making soy sauce but had been driven into bankruptcy by 'the democrats' during the years of Taisho democracy in the early twentieth century. Years later, his father had had a construction business, building roads for the prefectural government in Tochigi. But he had been ripped off by his business partner, an uncle for whom Tadi had nothing but scorn. Draining the last of the sake, he let out a long sigh. 'Japanese people are weak. They only think about material things. That is why Japanese families are always arguing.'

He told me about the novel he was trying to write. 'It is about upper-class university graduates and the way they dominate the job market.' This was his cue for an analysis of the ants and the bees of the world economy, the 'lazy' Italians, who, he said, seemed to have the right idea, and the 'industrious' Japanese, who were a nation of dupes, still working like dogs long after the country had made its money.

I agreed it made no sense. Fifty years after Japan's fertility rate first dropped below replacement level, its workforce is shrinking, and every sector of the economy is beset by labour shortages. If there was ever a time when workers could afford to stick their necks out, it is now, when their value to employers is at an all-time high. But Japan's trade unions lost their teeth half a century ago and collective action seems impossible, given that people are out of the habit of organizing in the workplace, and lead ever more atomized lives.

*

Perhaps it was Tadi's decision to move out of the share house that inspired me to get out, too. After three years tethered to my desk in Tokyo, I felt the need for some wilderness. I was tired of the capital, which the pandemic had only made more solitary and subdued. Some weekends, I would take a train from Shinjuku to the western edge of the city and hike up the first mountain I came to. From the ridgeline of Mount Takao, I would look wonderingly across the expanse of empty, forested mountains to the west. Then I would turn around and head back down to face the megacity again.

This time, I told myself, I would keep going and really immerse myself in Japan's mountain landscapes. It was hard to believe, holed up in the metropolis, but mountains, including hilly terrain, account for about three-quarters of the country's total land area. Without a car they are hard to access, for they are generally steep and covered with forests; two-thirds of Japan is covered in trees, making it one of the most forested countries in the world.

Travelling in rural Japan wasn't just an escape – it was a crucial part of my research. My time in Tokyo had given me precious insights into the origins of Japan's demographic problems, but I knew that to see the sharp end of its reproduction crisis I would have to venture into the countryside. Between 2000 and 2005 alone the number of people living in small towns and villages across Japan had fallen by 10 million.[19] The older ones had aged and died, and the rest, who tended to be young, had moved to the cities. As a consequence, as of 2022, 85 per cent of Japan's municipalities have a shrinking population, and the Japan Policy Council says that nearly half of them are 'at risk of extinction' by 2040.[20]

I also wanted to see the folksier, earthier side of Japan. I knew it was out there somewhere, and sensed that it would be an antidote to the highly regulated, sanitized life I was living in Tokyo. Before I left, I went to the city's largest bookshop to look for a book about the nature of Japan. I wanted to find out more about its rivers and mountains, wild animals and plants. It was nigh-on impossible to find one. The English-language section had plenty of guidebooks, but they all focussed on Japanese culture – its Buddhist temples and kimono-clad geisha, neon-lit maid cafés and fantastical manga characters. The only book that might give me a sense of what Japan was like before the humans showed up was Mark Brazil's *Japan: The Natural History of an Asian Archipelago*. I bought a copy and went home to research my trip.

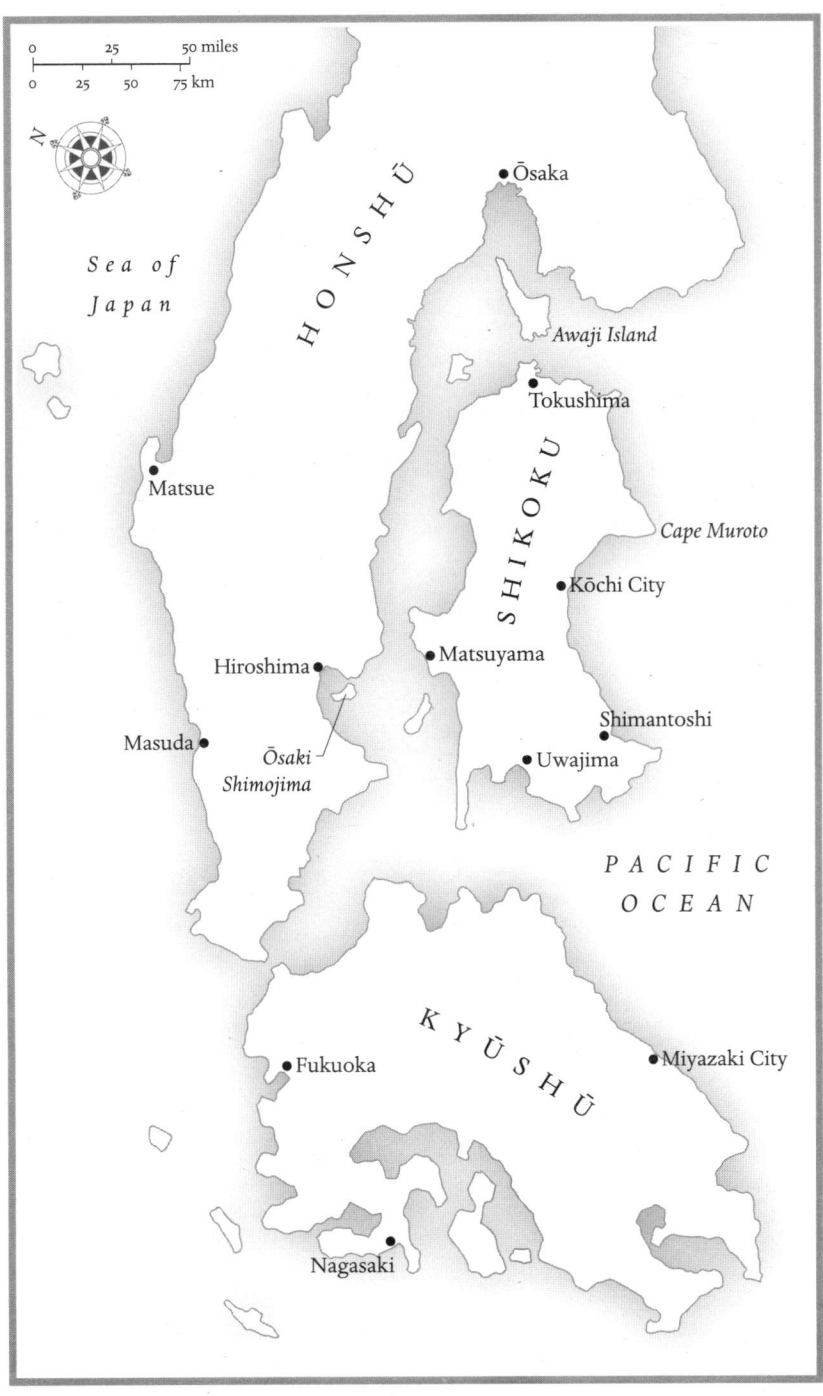

0   25   50 miles
0   25   50   75 km

N

Sea of
Japan

H O N S H Ū

● Ōsaka

Awaji Island

● Tokushima

● Matsue

S H I K O K U

Cape Muroto

● Kōchi City

Hiroshima ●

● Matsuyama

Masuda ●

Ōsaki
Shimojima

Shimantoshi
●

● Uwajima

P A C I F I C
O C E A N

K Y Ū S H Ū

● Fukuoka

● Miyazaki City

● Nagasaki

The Country

7.

Tokushima: A Provincial City on the Wane

What was happening in the rapidly depopulating countryside? It was hard to know where to start, but Shikoku grabbed my attention. It is the third largest of the 430 inhabited islands in the Japanese archipelago – there are over 14,000 in total – and lies south-west of Osaka. The blight of empty houses afflicting the countryside is particularly pronounced there: more than one in five houses on the island stands empty and more are abandoned with every passing year.[1] Kōchi prefecture on the south coast of the island looked interesting. It has more single men than any other prefecture, a sure sign that eligible women are moving to the city in search of work and opportunities, leaving eligible men behind to pull their hair out in the countryside.

One evening, I cycled down to the ferry terminal in Tokyo Bay, where I boarded an overnight ferry that would take me to Tokushima, the largest city on the east coast of the island. The ship was freshly painted in white and lime green, a nod to the citrus fruit for which the countryside around Tokushima is famous. The white lino floors were no less pristine, so the first thing everyone did on boarding was head to their cabins to drop off their luggage and change into slippers.

About half of the passengers looked to be soldiers from the Self-Defence Forces. They seemed as surprised to see me as I was to see them. Below the main deck, there was a communal area with a row of vending machines selling pot noodles, beer and soft drinks, and, opposite them, a table with six or so microwaves. The soldiers milled around the machines, bought some dinner and ate as fast as possible. Some of them were lounging in sportswear, engrossed in their phones. One was sitting cross-legged on his chair. He was wearing black nail varnish and looked a bit too sensitive and solitary to be a soldier.

Another was hunched over a bowl of curry udon, hoovering up the unctuous gloop, his powerful shoulders moving under his shirt. He stared straight out to sea and sniffed hard. In profile, his plucked eyebrows put me in mind of a *kabuki* performer. The combination of toughness and theatricality was quite striking, but when I saw him again later, face-on and in glasses, his thespian air had evaporated, and he could have passed for a regular *salariman*.

Back in the 1990s, nobody could have predicted that a quarter of a century later, the LDP would be echoing the nationalists' call for Japan to ditch the pacifist constitution foisted on the defeated nation by the American occupation administration in 1946. Much of the world still thinks of Japan as a peaceful country, but hostility to China and Korea had only risen in the time I'd been away, and its peace constitution is rapidly becoming a thing of the past. In response to the growing risk of 'deterrence failure', Japan plans to develop 'counter-strike capabilities', the better to stand up to a rising China.[2] In December 2022, the National Security Review recommended doubling defence spending within the next five years.

Japan's demographic woes pose huge challenges for the military. In the future, there will be less need for soldiers, as effective warfare will rely on AI, swarm technologies, drones and cyber warfare. However, these technologies are not going to be in place for another ten years, so conventional military strength is still what matters, and this is where demography comes into play. Greying populations are changing the parameters of the tense rivalries that characterize this part of the world. All of the countries of North-East Asia – Japan, South Korea, North Korea, Taiwan, Russia and China – are ageing fast, and they are all running short of soldiers.

Japan's Self-Defence Forces (JSDF) haven't been able to meet their recruitment targets for the past 20 years.[3] In response, they have raised salaries, extended the maximum age for entry to 32 and raised the retirement age of serving personnel. Meanwhile, the Ministry of Defence is increasing the number and depth of its security alliances with countries with younger populations, like India and Indonesia. Birth rates are in decline there as well, but the impact will not be felt for a couple of generations and, for now, the countries of South and South-East Asia are enjoying a demographic dividend. With a combined population forecast to increase by 582 million between now and 2050, the region is a rich source of young recruits.[4]

It was dark by the time I made it to the ferry's onboard *sento*, so I couldn't see much of Tokyo Bay out of the window. A few soldiers were lounging in a low tub about 4 metres long and 2 metres wide. Easing myself into the hot water, I was feeling delightfully light-hearted about the trip that lay ahead. My plan was to spend two weeks following the Buddhist pilgrimage route around the southern half of Shikoku, from Tokushima on the east coast to Matsuyama on the west coast. The route was made famous by Kōbō Daishi, the founder of Shingon Buddhism in Japan, who spent decades in the late eighth and early ninth centuries wandering around Japan as an ascetic and trained at some of the island's temples. I too was wandering, though seeking a different kind of enlightenment. I wanted to visualize what happens to a country when its people stop having children.

After my bath, I donned the complimentary *yukata*, had a smoke in the ferry's little smoking room and turned in for the night. With its bright green paintwork, gleaming white floor and little round cubby holes, the cabin looked like a dormitory for infants. The men from the JSDF didn't seem to mind. We slept in two-storey bunks. Ensconced in plywood, hidden behind a little curtain, it was lovely and warm. I made a start on *Japan: The Natural History of an Asian Archipelago*. It was full of surprises. I would never have guessed it living in Tokyo, but apparently Japan has more species of trees and insects than all of continental Europe put together. This is because it was spared most of the ravages of the last major ice age, when northern Europe was almost entirely covered in ice. Many habitats and species survived, and they have had more time to evolve into endemic species and subspecies.[5] A great deal remains to be discovered in its mountains. The Mikawa salamander, for example, was unknown to scientists until 2017.

Another native creature that grabbed my attention was the solitary snipe, a bird that 'lives alone beside cold, fast flowing mountain streams, typically between snow-covered banks. The cold brown and grey tones of its plumage combine with its slow-motion creeping behaviour to make it difficult to spot. It crouches for minutes on end, barely moving apart from to rock back and forth on the spot.'[6]

Mark Brazil's description of the solitary snipe put me in mind of all the incorrigibly solitary men and women I had met during my time in Tokyo, and their quiet, stubborn ways. On reflection, they seemed content enough, but their failure to reproduce made their future unsustainable. Demographers are inclined to think of people as rational actors, who get married, have children and get divorced for rational, measurable reasons, but the collective reluctance to reproduce may be unconscious. I wondered what Charles Darwin would have made of Japan's fecundity fix. An evolutionary psychologist might argue that spurning childbirth is an instinctive response to overcrowding. It is probably no coincidence that every developed-world country with high population density also has a low fertility rate.

Only when my head came to rest on the pillow did the deep roar of the ship's engines reach my ear. Combined with the gentle pitch and roll of the vessel, it made me feel as if I were sleeping on the bonnet of a truck as it glided gently down a long and winding road.

*

Early the next morning, I went up on deck to get my bearings and some fresh air. The winter sky was blue from horizon to horizon, the sun was bright and a brisk wind was whipping up white tufts from the sea. Around us were masses of fishing trawlers, bigger than I'd imagined, with big beams suspended over their decks to haul in their nets. A nation of hungry fish lovers awaited their return to port.

Shikoku came into view later that morning: ranges of mountains retreating into the distance, each a distinct shade of misty blue or grey, like the painted flats of a stage set. As we approached

Tokushima, they gradually turned green and brown, and I could make out a long line of concrete polyhedrons. In the name of flood control, a third of Japan's coastline has been lined with these concrete blocks, a glaring example of successive governments' addiction to public works.

There is good reason for their obsession with pouring concrete. One of the remarkable features of the Japanese archipelago is its tendency to self-destruct. No other country is as prone to volcanic eruptions, earthquakes and tsunami. It is said that within the next 30 years there is a 70 per cent probability of a magnitude 7 or 8 earthquake, potentially directly under Tokyo. If such a powerful quake were to hit the capital, the consequences would be catastrophic. When it last happened, in 1923, 100,000 people were killed.[7]

The threat of natural disaster keeps people in a state of watchfulness and lends the act of pouring concrete the aura of a sacred ritual. In the boom years, the national effort to limit the threat of disaster bordered on the pathological. The government had the money, so it set about building embankments, enclosures and hoardings to stop the country's rivers from flooding and its mountains from collapsing. The primacy of safety occupied a generation of planners, engineers and builders, who strived to anticipate every possible mishap and prevent every possible injury. In the process, they created the safest roads in the world, but they also erected no end of warning signs, railings, barriers and bollards.

The mania for public works grew most acute when the economy stopped growing in the mid-1990s. Determined to give it a Keynesian kickstart, the government set about bestowing the benefits of modern infrastructure upon the countryside. Masses of bypasses, flyovers and airports were built, as well as several bridges to nowhere, tunnels without exits and ports without ships.

Although often of dubious value, these projects went ahead thanks to the 'Iron Triangle' of politicians, bureaucrats and construction companies. Their backroom deals essentially enabled bureaucrats to channel the population's life savings into a wide range of debt-encrusted public bodies, which in turn funnelled them into high-profile infrastructure projects. Local governments loved them because they associated construction with development. The public were happy because, in return for their votes, the politicians gave them lots of shiny new infrastructure. And the bureaucrats were happy because they got lucrative, post-retirement sinecures with the public bodies that oversaw the projects.

But these infusions only served as steroids, bloating rather than strengthening the rural economy. They also took a terrible toll on the environment. In the course of building Japan's 102 commercial airports, and its 1.2 million kilometres of roads, 90 per cent of the country's tidal wetlands have been drained and lost, and its groundwater has been drastically depleted. Of Japan's 30,000 rivers and streams, all but three have been dammed and had their banks encased in concrete.[8]

Japan's fauna has been especially hard-hit. According to the Ministry of the Environment's Red Data Book of Japan, 36 per cent of the country's mammals, 24 per cent of its freshwater fish, and 19 per cent of its birds are extinct, endangered, rare or localized. The plight of the national bird – the crested ibis or *Nipponia nippon* – is emblematic. Habitat degradation and loss depleted its numbers until it only survived on the island of Sado. Finally, it died out there too, and it was only thanks to a donation from China that a captive breeding programme was able to get underway. The national and prefectural governments went to great lengths to redress the situation and there are now 350 crested ibis living on Sado.[9]

Until recently, it seemed Japan would never wean itself off its addiction to building, for, as well as being immensely powerful, the Iron Triangle was opaque and unaccountable, and that made it hard to reform. As late as 2012, the construction sector employed one in ten workers and the Japanese government was spending the equivalent of 8 per cent of GDP on public works, two to three times the sum spent in other industrialized countries.[10]

However, in the last decade, the Iron Triangle has started to look decidedly wobbly. With the workforce shrinking as a proportion of the overall population, the revenue the government gets from income tax has been dwindling. It is no longer able to fund out-size construction projects, and this has fundamentally altered its relationship with the regions. Having no choice but to cut local government loose, it has granted the regions a measure of autonomy they have never had before.

Small-town officials, long accustomed to doing the bidding of bureaucrats in far-away Tokyo, are having to think for themselves. Given the choice, they would have carried on pouring concrete for a thousand years, wedded as they were to the pro-growth agenda that held sway for most of the post-war years. But the regions have had environmentalism and post-growth economics thrust upon them by long-term economic stagnation, dwindling budgets and swinging cuts. As a result, the very meaning of 'growth' and 'development' is being called into question.

★

The ferry came into Tokushima harbour, and I caught sight of a big road-bridge and white concrete apartment blocks. High on a hill overlooking the city, I could make out the quarry that supplied the raw materials for the cement of which the city was made. Closer to the water was the cement factory, which was emitting a beautiful plume of thick white smoke.

Walking the streets of Tokushima on a mid-week morning was a curious experience. Even in the prefectural capital, the streets were empty and most of the shops were closed. Still, it would be nice in the summer, when the tourists arrived, I said to myself. The main street was lined with palm trees and, although the weather could hardly have been called balmy, the smell of the island suggested a warm land in hibernation, something spicy that might have been camphor laurel trees. It was a fitting motif for my first visit to the margins, as solid camphor is often placed in tool sheds to protect tools against rust.

Tokushima is famous for its *awa odori*, an annual festival when the people of the city dance in the streets. It is an interesting vestige from pre-modern Japan. I liked the festival's motto – 'You're a fool if you dance, and you're a fool if you watch, so you might as well dance.' I took it as an emblem of the more ribald, licentious past preserved in the country's traditional festivals, called *matsuri*.

Unfortunately, I had come at the wrong time of year to see the *awa odori*, but a kindly old woman at the tourist information centre said that they staged a mini re-enactment of the festival for tourists every day at the civic centre, so I went along for the potted version. Our guide was an OAP, as was practically everyone in the audience. The *awa odori* was a graceful dance performed to the sound of a drum and a bell, with a nice lilting rhythm I could imagine getting drunk to. It was punctuated by more frenetic dancing by the younger, more active members of the community. They were the kind of young people that OAPs like to see – not twitching *otaku* or scowling *hikikomori*, but acrobatic ninja warriors and graceful maidens.

I remembered a woodblock print of a *matsuri* that Maki Hirayama had shown me when I went to see her at Meiji University. It had been made in 1868 and depicted an Obon festival in a town called Kuroishi in the far north of the country. It was a light-hearted scene, much like a cartoon, of a procession of people, some wearing huge masks of bears and cats, winding their way past a shrine. Some of them were carrying umbrellas, and some of the men were wearing women's kimonos.

Maki considered it an example of an early forerunner of cosplay. The word comes from the English words 'costume' and 'play', so it's easy to assume that dressing up as your favourite manga character is an instance of Japan imitating the West. But donning a mask in order to lose yourself in a fictional character has deep roots in Japan. Like manga and maid cafés, cosplay is a feature of modern city life that we assume to be modern, or even post-modern. However, it has its origins in pre-modern times.

Like the carnival tradition in Europe, the *matsuri* was the one day in the year when there were no rules. For most of the year, commoners lived by the rules of monogamy, but come the summer festival, many of them enjoyed free sex. I had asked Maki if there had been *sōshoku danshi*, or 'herbivorous men', in the Edo period. 'I don't think so,' she told me. 'Most men loved sexual and erotic matters.' She was convinced that the Edo era was a more liberated one than our own, both creatively and, apparently, sexually.

'In pre-modern Japan, what mattered was not sex per se, but baby-making. A samurai was expected to marry, and the marriage would be arranged by his parents. In this regard, at least, the samurai lived by strictly monogamous norms. Their sex lives were governed by rules, but these could be bent; many men patronized geisha houses, which often doubled as brothels.'

Divorce was just as easy: if a man wanted to divorce his wife, he just had to write three lines saying he wanted her to leave the household (if he was illiterate, he just drew three lines). In the Tosa domain, there was even a law stipulating that a man could divorce *no more* than seven times. Small wonder, then, that for much of the Edo period, Japan had the highest divorce rate in the world. At its peak, it reached 4.8 per 1,000, which is higher than Russia, the country with the highest divorce rate in the world today.[11]

★

In Japan, night-life is synonymous with the sex trade, and even the smallest town has a redlight district. That evening, I went out to have a look around Tokushima's little nightlife area, but despite it being a Friday, Sakaemachi – 'Prosperity Town' – wasn't looking very prosperous. Stealing a peek through the windows of the few hostess bars that were both open and had a window to peep through, I only saw a couple of elderly patrons.

Prostitution was outlawed in 1957, and thereafter Japan made a transition from what might be called 'prostitution culture' to 'love culture'. But paying to spend time in a woman's company is still ubiquitous. The hostess business, for example, is everywhere and likely bigger than the licensed sex trade.* Like all hostess bars, the ones in

---

* Prostitution is illegal, but the ban only applies to penetrative sex, and other forms of sex work do go on, albeit discreetly.

Sakaemachi weren't offering sex openly, but a sign outside one bar said there was a ¥1,000 charge to choose a girl.

To be clear, the job of a hostess does not include sex work, whatever else a specific hostess may do.* She is expected to light a customer's cigarette, keep his glass topped up, laugh at his jokes and sing karaoke with him. Groups of office workers often visit hostess clubs after work, looking for entertainment, and plenty of businesses are happy to pick up the tab in the belief that it is a good way to entertain clients and build trust between male co-workers.

Paying women for the pleasure of their company (and sometimes of their bodies) has been part and parcel of the nightlife of Japan for hundreds, if not thousands of years. 'In Japanese culture, the power of sexuality has always been thought to be very great,' Maki Hirayama had told me.

> People celebrated sexuality in the *matsuri*, and it was celebrated in Shinto too, for sex was thought to be sacred. It was the most precious thing in life, and it was not always confined to marriage. Prostitution has its origins in religion and the sacred power of sexuality. Originally, the shaman was a woman, and she was also a prostitute.

The idea that the first Shinto priests were women will come as a surprise to traditionalists, and the idea that they were also prostitutes is shocking. But sex and religion have always been closely entwined in Japan. Following the arrival of Buddhism in the sixth century, prostitutes set up shop around temples. Male prostitution was also common, particularly around larger temples like Sensō-ji, the oldest temple in modern Tokyo.

After 1603, when Edo became the seat of the Tokugawa shogunate and the de facto capital, the sexual activities of the samurai class were closely regulated within the four walls of the Yoshiwara,

---

* Hostess clubs are classified as food and entertainment establishments and regulated by the Businesses Affecting Public Morals Act, which prohibits any form of sexual contact between employees and customers.

the best-known of Edo's licensed red-light districts. But the authorities were less concerned by what other classes got up to, and there were plenty of other, less well-known pleasure districts in the city. Whenever harvests were bad and food stocks ran low, poor farmers sold their daughters into prostitution as a matter of course.

When the American writer William Elliot Griffis came to Japan in 1870 to help reorganize the educational system along American lines, he was amazed to discover that even the rooms in the grounds of Sensō-ji were used for prostitution. His description of what he saw is more reminiscent of a hostess bar than a brothel.

> They bring you tea, smile, talk nonsense, and giggle; smoke their long pipes with tiny bowls full of mild, fine-cut tobacco; puff out the long white whiffs from their flat-bridged noses; wipe the brass mouth-piece and offer it to you, and then ask you leading and very personal questions without blushing . . . Full grown, able-bodied men are the chief patrons of these places of pleasure, and many can find amusement for hours at such play.

Learning about the vast scale of the sex trade in Edo-era Japan, and the perfunctory nature of most conjugal relations, made me wonder again about the present. Was all the the romantic idealization of monogamy really a foreign idea? Maki certainly thought so. 'In the *Tale of Genji*, the hero, Hikaru ("Shining") Genji, has only one formal wife, but he has many sexual partners.' It is hard to overstate the importance of Murasaki Shikibu's *Tale of Genji* in Japanese culture. As well as being one of the first novels ever written (in the early eleventh century), it was probably the first novel written by a woman, and certainly the first to win global recognition. 'For hundreds of years, Genji was thought to be the ideal man. This suggests that people didn't mind that he changes his mind so often.'

Maki was keen to stress that, in Japan, marriage was never believed to have the divine sanction that gave the institution such strength in the West. 'Unlike in Western countries, in Japan marriage is not based on religion. God does not sanctify the marriage. It is a secular matter.' This has had a big impact on the institution's durability. 'Unlike Western people, the Japanese don't have the ideal of being a couple, meaning a man and woman being equal and united. This is the ideal, but it is not very familiar to the Japanese.'

The monogamous norm only became stronger in the twentieth century, under the impact of Western ideas and modernization. Thereafter, practically everyone married at least once, and sex in marriage was thought to be very important. 'At that time, not many wives worked outside,' Maki went on. 'They depended on their husband's income, so they could not refuse his demands. Having sex with their husbands was just like their job.'

Most people only got married because they felt duty-bound to have kids. Marriage was a functional arrangement to suit the needs of children, not a realm of conjugal intimacy, and men did not expect their sexual urges to be entirely satisfied at home. There was a double standard at work, with women expected to remain chaste after marriage while men were allowed, and often encouraged, to use prostitutes.

I had asked Maki if hostesses had existed in the Edo period. 'They existed, but in quite different conditions,' she told me. 'Geisha were like hostesses. The politicians of the Meiji era, like Ito Hitobumi, the first prime minister of Japan, married geisha because they needed to meet Western politicians. Ordinary wives were not used to hosting guests. The geisha were the experts.'

I asked Maki about the enduring appeal of the hostess.

In the era of modernization, the strongest bond has not been between the couple, but between the mother and her child. Men's ideal is to be loved and cared for by their mothers. I think that is why they like *kawaii* women so much. It makes it difficult for them to have an equal relationship with a woman.

This has had positive and negative effects on sexuality even today. Sexuality is thought to be sacred, and because of this, Japanese people accept prostitution. A man can easily purchase sexual services, and the sex worker provides him with anything he wants. But from my perspective, they depend on prostitution too much, and they don't work on improving their sex lives in an equal relationship. Couples need to change their sex lives, but the men don't have any idea how to improve their sex lives with an equal partner, and women don't have any idea either.

In the past, having sex with their husbands was just like their job. But now women have more power, so they can refuse, and gradually sex in married life is becoming less important.

As more women get a higher education, enter the workforce and earn salaries that give them financial independence from men, they too are turning to the market for emotional (and sometimes sexual) gratification. In recent years, female empowerment has spawned host clubs, where a woman can pay a good-looking young man for the pleasure of his company. I had seen ads for these clubs on illuminated hoardings while walking the backstreets of Kabukichō in Tokyo. They featured blow-ups of androgenous man-boys with doe eyes, bleached hair and mid-Pacific names like Kaz, Sho and Taka.

Hosts are expected to have a variety of skills, be it magic tricks or the gift of the gab, and some clubs have a dedicated stage where they dance or do comedy routines. 'It is often a girl's dream to assume the role of taking care of a man and to be loved back,' says Yoko Tajima of Hōsei University. 'But because of the way the family works here, their dreams are frustrated. Their fantasy, however, becomes a reality, albeit temporarily, at the host clubs.'[12]

The rise of the host club suggests that, as the appeal of the nuclear family wanes, people are reverting to the more fluid norms that governed sex lives in the past. But there are still obstacles; with an evening of non-sexual entertainment and banter with a host costing upwards of ¥80,000 (£400), the pleasures of the host club are out of bounds for most women. As Maki put it, 'The wage gap between men and women is still big, so their roles are determined.'

★

The following morning, before leaving Tokushima to start my tour of Shikoku, I went to the nearest *konbini* for a regulation-issue coffee and pastry. I headed for the park over the road, where a group of OAPs in white shirts and plimsolls were doing stretches. Every morning, millions of elderly men and women gather in parks across Japan to follow NHK Radio's group calisthenics programme.

On the face of it, there can be no better measure of Japan's postwar success than its declining mortality and growing life expectancy. Life expectancy at birth is the highest in the world. In 2020, it stood at 81.6 years for a man and 87.7 years for a woman.[13] That the average Japanese person lives so long is a remarkable achievement when you consider that, as late as 1947, life expectancy was just 50 years for a man and 54 years for a woman.

No less important than life expectancy is healthy life expectancy, which is to say, 'the average period of time spent without any limitation in one's daily activities'. In 2016, healthy life expectancy at birth was 72 years for men and almost 75 years for women, and improvements are being made every year. As people live longer, healthier lives, the very meaning of words like 'aged' and 'elderly' is changing. The Japan Gerontological Society states that it is no longer accurate to describe someone over the age of 65 as 'elderly', and suggests that the term be reserved for those aged over 75.

Heading south out of Tokushima on my bike, I passed some spry 80-year-olds hoeing, tilling and harvesting crops. A little further on, a frail old woman with legs like matchsticks was folded up on the gravel outside her house, doing some weeding in a wide-brimmed sunhat. It was good to see the old people staying active, I thought – as the rest of the world grows older, I daresay we can all learn from Japan's ageing citizens.

National Geographic reporter Dan Buettner has made documentaries about what have been dubbed the world's Blue Zones, those regions where people live significantly longer and healthier lives than average, often living for in excess of 100 years. He believes that one of the reasons for the longevity of the people of Japan is the importance they attach to having *ikigai*: a sense of purpose in life. The way Buettner sees it, they have less desire to retire, as they enjoy working and go on doing it for as long as they can. The facts bear him out: according to the Cabinet Office's Annual Report on the Ageing Society, 70 per cent of people aged 60–69, and about 50 per cent of those over 70 either work or take part in volunteer activities, community activities and hobbies.

The report also shows Japanese seniors tend to have higher cognitive abilities than elderly people in other rich-world countries, which may be because they tend to stay active for longer. 'Compared to 10 years ago, Japanese seniors are healthier, and have a higher quality of living,' says Yuko Oguma, associate professor in Health Management Research at the Keio Sports Medicine Research Centre. 'This is thought to be down to a combination of improved healthcare and a better understanding of how bodies age. Recently, there has been evidence that muscles can continue to strengthen, even in old age, which is contrary to what we used to believe.'

Although Oguma admits it is hard to prove, she believes that having peers that look out for each other is another, often overlooked factor in healthy ageing. 'Often it is the senior citizens themselves that put together programmes within the community. They work among themselves to provide activities, to be more fit or to be included socially. It is this proactiveness that strengthens them.'[14]

Staying fit and active is all to the good, but cycling through the suburbs of Tokushima, it occurred to me that Japan's OAPs might be staying active because they feel guilty doing nothing. Perhaps that was why the women seemed to be constantly sweeping. People looked to be intensely purposeful with their free time, but they were also intensely private and often spent it with their pets. I passed an old man who was walking a decrepit poodle that was wearing little felt booties. A few miles further on, I passed a man who was taking his cat for a walk. The only creature I saw who was content to just watch the world go by was an old two-legged dog, who was wearing a nappy and sitting in a doggie wheelchair in the doorway of a run-down coffee shop.

Gradually, the *konbini* and suburban shopping centres began to thin out, and things started to get baggy. There were more empty houses, fewer people and more cars. Then the cars, too, died away and what was left of the people grew older still.

That night, I stayed at a *minshuku* (guest house) in a hamlet called Aratano, run by a farmer and his wife. Mr Kitamura cleared a space for my bike in his barn, which was stacked to the rafters with tins of bamboo shoots, and I followed him into the house. Although he looked flustered by his foreign guest and in a rush to get back to his bamboo shoots, I was delighted to be spending the night in such a normal household. The Kitamuras' *minshuku* felt homely and relaxed, even a little neglected. I noticed there was something smeared on the kettle, and dust on every flat surface.

Shortly after I arrived, Mrs Kitamura came into my room wearing a woolly beanie, and served me some snacks on a tray. It was January, which meant it was the season to pick strawberries and mandarins. She served me some salty mushroom tea, which was delicious, and I noticed that her hands shook. Neither she nor her husband used the polite *keigo* form customarily used to address guests, which was a welcome dose of familiarity.

They didn't even wear face masks, which also made an agreeable change. Everywhere I had been, everyone was wearing face masks, even outside, even after the pandemic was over, and even in the depths of the countryside. I might have put this down to a customary excess of caution, but then I would go into a busy *izakaya* at night, the ideal breeding ground for the virus, and no one would be wearing a mask. Its function was clearly more social than medical. People wore them out of consideration for others, and in the evenings, when they had done their duty for the day and were relaxing with friends, they took them off – and promptly gave one another the virus.

That evening, I went for a walk around the village and soon found myself in the grounds of a temple, which was overshadowed by giant cedar trees with thick straw ropes around their girths. After so long in Tokyo, I welcomed the deep quiet and the dearth of distractions. The only sounds were the breeze moving through the bamboo grove, the trilling of an unseen bird and the gurgle of the brook running past the temple.

Although it had only just gone nine, the only light to be seen came from a farmhouse, where a group of teenage girls were chatting loudly. I hadn't heard anyone be so garrulous and carefree for a long time. One of them came out with a bowl of washing in her hands and even started singing. What would become of them? I wondered. Surely there was no work for them here, nor much chance of finding a partner. Once they'd finished school, they would most likely leave for Osaka, the nearest big city.

★

I was still half asleep when I saw the pilgrim in the room next door set out early the following morning. He was wearing a conical hat made of sedge with the words *dōgyō ninin* – 'two people walking together' – written on it. It was a reference to Kōbō Daishi, in whose hallowed footsteps all pilgrims walk. There are references to people making the pilgrimage around Shikoku as long ago as the twelfth century, although it did not become a well-known route until the first guidebooks were published in the late seventeenth century. Today, hundreds of thousands of people from all over the world make the pilgrimage – although, this being mid-winter, I would only spot a handful.

Half an hour later, I too was back on the road. From Aratano, I cycled up a moss-covered, single-track forestry road that wound its way through bamboo groves before cresting a low range of mountains and meandering back down to the coast. Along the way, I passed old wooden fishing boats that had been left to rot in the mountains and noticed how the road markings were starting to crack and crumble.

Shikoku is a mountainous island, and this goes a long way in explaining why it is relatively poor, for the Japanese have always depended on rice for sustenance and rice paddies have to be flat. Even on a slight slope, stone walls have to be built to create terraces

143

on which to grow the crop. Back on the coast road, I passed plenty of abandoned rice paddies, which the *susuki* (pampas grass) had taken over. At one, I stopped to watch a *tsuru* (crane) take flight from a riverbank and fly over the *susuki*. It was a shame to think of all that work gone to waste.

I passed through countless tunnels, climbing hills to their mouths, gliding through their smooth concrete bodies and emerging into valleys on the other side that were invariably a little bit wilder than the one I had just left. One of the delights of Japan is that, while the system of manners can be oppressive, what people do behind closed doors is considered their business. In remote parts of the country, when there is no one around, they even venture outside to do them. Entering one tunnel, I could make out the distant sound of music, which gradually grew louder as the prick of light up ahead grew larger. After several hundred metres, I emerged to a vista of steep cliffs, a sandy beach and a man idly strumming a ukulele outside his surf shop. Further down the hill was an abandoned beach resort, where grass was growing up around the seating under a gazebo. By now, the mildew on the road signs had turned to moss.

Outside the next *konbini* I came to, in a village called Mugi, there was a sign that read 'Do not feed the cats.' I would have liked to pet a cat, but I couldn't see one, so I walked around the shop to the back, which looked out over the muddy estuary of a broad river. One, and then two little cats emerged from behind the wall of the embankment, followed by a third and a fourth, until I was being watched by ten pairs of mistrustful eyes. Then a woman emerged from the house next door to the store with some scraps for them, and they all dashed away.

I had taken the house next door to be abandoned, as the front garden was overgrown and the walls were covered in mildew. But the distinction between an inhabited house and an abandoned one, I realized, is not always clear. Even an inhabited house can look abandoned if its occupant is too frail or infirm to weed the garden. Usually, though, the rot starts from the inside, when the resident of a house dies or goes to live in an old people's home. The outside of the property is maintained by relatives, and the neighbourhood by the municipality, but the absence of an occupant creates a void, and it is only a matter of time before the attempt to keep up appearances starts to falter.

As the older generation dies and the population of Japan shrinks, houses are being abandoned nationwide. This is because when someone dies, there is invariably no one to take her place, for her children moved to the city long ago and have no interest in returning to the countryside. Lumbered with an unwanted inheritance, the reluctant heirs may try to sell their mother's house in order to meet the cost of inheritance tax, but in most cases, they will not find a buyer. The tax on land goes up sixfold as soon as the building that stands on it is demolished, so they usually just let the house stand empty.[15]

In many depopulated areas, entire neighbourhoods have become unsellable, and the property market has collapsed. In 2024, Japan's Housing and Land Survey logged a record 9 million *akiya* (empty houses), meaning that, nationwide, 14 per cent of houses are unoccupied.[16] That is enough to accommodate the entire population of Australia at three people per dwelling. Some forecasts predict that by 2040 the vacancy rate could be as high as 40 per cent.[17]

Although it was a weekday, the street running through Mugi was deserted, bar a little old woman with a stoop. There was a ramen restaurant, but it was closed, as were the petrol station, the hairdresser's shop and the estate agent. Many of the shops had a sign in the window that read '*junbichū*' ('getting ready'), a refusal to admit defeat that I found poignant at first, but soon came to seem ridiculous. Nobody was getting ready to do anything, apart from die.

The only shop in Mugi that was open for business was the *konbini*. Convenience stores would become my saviours on my trip around Shikoku, sources of nourishment but also havens from the forlornness of the dying villages I passed through. There was talk of automating the country's *konbini* as a way of addressing the chronic shortage of labour. It was a superficially appealing idea, but one that would leave young people in rural Japan with no work apart from farming, which few young people, whether Japanese or Javanese, seem to want to do any more.

After a few more hours of cycling south through desolate villages, I came to a village called Kaifu, and made my way to Fuku-chan's, a new, clean, warm and comfortable *minshuku*. The ground floor was open plan, with a sunken kitchen at the same level as the *genkan* (vestibule), and the rest on a raised wooden floor, bar a living room with tatami mats at the far end. Floor-to-ceiling windows ran all the way along the front of the house.

I was the only guest. The owner, Ms Fukushima, was the kind of capable, public-spirited organizer that holds these communities together. She was middle-aged, unmarried and lived with her ageing mother, Fuku-chan. She showed me a family photograph taken when she was a girl: it showed mum, dad and eight kids, all dressed in kimonos, posing in the back garden on a summer's day.

I didn't want to pry into Ms Fukushima's marital status, so instead I asked her about the depopulated villages I had passed through since leaving Tokushima that morning. 'Isolation is a quiet experience,' she told me. 'It can make people strange, particularly once they have retired. Without jobs and often without families, their minds wander. It was other people who gave them a sense of purpose, you see.'

8.

The Only Way Is Down: On the Narrow Road to the Deep South

Early the next morning, I had a look outside, where a small garden led down to a wide, slow-moving river. Upriver, a string of houses on the far bank was reflected in the still water. The hills around were green and incredibly quiet, save for the sound of birds talking to one another.

The headline on the front page of the *Yomiuri Shinbun* that morning brought news that the government was about to introduce a new policy to address the problem of abandoned houses. As I struggled to decipher the *kanji*, slowly reading the words under my breath, I could hear old Fuku-chan reciting the sutras in front of the *butsudan* (shrine) in the front room. The calm, sing-song tone of her voice suggested that it had become a ritual for her a long time ago.

When she had finished, she rang a little bell and, after a moment of silence, I heard the sound of the TV. It seemed to be a discussion programme, quite a rarity in Japan, and the participants sounded like they were openly disagreeing with one another, which was rarer still. I hadn't heard a raised voice for a long time, and I found the experience a bit unnerving. I wondered if, as Japan's shrinking crisis grows more acute, the people of what must be the most conflict-averse country in the world would start to argue among themselves.

On the way out of Kaifu, I stopped to watch a pelican glide over the sand dunes at the mouth of the river and noticed the prints of an animal in the sand, a hint of the overlooked fauna that I had been reading about. I pressed on, passing over miles of flat ground that might once have been precious rice paddies, now abandoned to *susuki* grass. After a while, I encountered what had once been a house: there was no trace of its timbers, just some broken roof tiles in a disorderly pile. Until the 1950s, when the government began to work its economic miracle, Japan was largely a land of wooden buildings. But the jungle climate rots uncovered wood very quickly, especially in the summer months, when the monsoon rains come, the air turns sultry and the temperature climbs into the high 30s.

I didn't go far that day. I spent the afternoon in the *onsen* of a hotel in Shishikui, looking out to sea. I had the place to myself, which was rather eerie, as was the *minshuku* where I stayed that night. It was of a type I was coming to recognize: worryingly austere, with no decorations on the walls and no attempt at creating cosiness. There were tatami mats on the floor, but, that aside, most of the furniture and fittings were of a pseudo-Western style and dated from the 1980s. Seeing the decade as a museum piece like this, I was reminded of how fashionable fakery had been in those days: the veneer on the doors was of imitation oak and the linoleum had been made to look like pebbles. Both looked to have been polished daily, unforgivingly, until they positively gleamed. Looking at them, I remembered something Ms Fukushima had said the night before about living in a community on its last legs. 'People no longer feel that they are being propelled into the future. Without propulsion, time slows down. Sometimes it stops, and it can even start to run backwards.'

*

The next village I came to was Toyo, a little fishing village where the River None came down to the sea. The barriers on either side of the bridge spanning the river had given in to rust and collapsed. A barrier that had not only been allowed to collapse but also to go unrepaired was quite a sight in a country so keen to efface the first sign of ageing.

I stopped to drink some coffee from my thermos flask. In a giant car park where warehouses might once have stood, five old men were sitting in the sunshine, each ten yards from the other, silently mending a giant fishing net. It was a starkly beautiful place, even in its decline. There were charming alleyways zigzagging away from the waterfront, lined with creosoted wooden houses, each with a row of flowerpots arranged around the front porch. Buzzards and kites took the place of seagulls, perching on telegraph poles or gliding over the mouths of little streams coming down from the mountains.

I spent the rest of the morning wending my way down the coast to Sakihamachō. There were no settlements between there and Cape Muroto, in the south-eastern corner of the island, just a little-used road that followed the coastline, with steep mountains covered in virgin forest on one side and the Pacific Ocean on the other. The land was drier here, and cacti and agave grew at the roadside.

Mid-afternoon, I passed two macaques playing on the roof of an abandoned warehouse. Next door was a derelict hotel, where the sea air was eating away at the air-conditioning units, turning them a rich shade of copper. The technology was still fresh: not the once-vaunted, all-too-soon obsolete VCRs, mobile phones and outsized desktop computers of the 1980s, but an entryphone with a built-in camera. It was one thing to see the timber houses of pre-modern Japan rotting into the ground, but quite another to see twentieth-century Japan going the same way so quickly.

Rounding Cape Muroto, the light faded from the sky and the traffic picked up, and by the time I got to the small town of Hane the roads were crowded with the tiny cars of local residents and trucks carrying fresh timber down from the mountains. There was a post office and a small supermarket, where I stopped to eat, but that was about it. The cashier in the supermarket was a kind woman who gave me some pot noodles, let me use the microwave, and invited me to sit down at the table and chairs provided to eat. A few late-night shoppers dropped by while I was eating, chatty people with none of the reserve or excessive politeness I'd come to expect living in Tokyo. They looked me in the eye and returned my greetings with a hearty '*Konnichi wa*' and a smile.

A girl came in with her mum, the first child I had seen since leaving Tokushima. 'The population of the town has been ageing and shrinking for some time, but the shops only closed recently,' said the cashier. 'Five years ago, my boss opened a supermarket in Hane, but it was too big, so he closed it and moved into this place only a couple of years later. He runs it as a not-for-profit venture. It's the only place in the town where people can meet.'

That night, I stayed at Minshuku Ouchishuku. The owner, Mrs Shidao, let me use the kitchen in her old house, where she had lived before building the new house next door. 'There is a travelling sales-man staying in the dining room, but he won't be back until late,' she said. His suitcase and a neatly folded stack of shirts awaited his return. The kitchen was spotless, and reminiscent of the post-war years. I was halfway through a cheese and ham sandwich that I'd bought in the supermarket when Mrs Shidao came back with a plate of fried rice and a delicious potato, cabbage and cucumber salad. For afters, there was *haruka*, a native citrus fruit that is tarter than *ponkan* or *mikan*.

She said her neighbour had given it to her. 'People on the coast are accustomed to sharing food amongst themselves. The fisher-men often give some of their catch to local farmers in return for rice and vegetables.' This kind of non-monetary exchange used to be common in the countryside, and, though it waned in the second half of the nineteenth century, it never entirely went away. Now it is making a comeback, partly because there are so few shops left in places like Hane, but also as a way for people to make themselves useful and stay in touch with their neighbours.

'Depopulation is killing this place,' Mrs Shidao told me.

My son went to the local school. When he left, he moved to Osaka to find work, but he moved back recently to farm chickens. He said he was shocked to see how the lifeblood had drained away from the place in the time he had been away. When he was at school, there were twenty kids in his class. His daughter has just enrolled in the same school, and there are only six kids in her class!

In a fifth of Japan's municipalities, most of them rural commu-nities like Hane, the number of schoolchildren shrank by upwards of 30 per cent in the ten years to 2020 alone.[1] The dearth of children is having a dramatic impact on the education system. Across the country, municipal authorities are closing more than 470 schools every year.[2] 'The only hope for Hane lies in other city dwellers getting tired of city life like my son did and deciding to come and live here,' Mrs Shidao said forlornly.

The same shrinking process is playing out all over rural Japan. The hollowing out of the countryside starts with the abandonment of private houses and the closure of schools, but it soon spreads to local businesses. Across Japan, entire shopping streets have been abandoned, leaving thousands of retail and office spaces standing empty. Once they're gone, rural communities become greying islands, with little to entice locals to stay or outsiders to relocate.

As the number of rate payers goes down, municipal authorities run out of money and are forced to reduce funding for public services, which only encourages more migration to the cities. Public transport is cut back, which forces the remaining residents into cars. This disproportionately affects older people, many of whom have mobility restrictions and are no longer able to drive. All too often, it falls to their ageing children to ferry them to the shops and the doctor's surgery.

Pragmatists see this process as part of a cycle. They say that for every independent trader who pulls down his shutters, there is a thriving out-of-town retail park with a freshly tarmacked car park. What they don't realize is that over the next two decades, as the remaining ageing residents get to the point of needing regular medical treatment, they too will have to leave the countryside for the nearest town. Once they've gone, the retail parks that drove local shops out of business in the boom years are going to fall victim to the same slow process of suffocation. And when the last of the residents has left, it will no longer be feasible to maintain the supply of water and electricity to their villages. Once that happens, life in rural areas will become unsustainable, and the countryside will effectively become uninhabitable.

I went outside to have a smoke. Mrs Shidao had a lovely collection of succulents in her yard, much more colourful than the ones I was accustomed to seeing on the British coastline. The travelling salesman, just back from work, came out to join me. He seemed pleased to see me peering at the little plants, getting intimate with diminutive things being a very Japanese pastime.

He said he lived in a small town just north of Tokushima. He was surprised when I said I hadn't been to any of the temples that pilgrims usually visit as they make their way around Shikoku. 'You must visit them,' he said, not so much recommending as commanding that I go. He dragged on his cigarette with some ferocity, and I found myself wondering at the shape of his head. It was square, hard and unyielding like a bullet. With him for a parent, I could see why a country kid might leave the island for the bright lights of Osaka.

I made my excuses and went upstairs to my room, where I settled in for an evening in front of the telly. NHK was showing a history programme about the development of the umbrella in Edo-era Japan. TBS was screening a programme about an ageing couple who had been feeling a bit listless until they discovered the revitalizing wonders of eating ginseng flowers ('not the root, as customarily thought,' a university professor in a white coat informed us).

Meanwhile, Fuji TV was showing a soap opera about a good-natured everyman who lives in Monzennakachō, the kind of old-fashioned downtown Tokyo neighbourhood where everyone eats *monjayaki* and spends his evenings talking to his neighbours in the local bar.* The drama centred on a bespectacled, middle-aged man everyone called *shachō* ('boss'), who was lamenting his company's latest financial woes and desperately sinking glass after glass of *shōchū*. As befits the good old days, the customers were all men, and the *mama-san* was a maternal, yet still beautiful, middle-aged woman. Dressed in a kimono, she kept the menfolk supplied with

---

* *Monjayaki* is a type of pan-fried batter popular in Kanto, the eastern region around Tokyo. It is similar to *okonomiyaki*, but runnier.

delicious home-cooked food and sake, consoling them without interrupting the flow of manly chat.

During the frequent breaks, I saw several ads for care homes, and lots selling products aimed at the 'grey yen': wigs and walking frames, supplements for people with osteoporosis, and all manner of goods promising to make the nation's bathrooms and kitchens even cleaner. Unsurprisingly for a country that spent 40 years making a lot of money and then 30 years making very little, in Japan, 80 per cent of financial assets are held by people over the age of 50.[3] This is good news for the country's 'silver businesses', which range from leisure and education to healthcare and housing. Among the innovations they have come up with are talking dolls that promise to make you feel less lonely, and diagnostic toilets that analyse your stools and give you advice on how to improve your diet.

The growth of the grey economy is particularly good news for Big Pharma. Japan's pharmaceuticals market was worth $105 billion in 2020, up from $76 billion in 2008.[4] Much of this growth is driven by rising demand for drugs used to treat geriatric ailments, from Alzheimer's to erectile disfunction, bedsores and diabetes.

Some businesses have managed to adapt to the ageing society successfully. One of Japan's largest nappy makers has announced that while it will continue to make nappies for babies in Malaysia and Indonesia, it will stop producing them in Japan and, instead, focus on the market for adult-sized nappies. Sales of adult nappies have been outpacing those for infants for more than a decade. This market is estimated to be worth more than $2 billion a year and is only expected to grow in the years to come.[5]

For most businesses, however, an ageing population can only be bad news. In 2010, the head of General Electric Japan, Yoshiaki Fujimori, noted with exasperation that his company had not grown in the past five years. Elderly people tend to go to bed earlier than other demographics, so they use less electricity.[6] It's not just a matter of elderly people consuming less than younger people. An ageing population is the first sign of a shrinking population, and as the number of people goes down, so does the demand for goods and products. Nobody wants to invest in a venture that can only promise diminishing returns.

In the course of my research, I found no studies of how companies can make money investing in a shrinking market. For now, what concerns governments most about the shrinking process is not post-growth economics, but the dependency ratio, which is to say the ratio between those who are economically active and those who are not (children, the retired and the sick). Japan's working-age population went from 50 million in 1950 to a peak of 87 million in 1995. That year, 70 per cent of Japanese people were of working age. Savings boomed, and the banks lent that money to the country's companies, which channelled it into breakneck growth. Since 1995, however, the working-age population has been falling sharply, and by 2050 it is likely to be back to 50 million, forming a perfect bell curve over the course of a century.[7]

By then, the likelihood is that 40 per cent of Japanese people will be over 65, and that is going to put a terrible financial burden on working people. Workers pay income tax, but the retired do not, so as the proportion of retirees goes up, government revenue from income tax goes down. In 1960, there were eleven workers supporting each retired person.[8] By 2020, there were fewer than two, and the NIPSSR predicts that by 2050 the working and non-working populations will be almost the same size.[9]

This state of affairs is unprecedented. The fear is that, as Japan's economic power and global competitiveness continue to wane, its lopsided dependency ratio will immiserate the government, leading to the breakdown of its ability to provide social services. Before that happens, the dependency ratio may provoke a political crisis, or even a revolt against the gerontocratic LDP. The government currently apportions 70 per cent of the welfare budget to pensions and medical services for the aged. Only 4 per cent is spent on child benefit and childcare services.[10] For the time being, voters seem happy to see so much of their taxes being spent on the elderly. They will be less happy if that means cutting back on social services that they and their children use.

Optimists argue that while the problems created by an ageing society are worrying, they are not unique to Japan, and the Japanese government has fared no worse than those of other countries. Despite thirty years of anaemic economic growth and stagnating wages, it has managed to maintain standards. So far, say those resisting the doomsayers, the ageing society has not caused political problems. Most elderly people accept that the country's best days are behind it, but that doesn't mean that it is about to fall into an abyss.

Moreover, Japan may already be over the worst of its shrinking pains. The most dramatic rise in the elderly population occurred between 1990 and 2010. In the next decade or two, the proportion of elderly people is likely to rise from 30 per cent to 40 per cent of the population, but as long as the fertility rate falls no lower than 1.0 it is unlikely to rise much further.

Besides, an ageing society needn't be a problem if elderly people continue to work and pay taxes. Of course, for that to happen, the retirement age will have to rise, which is unlikely to be a popular move. While I was cycling around Shikoku, the French were striking in protest at President Emanuel Macron's proposal to raise the retirement age from 62 to 64. In the UK, the pension age is already 66, and it is set to rise to 67 from 2026. It is expected to rise to 68 from 2044, and researchers are already saying that this is not going to be enough and that anyone born after April 1970 will likely have to work until they are 71 before they can claim their pension.[11]

In Japan, the picture is rather different. The percentage of over-65-year-olds who would like to do (or continue doing) a paid job is, at 40 per cent, far higher than in other rich-world countries.[12] The elderly are happy to keep working, often voluntarily, because they believe it is good for the country, and because it is what Japanese people have always done. They also want less stuff, presumably because their appetite for accumulation has waned in tandem with their ambitions; for many, the prospect of renumeration is no longer what motivates them to go to work.

Town halls run all kinds of volunteering programmes to keep elderly residents busy. Unfortunately, this does nothing for the state's coffers, which are crying out for more revenue from income tax. In 2021, the Diet approved bills requiring companies to retain their workers until they are 70 years old, effectively raising the retirement age from 65.[13] Reformers say that, in future, the retirement age should be linked to life expectancy; perhaps, in time, it will have to be raised to 75. Perhaps, in time, the rest of us will have to follow Japan's example.

*

I couldn't help feeling a bit forlorn witnessing the decline of the towns and villages I was passing through, but I was enjoying the peace and quiet of Shikoku. I spent the following day travelling west along the coast road from Hane to Kōchi city, past huge empty beaches, breathing in the air coming ashore through the pine trees. Coming into the city as the sun set into the sea, the sight of a customer in a shop seemed quite a novelty, its light a beacon in the suburban wilderness.

I spent much of the following day traversing the inclines of a mountainous peninsula called Yokonami, where high cliffs overlooked little coves, offering spectacular views over the Pacific Ocean. Towards the end of the day, I finally had a chance to see a *daruma* sunset, a natural phenomenon particular to Kōchi prefecture, in which the setting sun appears to resemble a traditional *daruma* doll. It occurs when warm air near the surface of the ocean meets cooler air higher up and refracts the sunlight, creating a unique, doll-like silhouette.

I ended the day in Susaki, an industrial town dominated by an enormous cement factory. I was by then growing accustomed to such stark contrasts between natural beauty, industrial development and mass suburbanization. On the outskirts of the town, I came to a giant hypermarket with a vast, almost empty car park. It looked to have been built for a much busier city.

I went inside to have some *tonkatsu* in the food court, passing a woman around my age who was helping her ageing mum get from her walking frame into the passenger seat of the car. Wandering the aisles with the handful of elderly couples doing their weekly shop was a bit like walking the streets of Tokyo at night; it felt liberating to have such a huge, prosperous place all to myself. There were all kinds of nursing-care products on offer: aprons for use while bathing elderly parents, disposal bags for all those adult nappies and bags of thickening powder, called *toromi*, that old people put in their drinks to stop them choking.

After my cutlet, I went to the nearest coffee shop to immerse myself in some of the data of demographic decline. When I got there, they were playing Aha's 'Take On Me'. It was a strange place to find myself being dragged back into the soundtrack to my youth, but I had heard a lot of 1980s pop in sleepy margins since coming to Shikoku. The 80s were Japan's golden years, and everywhere I had been I had heard orchestral cover versions of classics like 'Dancing on the Ceiling' and 'Girls Just Wanna Have Fun'.

I was served by a robot waiter. I could hear him coming because a plinky-plonky tune was emanating from the top of his head and his little plastic wheels screeched on the lino every time he went around a corner. When I told him I wanted the 'drink as much coffee as you like' option, he replied, 'Fine, help yourself,' and skidded away with a good-natured, pixelated smile on his customer interface.

The only other customer in Café Gusto that evening was a man about my age. He wanted to practise his English but struggled to make small talk. 'I have been to fifty-five countries,' he told me with a stutter. 'I liked England, Holland and Germany best.' Ah yes, I thought, steeling myself for the customary harsh words about China and Korea. 'I liked Vietnam too. It's an exciting place – on the way up. Not like Japan. Brazil was very dangerous,' he went on. 'And I hate China and Korea.' When I queried his prejudice, he admitted he had been to neither.

I asked him how he liked Japan and he looked deflated. 'It's better than the rest, but the government . . .' He scowled. 'The economy is stagnating, and no one is having kids.' When I asked him if he was married, he said he was not. So here was one of the famous single men of Kōchi prefecture that I had read about before coming. I asked him why he had chosen to remain single. He just said that life was easier that way.

I'd have liked to talk to him more about Japan's demographic crisis, but I found his stillness unnerving, and the sound of the robot waiter's squeaky voice echoing through the empty coffee shop only added to the air of unreality. We sat together without saying a word until the tension got too much and I took my leave.

*

From Tokushima in the north-east of Shikoku, I had made it to the little visited south-western corner of the island. Beyond Susaki, the cliffs rose right out of the sea, and the road builders had had to carve out a wild little road and build a roof for it. By now, the landscape was not so much depopulated as unpopulated. There were no settlements in this part of the island until the road turned inland at Kotohira shrine, where a river came down to the sea and I found a little village. It felt like a hive of activity after so many miles of solitary cycling, although in fact the only people I saw outside the village shop were a stooped old woman in a pinny perusing some vegetables and a couple of fishermen in thick plastic macs.

When I asked the old woman if there was somewhere I could find some lunch, she gestured towards a door in a nondescript concrete building. Inside was plain too: no decorations on the wall and a sticky floor that slurped at me as I made my way to the counter. The walls were stained with grease or maybe nicotine and there was a rancid smell. I was the only customer.

Two men, who I took to be father and son, looked up from behind the counter. They both looked like they'd just got out of bed, but the older man gave me a hearty enough welcome. A woman, who I took to be the older man's wife, appeared and I ordered sashimi – octopus, salmon, yellowtail and tuna – a tomato salad, some gyoza, a bowl of rice and a cold beer. The food was excellent, and the people turned out to be nice too.

I was learning to recognize the manners of the older generation of country dwellers. They were remarkably tough and prosaic people, the men of few words who loved hard work and their more voluble wives, who fussed about good-naturedly. The woman was slow and steady. 'There are only a few old fishermen left here now, and they're getting on a bit,' she told me. 'There are still a few kids in the local school, but they all leave for the city once they're old enough to work.'

She wasn't a great one for small talk either. The TV was on, as it always was. In a country so little given to discussion, it was ubiquitous, and when it was not showing a baseball match, it was usually showing a programme about food, preferably one in which a celebrity was sampling some regional specialities. Food and drink are what people liked to talk about – nobody can argue about food. Yet I always felt distracted by the fear underlying the endless pleasantries: the fear that people might argue, as if a raised voice were only a step away from a riot.

After lunch, I followed the little road up the valley past terraces of rich black soil planted with beautifully tended rows of radishes, onions and cabbage. The terraces, the road, the valley and the people who lived in it were all diminutive. Even the flatbed minivan that crawled past me, rallying support for the Japanese Communist Party from a megaphone, was tiny. '*Heiwa to kurashi o mamoru*' ('Defend peace and livelihoods') went the pre-recorded speech, which echoed around the valley in the pauses between the lines.

It was a long, hard climb over the mountains, and by the time I reached Shimantochō I was all but done in. It was getting dark, so I decided to take the local train for the final stretch to the neighbouring town of Shimantoshi. I made it to the station just in time for the last train of the day. The young driver hurried me aboard and kindly showed me how to tether my bike to the handrail, before donning his white gloves and dashing back to his cabin.

It was a cosy single carriage decorated with anime characters, with little curtains in the windows, and I was the only passenger. As we set off, the night closed in, and the rain began to fall on the bamboo groves. We were still in mountainous country, and I lost count of the number of tunnels the train passed through. It is easy to bemoan the extravagant expenditure on infrastructure, but as Japan's high-growth years recede in the rear-view mirror, I couldn't help marvelling at how well the government had spent the money when it had it.

Half an hour later, we reached Shimantoshi, where I checked into a *minshuku* and went straight to the local *onsen* to warm up. The locals craned their necks to look at me when I arrived, but politely ignored me thereafter. It was the most rudimentary public bath I'd ever visited, with none of the facilities I'd come to expect: no free soap or shampoo, and no sauna or jacuzzi. The artificial leather covering the massage chair in the dressing room was worn, and the lino was curling up from the corners of the bare changing room.

I'd been told of *onsen* where the water was so hot that nobody under the age of 65 could bear to sit in it. As my skin turned lobster pink, I comforted myself with the thought that I'd finally reached the austere heart of the Japanese countryside, a place untouched by the niceties of service-obsessed urban culture. To celebrate my arrival, I did something I'd never dared to do before: I sat in the electric bath. The belief that a mild electrical current is good for the heart is a peculiarity of Japan's bathing culture that I had, until then, been happy to leave to the stoical old men and women of the baby boom, for whom 'no pain, no gain' is practically a mantra. It was a deeply disconcerting experience; only by exercising the power of mind over matter could I convince myself that by electrocuting myself I was doing my health the world of good.

Afterwards, I followed the old timers' example, and bought a bottle of milk from the vending machine outside. Both the machine and the bottle looked to date from the 1970s. I sat on a bench and listened to the strangely comforting sound of the klaxon at the level crossing, warning that the barrier was about to come down. Through a gap in the wall of the *onsen*, I caught sight of a cat warming herself on a hot pipe, and the manager's hand slowly tickling her under her chin. It had been so long since I'd seen any display of physical affection, even towards a cat, that there was something almost illicit about the scene.

*

I'd been lucky with the weather until then, but it caught up with me that evening, when the temperature suddenly dropped to zero. The following morning, I made the decision not to go any further south. Instead, I would get back on the train and head north to the castle town of Uwajima.

A couple of hours later, I was sitting in a tempura restaurant in the town's very long and practically deserted shopping arcade, watching the wind blow flurries of snow through the empty streets.

When it stopped snowing, the wind died down, the sun broke through the clouds and I walked up a steep wooded hillside to have a look around the town's castle. From the top floor, I had an impressive view of the snow-dusted islands in the bay. It was no weather for cycling, so I decided to call it a day. I would get the train north to Matsuyama the next day, and then fly back to Tokyo.

I spent my last night in Shikoku in a grotty business hotel at the foot of the castle's ramparts. My first taste of neglect, at the Kitamuras' place in Aratano, had made a welcome change from the fastidiousness I'd grown used to in Tokyo. By now, however, the novelty had worn off. The kettle was dirty, the floor hadn't been vacuumed and the heating didn't work. I complained to room service, and the elderly proprietor tottered to my room to apologize. Quivering behind her was her middle-aged son, who came bearing an electric heater. She appeared to be losing her marbles and he didn't seem to have the wherewithal to help her.

This set-up is not unusual. Households consisting of an unmarried man in his forties or fifties and his elderly parents are on the increase, particularly in depopulated rural areas. Many sons don't leave the family home until they get married, and when that doesn't happen, many of them spend their entire lives dependent on their mothers to do the cooking and cleaning.

As long as the parents remain healthy, all is well, but problems arise if they become bedridden or need care, for the son is usually unable to provide for his own daily needs, let alone theirs. There have been many cases of abuse reported in the media, committed by sons whose aggression is often borne of frustration and/or depression brought on by the role reversal that takes place when ageing parents are no longer able to look after themselves.

The situation is worse for middle-aged daughters because many elderly people still expect their daughters to take care of them in their dotage. This is where Japan's informal welfare system, which men have taken for granted for millennia, collides with the reality of a shrinking workforce. The government says that it wants to raise the fertility rate, but it also wants more women to join the workforce, in the hope that they reduce labour shortages. This is a hard circle to square, as many working women are too busy looking after the older generation to think about raising a new one.

*

The plane back to Tokyo flew north over the mountains of Shikoku towards the Inland Sea and then east along the Pacific littoral. Looking out of the window, the general impression was of intensive farming, but there were quite a lot of abandoned fields, and plenty of solar panels on land that would have been given over to farming a generation ago.

This is not new, of course. Japanese people have been moving off the land and into the cities for generations. What *is* new is the collapse of the domestic tourist trade, which the government pumped billions of yen into in the 1990s in an attempt to generate jobs for people living in the rural hinterland. Reflecting on my trip to Shikoku, it occurred to me that wherever I had been, practically all the roadside eateries, coffee shops and lodgings I passed had been closed.

Peering through the dusty window of a roadside travel lodge had been like looking back in time to the 1980s, when all was right with Japan. People had lived in families back then, and they'd taken their holidays together. Midway through the third decade of the twenty-first century, however, the family ideal has come to look distinctly passé, as has that of the happy couple. The holidays ads I'd seen on the metro in Tokyo invariably featured young women – either girls with other girls, or girls all by themselves. The changes in tourism are economic as well as demographic: the younger generation is divided between those with proper jobs, who would rather holiday abroad, and the rest, who don't have money for any kind of holiday. As a result, the domestic tourist trade has all but dried up.

It wasn't just that the towns and villages I'd passed through in Shikoku were economically moribund; most of them had been deserted. Yet the pragmatist in me had to ask: so what? The depopulation of the countryside is just one facet of the ageing and shrinking process. In other ways, being elderly in Japan is great. Generally speaking, the younger generations pay OAPs a great deal of respect, partly because filial piety is still strong and partly because those ageing baby boomers are the ones who got the country back on its feet after the trauma of war, defeat and occupation. Without them, Japan would not be the safe, prosperous and eminently stable country it is today.

The evening news occasionally reported on problems associated with mass ageing, such as the rising number of traffic accidents caused by elderly drivers, but the tone was always caring and affectionate, for the nation's grandparents are considered to be beyond reproach. Living in a land of old people might be strange, but it is still comfortable, just as it is in remote parts of Scandinavia and North America. The question is, for how much longer can the state afford to subsidize them? Currently, the Japanese government's biggest problem is not the ageing population per se, but the huge debt that it is accumulating to pay for their healthcare and pensions.

It is easy to assume that this ballooning debt is down to the multitude of 'bridges to nowhere' that the government built in the late 1990s. But it stopped approving that kind of big stimulus package two decades ago, and these days state spending is not especially high. In 2024, Japan's government spending was the equivalent of 44 per cent of GDP, which compares favourably with the UK, where it was 45 per cent.[14]

National debt has grown, not because the government spends too much, but because tax revenues have halved since 1990.[15] This is extraordinary, but hardly surprising: after three decades of economic stagnation, the pay of many workers has fallen below the income tax threshold, corporate tax revenues have dropped and the slump in land prices has hit revenue from inheritance tax.

As a result, the government has had to borrow money. Back in 2005, for every ¥100 it spent, it had to borrow ¥40. By 2012, that had risen to ¥50, and public borrowing had ballooned to 230 per cent of GDP, far and away the highest rate of indebtedness in the OECD. For now, at least, the international money markets still regard Japanese government bonds as a safe haven rather than a ticking time bomb. This has allowed successive governments to borrow money for ten years while paying interest rates of less than 1 per cent, a cheaper supply of money than any government has enjoyed since Babylonian times.[16]

Unfortunately, rising interest rates are pushing up the cost of borrowing, and in the years to come, declining tax revenues will leave the government with no option but to take on even more debt. Japan's debt-to-GDP ratio will become even more distended, and this will inevitably affect its credit rating. Fortunately for the Japanese government, it is able to borrow most of the money it needs from its own people, who accumulated huge savings in the years of high growth. Japan Post is said to be the largest holder of personal savings in the world, and it holds about a fifth of the country's national debt in the form of government bonds.[17]

The government uses this money to pay for pensions and healthcare for the elderly, but it also funnels it into chosen industries, and this steady flow of cash is the grease that keeps the LDP's re-election machine on the road. It is no coincidence that, as well as being the government's favourite lender, Japan Post is also the nation's largest employer, with over 400,000 employees. Most of them vote LDP and, like the ruling party, they value state paternalism, informal social welfare, risk avoidance and predictability.[18]

This approach might have worked in the boom times, but unfortunately for the nation's conservatives, nobody has any money any more. Before the financial meltdown of the early 1990s, the savings rate was running at more than 20 per cent of disposable income; by 2023 it had dropped to just 0.1 per cent.[19] For now, this precipitous decline is offset by a strong rise in corporate savings, which is why Japan continues to run a comfortable current account surplus. But as and when it turns negative, doubts about the sustainability of Japan's debt financing are sure to grow.

As Japan Inc. frets about the future of the domestic economy, it is investing ever larger sums overseas. Japan remains the world's richest country in terms of net foreign assets, but a nation of wealthy companies and ageing, impoverished workers is not sustainable. If the shrinking economy convinces Japan's multinationals to stop investing at home altogether, the government will have to start borrowing money from abroad. Once that happens, its current account surplus will soon vanish.

That is an eventuality the government will go a long way to avoid, and so, rather than resort to borrowing from abroad, it is more likely to progressively push up the consumption tax, cut back on social security benefits and possibly even inflate away its debts. That would mean, in effect, partially defaulting, not on its debts to financial markets, but on its obligations to society. That is bound to cause political strife. The question is, how much squeezing will the Japanese people put up with before the pips start to squeak?

9.

'Quality over Quantity': Three Farmers in Miyazaki

My trip to Shikoku left me with the impression of a little-visited museum: curling at the corners and on the brink of shutting down for good. Still, I knew that by sticking to the picturesque coastline, I had only skirted the issue. To see the most severe consequences of Japan's demographic woes, I would have to venture into the interior, to the uplands and mountain valleys that are home to its more remote communities.

I also needed to talk to more people, particularly those actively grappling with the seismic shift in thinking that a shrinking population demands. Some of them were sure to see things as starkly as I did. I wanted to find out what they were doing to rise to the challenge. Fortunately for me, the Japanese government is well aware of foreign interest in its demographic difficulties and is keen to show journalists what it is doing to tackle the problems associated with childlessness and mass ageing. Shortly after my return to Tokyo, I got word that the Foreign Press Centre was organising a trip for journalists to visit some farmers in Miyazaki prefecture and I decided to tag along.

The ageing society is having a dramatic effect on farming in Japan. The average age of a farmer is 69, making Japanese farmers the oldest in the world.[1] With the number of farmers declining even faster than the overall population, the agricultural sector is beset by a shortage of workers, especially come harvest time. Depopulation is changing farming in less expected ways too. Demand for food is declining because older people need fewer calories than the young. Plus, the Japanese palate has changed. The young eat less rice and more wheat and meat products than their grandparents, and most of these have to be imported. Combine that with the shrinking population, and you can see that even more fields are going to be abandoned in the years to come.

The government says that it doesn't have to be that way. The LDP has laid out its 'Vision for a Digital Garden City Nation' and the 'Green Transformation' has been a key policy for successive LDP governments. The way the prime minister's press office sees things, rural communities are at the forefront of the digital transformation. By 2025, 'almost all farmers in the country will practice "smart agriculture" with advanced technology – including AI, robots, and the IoT [Internet of Things] – for improved efficiency and productivity in the face of labour shortages due to an aging population.'[2]

Prior to joining the press trip, I was given lots of glossy brochures, illustrated with photos of robots, GPS-guided drones and smiling old folk, hyping up the government's plans for farming communities. There were no abandoned fields in its vision for the future. Instead, there were automated combine harvesters, controlled remotely by enthusiastic young farmers in white coats.

I was looking forward to seeing these high-tech solutions for myself, and Miyazaki was the place to see them. Lying on the eastern half of Kyushu, the big island in the south-west corner of Japan, the prefecture is farming country. Thanks to the volcanos that created the island, the soil is dark and rich, which explains why Miyazaki is the country's biggest producer of cucumbers and is number two for green peppers. Some years, crops are destroyed by typhoons, and other years by floodwater, but farmers replant as soon as the water recedes, and many of them are able to get two harvests a year.

We flew from Tokyo to Miyazaki and then boarded a minibus, which took us inland. We were to visit three farms. The first was a family business called Ishihara Foods, a major producer of frozen vegetables on the road to Miyakonojō. The company produces, packs and freezes 2,000 tons of vegetables a year, more than half of which is spinach, plus edamame, carrots, burdock, yam, broccoli and radish.

Its offices were decorated in mushroom, which set a reassuringly utilitarian tone after the endless brightly lit offices of white-collar Tokyo. The president of the company was 35-year-old Shoko Ishihara, a friendly farmer with a brisk and business-like attitude. The European journalists among us wanted to know what the company's employees thought about having a woman for their CEO. After all, Japan is a country in which women make up just 1 per cent of senior managers. 'I don't pay attention to that sort of thing,' she said simply.

Before taking over the family business in 2021, Ms Ishihara had been a social worker in a town in Miyagi prefecture that had been devastated by the tsunami that hit the north-east of the country in 2011. She had acted as a bridge between the central government and local people, many of whom had lost everything. 'Seeing people leave the area after losing their jobs to the tsunami, I realized that welfare cannot do everything. Employment is the greatest form of welfare, and there have to be local businesses that can create jobs for people.'

Ishihara Foods used to be a traditional wholesaler, buying their vegetables from 300 local farmers, which gives you an idea of how small most Japanese farms are. Japan is blessed and cursed by having so many smallholders, often a man and his wife. On the one hand, it means that farmers are independent; on the other, it makes for higher costs.

Ms Ishihara's father used to bring the vegetables from his suppliers' fields to his warehouse, where a team of women would sort and pack them. But then his suppliers started to get old and retire, so in 2003 he made the decision to move into farming himself and, one by one, he bought out his suppliers. 'Most of them were happy to sell,' said Ms Ishihara. 'Their sons and daughters weren't interested in farming, and until we came along, they'd been resigned to abandoning their fields to the weeds.'

Her father's intervention gave the local community a new lease of life, but the ageing process hampered his new venture just as it had the local farmers': within a few years, the fifty local women he employed to harvest, sort and pack the vegetables also retired. With no young people to take their places, and tight controls on bringing in immigrant labour, he had to think afresh.

'As part of my training to take over the business, my dad sent me to California to spend some time working on farms there,' said Ms Ishihara.

> Like many foreign visitors, I was surprised to see how dependent American farmers were on immigrant workers from Central America. But what really amazed me was how much work was still being done by hand. It was pretty ironic, given that Silicon Valley was only a few hours' drive away. But I guess my employers' dependence on cheap foreign labour had blinded them to the potential of the latest technical innovations.

When she returned to Miyazaki, she convinced her father to invest heavily in digital management and to mechanize as much of the food production process as possible. 'Now, we use smartphones to manage everything from growth conditions to work records and the agrochemicals we use on our crops,' she said. They had deployed sensors in the fields to monitor all the variables, from temperature to rainfall, sunlight, soil quality and fertilizer. From the comfort of her office, she could see who was working where, and with cameras installed in every field, she was able to monitor the damage done by pests and heavy rain.

Today, Ishihara Foods farms 500 hectares, spread out over 750 plots, all within a 30-minute drive of head office. Having so many plots to farm means they cannot achieve the economies of scale that make farming in Hokkaido so profitable. But by freezing their vegetables, they don't have to worry about being so far from their consumers in Tokyo, Osaka and Nagoya.

Although the company has automated much of the production process, it still has 116 employees, and is still bedevilled by labour shortages. Farming, forestry and fishing have sustained rural communities for millennia, but they are poorly paid and most young people don't want to do them, considering them to be *kitsui* ('hard'), *kitanai* ('dirty') and/or *kiken* ('dangerous'). 'I want to change the image people have of farming as being hard and dirty work,' said Ms Ishihara. 'My goal is "easy agriculture" where you don't even have to touch the soil.'

She took us out to the fields to show us one of their fully automated, air-conditioned 'robot' tractors. It looked like an ordinary tractor, but it was driverless and used satellite GPS to navigate its way around the fields. 'Burdock roots are almost 2 metres long. Digging them up used to take a long time, and the guy in the cab would often fall asleep while he was doing it,' she said with a laugh. 'Now we don't have to worry about that.'

Like Ms Ishihara, the visionaries at the Ministry of Agriculture hope that once dependence on manual labour comes to an end, popular perceptions of farming will change. Deploying high-tech solutions means that farming no longer need be hard work, they say. In the future, food producers will be more akin to engineers and technicians than farmers. They will be entrepreneurs who happen to produce food, their profit margins will grow and this will attract more young people into the business.

Once the dependence on rain, sun and soil is broken, food crops can be grown anywhere. They can be grown indoors, lit artificially and watered hydroponically, allowing them to grow at any time of day or night, without the need for soil. They can also be grown in towers to maximize the use of space, and these towers can be built in cities, reducing the distance between producer and consumer, and allowing everyone to enjoy fresher, tastier food. Transport costs will come down, reducing carbon emissions, as well as the cost of food.

My visit to Ishihara Foods gave me an exciting vision of the huge improvements in farming made possible by hydroponics. Put your faith in the power of technology, and you'll appreciate that Japan's farming sector may have no need for mass immigration to alleviate its labour shortages. But Ishihara Foods wasn't there yet. Ms Ishihara employed two 'technical trainees' from overseas (she said she was not allowed to call them 'immigrants' because, officially at least, Japan doesn't have an immigration policy for agricultural workers). One of them was from China and the other from Indonesia. 'The Chinese guy is really good,' she said. 'He can use a laptop and is always keen to do more.'

★

Back in the minibus, several of the foreign journalists I was travelling with were scornful of the Japanese farming model. One of them pointed out that Ishihara Foods was quite unusual, both for its size and its commitment to high technology. Most Japanese farms are smallholdings, lovingly tended by ageing farmers who are only still in business because the LDP subsidizes their production of overpriced fruit and vegetables in return for their support on election day. Japanese consumers should be voting with their wallets, and buying cheaper imported fruit and veg, argued another. Perhaps they should, I countered, but Japanese shoppers believe that domestic produce is of a higher quality and are happy to pay over the odds. It might not make much sense to a free trader, but it keeps the last of Japan's ageing farmers in business.

The second farm we visited was more illustrative of this model – and of the Galapagos Syndrome that critics blame for the domestically focussed, introspective turn that the Japanese economy has taken since the 1980s. The boss of Yokoyama Kajuen was Yoichi Yokoyama, who had left his job at a major grocery-store chain 11 years before, to become the third generation of Yokoyamas to run the family's mango farm on the outskirts of Miyazaki city.

Like Shoko Ishihara, Mr Yokoyama was committed to investing big in high tech. He grew his mangoes in polytunnels, which allowed him to keep them artificially heated at a constant temperature of 30°C. Guiding us into one of his tunnels, he told me that he tied each fruit into a position where it would get the maximum amount of sunshine, and cut the rest of the fruit off the branch, so that the 'only child' at the end got the maximum amount of nutrition. He had forty-eight trees and produced 5,000 mangoes a year, each of which sold for ¥6,800 (£34).

Why were they so expensive, I asked him. 'Well, I have five mango greenhouses, and each one cost me ¥48 million [£244,000] to set up,' he told me. 'The way we cultivate them is expensive too. I have six workers and we tend each fruit by hand every day.' Looking around, I saw a worker standing stock still, silently peering at a mango. This, I thought, is the Japanese way. I was reminded of the only other time I had visited a farm in Japan, when I had been impressed to see a worker watering grapes individually, by hand, with an eye dropper.

But still, who would pay £34 for a mango? 'We produce fruit for the corporate fruit market,' said Mr Yokoyama. He was referring to the custom whereby companies give premium-grade fruit to valued clients in spring and summer to mark the change of season. 'Companies give their clients fruit as a token of gratitude for their custom and to wish them prosperity,' he said. Mr Yokoyama's most prized variety was *taiyō no tamago* ('egg of the sun'). He was looking forward to the annual mango auction, and the 'celebratory prices' he would be able to charge. The first piece of fruit from his first crop of the season regularly went for ¥486,000 (£2,440). He gave me a slice of his standard, ¥5,800(£29)-a-pop Irwins to try. It was the sunniest shade of yellow and had a wonderfully fragrant aroma. I took a bite: it was indeed a perfect mango.

Mr Yokoyama was also keen to show us his avocados. 'They have only become popular in Japan in recent years,' he said, leading us from one hot and humid polytunnel into another. 'Almost all of the avocados consumed in Japan are a single variety imported from Mexico. When we learned that, we were determined to grow avocados that match the Japanese palate as well as Miyazaki's climate.'

With avocados said to be the most nutritious fruit in the world, Mr Yokoyama was confident of turning Miyazaki into a major producer. 'So far, we have tried growing sixty varieties. By a careful process of trial and error, we have whittled this down to fifteen.' He showed us his luxury variety, a massive avocado that he marketed as the 'Hinata Princess'. It was twice the size of a standard avocado and sold for ¥9,700 (£48). I could see that he put a great deal of time and energy into growing his avocados but, really, how could he justify charging so much? The Mexican avocados in my local supermarket in Tokyo went for ¥160 (80 pence) each, and even his regular avocados only cost ¥970 (£4.80) each.

The expression on Mr Yokoyama's face betrayed not a trace of cynicism. 'Mexican avocados spend 180 days on the tree. Ours spend 250 days on the tree. This increases their oil content, and gives them a butterier texture,' he told me patiently. 'And the avocado tree is fickle. Some trees give us a hundred pieces of fruit, while others give us none.' And who was paying these outsized prices? 'Most of our customers are high-class restaurants, mainly French, mainly in Osaka and Fukuoka,' he said. 'They are happy to pay premium prices for top-quality ingredients.'

★

One of the reasons why Japanese people are concentrating in the cities is the lack of interesting, well-paid jobs in the countryside. But as the systems of mass production and mass consumption are being increasingly called into question, a two-tier structure is emerging. A growing number of people want to know more about the provenance of their food, buy organic and support domestic farmers. This has created a secondary, smaller but more profitable market, in response to which a small but growing number of young people are opting to become farmers. Catering to the growing market for produce with a conscience gives them precious *ikigai*, and they like the relatively relaxed tempo of life outside the harvest season. Those that can integrate production, processing, marketing and online sales are able to make a passable living.

The third farm we visited, Katsuki Wines, was a good example of all of the above. It should be said at the outset that Miyazaki prefecture is not wine country. It rains constantly, the summers are hot and humid, and harvests are frequently destroyed by the typhoons that roll through in the autumn months. None of this, however, had deterred the owner of the vineyard, Yoshitada Katsuki. Like many 30-somethings, he had grown up determined to escape the rat race. He went to New Zealand as a backpacker and spent the next ten years working in its wineries. 'In Japan, people get bored in the countryside. They don't want to work in the fields with all those old farmers,' he told us. 'But when I was in New Zealand, I saw how exciting country life can be.'

Returning to his hometown of Aya in 2013, Mr Katsuki set out to produce fully organic wine from grapes sustainably cultivated on a hectare of land he had inherited from his father. It was far from straightforward. His first grapes rotted on the vine, so he learned to cover them with plastic sheets to keep the rain off. His first harvest was plagued by infection, so he ordered a tough variety of Chardonnay grape from Portland, Oregon and began experimenting with more infection-resistant types. But most of his second harvest was eaten by birds and bugs attracted to the sweet young fruit – after that, he learned to cover his vines with nets in July.

Only in 2018 was he finally able to bring in his first decent grape harvest. Despite being priced at ¥10,000 (£50) per bottle, the first 1,000 bottles of his 'miracle wine' sold out within a month. By the time of our visit, he was producing 6,000 bottles a year, most of which he sold online, though he also had a following among the bar and restaurant owners of Miyazaki, many of whom shared his philosophy and admired his passion. Come harvest time, some of them helped him to pick the grapes, and several had gone on to become friends.

Mr Katsuki's business was hardly thriving; he had racked up debts of ¥29 million (£145,000), and could not survive without subsidies from the prefectural government, which is keen to support anyone who looks like they might revitalize the farming sector in Miyazaki. 'I am still hopeful of building a thriving business,' he said, as the rain poured down around us. 'I am not trying to produce great wine. I just want to show young people what you can do with a bit of effort.'

Mr Katsuki was walking on a well-trodden path, looking for *satori* ('enlightenment') by seeking out and then overcoming adversity. In many ways, he could be said to have succeeded. He had a job he enjoyed and was a respected member of his community. 'I spend my free time drinking my wine with my friends,' he said with a broad smile. But it wasn't a path I felt tempted to follow him down. We were in Miyazaki, not New Zealand, much less the Mediterranean, and the native sensibility – shy, restrained, instinctively private – was still dominant. Even in springtime, when the air was fresh and the scent of ripening crops hung in the air, he and his new buddies preferred to sit indoors to drink his wine. Nobody at Katsuki Wines was going to be pulling out a guitar, striking up a tune and inviting passers-by to join them in an impromptu dance anytime soon.

Be that as it may, Mr Katsuki shared his excitement with everyone, and several budding entrepreneurs who wanted to make their own wine in the future had gathered to work for him, many of them urbanites looking to escape the daily grind of the office worker's life. He employed three young winemakers, all from other prefectures, who had heard about Katsuki Wines through social media. One of them was Motoki Sugino, who told me that he used to be an accountant in Nagoya. 'The working hours were long, and I didn't like my job, so I jacked it in and went to New Zealand. When I came back, I joined Katsuki Wines.'

In the course of my travels in the Japanese countryside, I would meet lots of young people like Motoki – migrants from the cities who were concerned that, unless more is done to revitalize moribund rural communities, there is a real danger that they will simply disappear. There are still a few traditional, rural craftspeople holding out, but if they go, much of what makes Japan distinct will go with them.

Many migrants want to breathe new life into the farming sector by creating high-value-added farm goods that can be marketed online and exported, building on Japan's reputation for top-quality, beautifully packaged consumer goods. While artisanal production will never be able to sustain more than a slither of people living in rural communities, it is certainly acting as a lure to a significant number of jaded young city dwellers.

*

Before we flew back to Tokyo, the team from the Foreign Press Centre had one more good news story for us: the regeneration of what was once Japan's premier honeymoon destination. Aoshima is a seaside resort just south of Miyazaki city. It is named after a tiny subtropical island that lies 200 metres off the coast. In the centre of the island is an ancient Shinto shrine that is listed in *Nihon Shoki* (*Chronicles of Japan*), the second-oldest book of classical Japanese history, as answering the prayers for happiness of those entering into arranged marriages. It has long been a pilgrimage site for women hoping for romance and marriage.

A stiff breeze was blowing as we crossed the bridge from the mainland, but the vegetation on the island was so thick that no sooner had we crossed to the leeward side than the wind fell away, and it became wonderfully still and quiet. The jungle on Aoshima island is said to be the most northerly in Japan, a vestige of the dense thicket that covered southern Kyushu before the land was brought under the plough.

The Nagatomo family have been head priests at the shrine for the past twenty generations. The current holder of the post, Yasutaka Nagatomo, met us in front of the plain red *torii* gate that marked the entrance to the shrine in a resplendent outfit of purple and white robes. He led us through the *torii* gate to the intricately carved gateway to the shrine, which was painted in beautiful hues of tropical yellow and orange. 'Some of the palm trees on the island date back to the Edo period,' he said, gesturing overhead. We walked down a carefully raked sand path to the shrine's inner sanctum, where we came to a rock covered with tiny seashells.

'Cowrie shells are the oldest charm in Japan. Pregnant women used to take one from the beach to the shrine to pray for a safe delivery,' he said, picking up a cowrie from the sand and handing it to me. It was part of a longstanding tradition of expressing one's feelings for one's partner through the gift of a shell. 'They are bivalved, you see, and come in endless shapes and colours. Just like a couple,' he told me, with a beneficent smile.

Over the generations, many members of Japan's imperial family have visited the shrine on Aoshima island. However, it only became a mecca for ordinary honeymooners after 1960, when Princess Takako, the fifth daughter of Emperor Hirohito, honeymooned in Miyazaki with her new husband. Hisanaga Shimazu was a commoner, grandson of the last *daimyō* of the Satsuma domain in modern-day Kagoshima prefecture. In marrying him, the princess became the first female member of the imperial family to marry someone from outside the aristocracy, a break with convention that cost her her imperial status and caused quite a scandal.

Paparazzi photographers followed the newlyweds to Aoshima island and the photos they took, of a defiantly modern couple relaxing under the palm trees at the shrine, inspired millions of young newlyweds to follow their example. This was several decades before cheap air travel brought Hawaii and Guam within reach and, with Okinawa still occupied by the United States, Aoshima was the closest most couples would ever get to a tropical paradise. By the time the little island's popularity peaked in 1974, over a third of Japan's newlyweds were honeymooning in Miyazaki. They all visited the shrine on Aoshima island, which received a million visitors a year.

Ironically, it was at around this time that Japan's fertility rate slipped below replacement level for the first time. The number of visitors to the shrine began to fall in 1990, as overseas travel became more affordable, and continued to fall as incomes stagnated and the marriage rate went into decline. By 2006, less than half a million tourists a year were coming to the island, most of them not newlyweds but elderly couples taking a trip down memory lane.

Determined to resist the onset of decrepitude, Mr Nagatomo got together with a group of local business owners and launched a public–private project to revitalize the town of Aoshima. They secured government funding to renovate local facilities, and when word got around that the waves off Aoshima were good for surfing, they organized competitions and beach events. The surfing community became a magnet for city dwellers looking for weekend breaks, and some of them stayed, lending the town an easy-going, laid-back vibe. Tourists started coming in the off-season and more hostels, spas and restaurants opened to cater to them. In 2018, the shrine on Aoshima island once again had over one million visitors. Not many of them were there on honeymoon, and there were more pet dogs than children, but the area started to recover some of its former prosperity.

I asked Mr Nagatomo how he felt about Japan's declining population: was he concerned by his countrymen and women's reluctance to procreate?

> Quality is more important than quantity. A shrine is the heart of a community. In the Meiji era, the population of Japan was just 30 million, yet they had the same number of shrines as we have now. It is up to our communities to decide what they want to be, but I believe that we should focus more on our communities and stop moving around so much.

I wondered if he was referring to the spiritual restlessness of modern life, or just having a pop at his island's rivals in Okinawa and Hawaii. It was hard to tell.

Back when Aoshima was the best-known honeymoon destination in Japan, there were several hotels for newlyweds to choose from. We crossed the bridge from the tiny island back to the mainland, and our escorts from the Foreign Press Centre took us to the site of what had once been the largest of them. The six-storey Tachibana Hotel opened in 1976, but when the marriage rate began to fall, so did bookings, and when the economy went into meltdown in the early 1990s, the hotel went bankrupt. The building was abandoned, and stood for the next 20 years as a sad reminder of the town's heyday, and an unofficial monument to the dwindling number of baby-makers in Japan. In 2017, as if giving up on the dream of restoring the country to fecundity, the municipal government demolished the Tachibana.

It leased the plot where the hotel had stood to a group of property developers, who replaced the Tachibana with something more appealing to the post-growth generation. The man from the development company showed us around Aoshima Beach Village, which opened in 2020. Masahiro Yamashita was a local and had fond memories of the Tachibana. 'My parents stayed there on their honeymoon,' he said bashfully.

If the Tachibana had been modelled on the hotels of Hawaii, Aoshima Beach Village had been landscaped to look like Arizona, with lots of white walls, abstract shapes and minimalistic concrete. The cacti plants made for an arid, cerebral vibe, and I couldn't help wondering how they would fare in the rainy season. All the signage was in English, instructing guests to 'surf' and 'chill', and there were several Airstream trailers, shipped over at great expense from the US. Further on was a barbecue area, and some raised beds where vegetables and herbs were grown for the on-site restaurant.

I could see no tourists, let alone locals, but it was still only April. 'The developers couldn't get a bank to lend them the money they needed to build a luxury hotel, so they financed the project by combining the beach village with a hotel-cum-holiday home,' Mr Yamashita told us.

The six apartments that comprised 'Not-a-Hotel Aoshima' had already been sold. He showed us around the largest of them, the 'Masterpiece'. Inside, there were no light switches. 'It works like a Tesla,' said Mr Yamashita, pulling out an iPad that controlled the lights. Unfortunately, the battery was flat, but I got the idea. The owners were a party of twelve, all from Tokyo, each of whom had chipped in ¥58 million (£291,000) for the right to stay in the apartment for thirty nights a year. When they weren't using it, they rented it out as a luxury suite for ¥500,000 (£2,512) per night. Despite the price, it was fully booked.

With domestic tourism recovering after the pandemic, and the return of regular flights from Asia, Mr Yamashita was confident that

Aoshima had a bright future as a rival to Hawaii and Okinawa. 'Some of our guests are wealthy CEOs of start-ups and IT companies from Tokyo, Osaka and Nagoya, but increasingly they are tourists from China, South Korea and Taiwan.' Just as the farmers I had met in Miyazaki had gone boutique, hoping to tap into the lucrative high end of a shrinking market, it looked like the prefecture's hoteliers were going the same way.

And who worked in the hotel, I asked – were they foreigners too? No, Mr Yamashita replied, they were locals. Was he concerned about labour shortages? 'For the time being, no.' And the future? He gave me a wan smile. 'Foreign workers won't be allowed into Japan in large numbers for another 10 or 20 years. The old people are very conservative.'

10.

Mitarai: 'The Wild Boar Have Eaten all My Oranges!'

Clearly, Japanese farming communities are rising to the challenges posed by the ageing and shrinking population in varied and creative ways. However, when I returned from my Foreign Press Centre trip to Miyazaki, my thoughts were not so much of the country's high-tech agricultural entrepreneurs as of the ageing farmers who far outnumber them.

I knew I didn't yet have a complete picture. We had stayed in the lowlands and hadn't strayed far from the officially sanctioned track. If I wanted to see the situation at its starkest, I would have to strike out by myself again, visit some of the islands and travel up into the mountains. Remote-controlled tractors are all well and good in the lowlands, but it is hard to achieve economies of scale in the mountains, where plots tend to be smaller.

As Mrs Shidao in Hane had said, if rural communities are not to die out, they have to attract more migrants from the cities. According to a Cabinet Office survey, 30 per cent of urban Japanese in their 20s say that they would like to relocate to the countryside.[1] Popular men's magazines like *Brutus* and *Tarzan* have run no end of articles extolling the virtues of the country life, waxing lyrical about organic kitchen waste, compost bins and shingle roofs with the same obsessive attention to detail that they once bestowed upon Italian silk ties, trouser presses and fuel-injection engines.

To paraphrase David Goodhart, these articles strike a chord with 'nowhere people' looking to become 'somewhere people'. Many 20-somethings are the children of *salarimen* and spent their childhoods moving from town to town, following their fathers, who were in turn following the diktat of their line managers. They tend not to have strong regional identities, and the countryside offers them the promise of a fresh start in a place they might come to call home.

Some urban migrants might like to imagine themselves as post-growth pioneers, and a few are looking to revive the ideals of the 'back to the land' generation that left city life behind in the 1960s. But most are only leaving the city because they are unable to square their desire for a better work–life balance with the reality of persistent low pay and overwork. Increasingly harsh conditions in the job market, combined with the effects of the financial crash of 2008, the Great East Japan Earthquake of 2011 and the coronavirus pandemic of 2020–23, have been pushing people out of the cities for the last 20 years.

*

Of those who make the jump from city to country life, many do so through the Rural Revitalization scheme, which the government launched in 2010 as a way of getting more urbanites to move to the countryside. In a bid to find out more about what was being done to resist the hollowing out of the countryside, I paid a visit to the Rural Revitalization office in Yūrakuchō, a business district near the Imperial Palace in central Tokyo. There were forty-seven desks, one for each of the prefectures of Japan, each flagging up the wonderful food and peaceful lifestyle awaiting anyone tempted to turn their back on the capital.[2]

The place was practically empty mid-week, so the staff had plenty of time to find contacts for me. With their help, I put together an itinerary for a trip that would take me back to the Inland Sea, then north from Hiroshima over the spine of south-western Honshu, the main island, to Masuda, a small town on the Sea of Japan. From there, I would head east for a few days in Osaka, before returning to Tokyo.

So it was that, a few weeks later, I found myself cycling along the Shimanami kaidō, a fantastic dedicated cycling route that runs 70 kilometres from Imabari, on the north coast of Shikoku, over a series of suspension bridges to Onomichi, on the south coast of Honshu.

This is the kind of tourist-friendly infrastructure the government is still happy to fund. The bridges afforded panoramic views of the islands of the Inland Sea and the crystalline waters that separate them. The scenery was reminiscent of the Mediterranean, with bright sunshine illuminating the dry, stony ground. This was a side of Japan that few foreigners are aware of; on Shodoshima, a small island to the east, there were even olive groves.

It was May, a lovely time of year to be cycling – the temperature 23°C, maybe 25 at midday, and the air still fresh and dry. Once off the last suspension bridge, I took a short ferry ride to Osaki Shimojima, a 5-mile-long, lozenge-shaped island, and followed the coast road as it wound through bamboo groves past little coves to Mitarai, the only town on the island.

I stayed in the town's old hospital, a fine wooden building dating from about 1910 that had been converted into tourist accommodation. From the outside, it looked Western: tall, with glazed windows in wooden frames and painted clapboard sidings that had faded to baby blue under the combined impact of strong sunshine and heavy rain. Inside, it was Japanese, with sand render on wattle-and-daub walls, plywood ceilings, and wooden stairs and bannisters worn smooth by a hundred or more years of passing hands and feet.

I was the only guest. Through the open window of my room, I looked across the grey-tiled roofs of the town and down into the shadows in the alleyway that separated the old hospital from its neighbour. The house opposite had a covered gateway that led into a beautiful ornamental garden, and the surrounding wall had apertures with wooden grilles. I could hear birds chattering and, from down the lane, the sound of someone earnestly thanking a neighbour.

Mitarai has not always been such a quiet town. In the Edo period, it was a busy port, servicing the maritime trade that carried goods from Osaka to the towns dotting the meandering coastline of the Inland Sea. In its heyday, 200 ships came through the harbour every day, waiting for the tide (*shiomachi*) or the wind (*kazemachi*) to carry them to the next port. While they waited, the ships' officers would amuse themselves with geisha in the teahouses ranged along the waterfront, which all had rooms upstairs to which a woman could take a customer. Ordinary crew members were not permitted to come ashore, so they had to wait for someone to row the unattached women of the town out to their ship. Once aboard, they would stay with the sailors, cooking, cleaning and providing sex for as long as their ship was in port.

That all changed once ships were motorized. Thereafter, maritime trade no longer depended on the tide or the wind, and ports like Mitarai became backwaters. People still came to the town to visit prostitutes, but after the sex trade was outlawed in 1958, there was no longer any reason to come. In a sense, the town's irrelevance was a blessing in disguise: in the 1960s, when bureaucrats in faraway Tokyo were considering where to build factories, they passed over Mitarai in favour of better-connected ports on the mainland. As a result, the town escaped the clamour of the high-growth era and survived as something of a time capsule from the Edo period.

The outside world only noticed Mitarai after a typhoon piled through the town in 1991. In its wake, the prefectural government dispatched a university professor from Hiroshima to assess the damage. When he returned with news of the wonderful wooden world he had stumbled upon in Mitarai, the town was designated a 'place of historical importance' and this made it ripe for rebirth as a tourist destination.

By the 2000s, the years of high growth and the frenetic urbanization it had fuelled were making Japanese people nostalgic for what had been lost. In Mitarai, the old geisha houses on the waterfront were renovated and converted, some into lodgings, others into restaurants. Come the summer, they would be thronged with office workers, who enjoyed nothing better than wandering down memory lane and communing with the spirits of their grandparents.

*

The staff at the Rural Revitalization office had put me in touch with Tom and Mai Miyagawa. They didn't have roots in the area, but had relocated to Mitarai from Tokyo five years ago, Mai as a representative of the Rural Revitalization scheme and her British husband Tom as a freelance photographer. Like many urban migrants, they had a young child and were looking for a quieter, more relaxed way of life.

The Rural Revitalization scheme paid Mai a small wage, in return for which she was expected to promote the area to urbanites looking for a weekend break and foreign tourists looking for a taste of the elusive 'real Japan' they had read about in guidebooks. She was expected to commit to a three-year stint in the countryside, but how she went about her work was up to her. 'I made a website and one couple who came for a weekend decided to stay permanently,' she told me. 'I also translated it into English and made an English-language map for visitors.'

Another part of her role was helping the locals. Just 200 people live in Mitarai, and three-quarters of them are over 65. 'One day, I overheard a group of old people reminiscing about the taste of udon. There were never many restaurants in Mitarai, but when the last of them closed down, they had nowhere to eat their favourite noodles. So I helped them to set up a cookery club so that they could cook udon together.'

Given how many orange and lemon trees there were on Osaki Shimojima, Mai had been surprised by how little the islanders used them in their cooking. So she found an Italian chef in Hiroshima and got him to come out to Mitarai and share some of his favourite recipes. After his visit, a group of local residents started making a variety of jams and marmalades. I tried a marmalade made from local lemons and whiskey; it was absolutely delicious. They sold their jams and marmalades to tourists at the island's *michi no eki*. These roadside service stations are often the only going concern in isolated parts of the countryside. Some of them have a local history museum and farm shop attached, designed to lure in tourists.

'Japanese lemons have become very popular,' said Mai. 'A lot of conscientious consumers want to support domestic producers these days.'

This is exactly the kind of small-scale, craft-based manufacturing that the Rural Revitalization scheme is banking on to rejuvenate Japan's small towns and villages. One of the country's most prominent exponents of post-growth economics is economist Kosuke Motani. In his 2013 bestseller, *Satoyama Capitalism*, he argued that as a result of demographic decline, economic growth is no longer a realistic hope for Japan. Instead, the government should focus on creating more resilient local economies that use resources sustainably and reinvigorate moribund communities.

Motani cited many examples of small enterprises that are functioning as incubation trays for all kinds of innovative projects. He celebrated them for being at the forefront of the country's transition away from an export-driven consumer economy. These small-scale entrepreneurial initiatives are quite a novelty in Japan, a country with a long history of highly centralized, top-down government and huge corporations.

When Tom and Mai moved to Mitarai, they set about looking for an *akiya*, or empty house, to buy. It turned out to be far from straightforward. Estate agents don't want to take on abandoned properties in depopulated parts of the country. The government puts a cap on how much they can charge in commission, and with many of them going for as little as ¥1 million (£5,025), selling them just is not worth their while.

Luckily for Tom and Mai, the Hiroshima prefectural government is well aware that the future of its outlying regions rests on their ability to attract migrants and has set up an online 'akiya bank' that lists empty homes for sale. Like many other local authorities in Japan, the prefectural government even helps new arrivals to cover the cost of renovating empty properties. The house that Tom and Mai found cost them just ¥1.5 million (£7,540). Renovating it set them back another ¥9 million (£45,220), but all the same, it was a bargain compared to buying a house in the city.

Many urban runaways are doing up dilapidated old houses in

the countryside. These houses often have a great deal of charm. In his paean to life in Japan's native, pre-modern culture, *In Praise of Shadows*, novelist Junichiro Tanizaki talks about the simple pleasure of watching the play of light and shadow on the materials of traditional houses: elm or cedar beams, straw tatami mats, wattle-and-daub walls. To anyone who has grown up in the city, knowing only twenty-first-century housing, these buildings are a revelation, not just for the senses, but for the imagination, offering newcomers a way of reconnecting with homespun traditions.

Though charming, they often come with some discomforts. Wattle-and daub walls generate a lot of dust as they age, yellowing tatami mats are often home to bugs, and it is not unusual to find a civet-cat living in your ceiling. But a renewed interest in doing things the Japanese way needn't mean jettisoning all the trappings of modern life. Twenty-first-century infrastructure allows migrants to maintain their connections to the city. Indeed, if you need high-speed internet for your work, the countryside is often a better place to be than the city, for connections are often faster, there being comparatively few users.

Some country towns have gone out of their way to create a welcoming atmosphere for newcomers. Shinya Ominami, the director of an NGO called Green Valley, has been working to turn Kamiyama, a small town in the mountainous interior of Shikoku, into a digital hub. Boosted by its fibre-optic cables, Kamiyama has become well-known for the cluster of 'satellite offices' that IT firms have established in renovated old homes. Many of their employees even go into head office one day a week, as the *shinkansen* (bullet train) is so fast, efficient and far-reaching that most country dwellers can get to Tokyo, Osaka or Fukuoka within a couple of hours.

Talking to my students in Tokyo, I had come away with the impression that most urbanites still associate the countryside with depopulation, stagnation and old people. But talking to Mai and Tom, it was clear that the character of the Japanese countryside is changing in the post-growth era. Being able to combine the best of both worlds has encouraged lots of jaded urbanites to move to rural towns like Kamiyama, many of them highly educated, entrepreneurial and determined to rescue the countryside from the perils of ageing and shrinking.

*

Tom Miyagawa was keen to give me a sense of the old community that he and Mai were hoping to revive, so the following morning he took me to meet Kazuyuki Sueoka, whose family have been farming citrus fruits in the hills around Mitarai for the last six generations. He lived in a grand old wooden farmhouse, approached through a covered gateway, with elaborate silver-black tiles on the roof and porch. There were sliding doors on the ground floor and sliding windows upstairs, bound by a low railing that was used to air the futons.

The house stood on one side of a yard, and there were outhouses stacked high with crates for the orange harvest running down the other side. In the middle of the yard was a dry pond, and around it a traditional Japanese garden of standing stones, stone lanterns and bonsai trees.

Mr Sueoka ushered us into his drawing room and went off to make us some tea. It was a room of dark wood, barely lit by a round fluorescent ring on the ceiling, with yellowing tatami mats on the floor, some worn leather chairs and a carved redwood table. He came back with tea and lit a cigarette. He was 71, a laid back, expansive man, at ease with himself and glad of some visitors.

I asked him about the Rising Sun flag pinned to the wall, which was covered with names written in black ink. 'It belonged to my father. All the villagers wrote their names on it to wish him luck before he went off to war,' he said. 'My father signed up to be a kamikaze pilot, but then Japan surrendered, so he came home. I was born shortly afterwards.'

He invited us into the next room, and we passed through a pair of paper sliding doors, over which were carvings in wood of Mount Fuji and pine trees. The room was dedicated to his forebears. On the walls hung pencil portraits of his grandparents, so fine that they looked like photographs. At the far end was a huge *butsudan* (household shrine) in gleaming black and gold lacquer.

'When the maritime trade dried up, my grandparents were stuck for a way to make a living. There was fishing, but there's no flat ground in Mitarai on which to grow rice. So they built terraces on the hillsides and planted mandarin trees instead.' For a time, Mitarai thrived on the back of the orange trade. Prices were high, and before long the entire island was covered with citrus orchards. 'At one point, almost half of the satsumas consumed in Tokyo came from this island,' Mr Sueoka said in wonderment.

He showed me a photograph of his father taken in the late 1950s. He was standing at the helm of a small sailing boat, and behind him was a hillside covered in orange trees. 'In those days, farmers had orchards on the neighbouring islands as well. They would sail out to them in the morning and come back with their cargos in the evening. Ozaki Shimozima was practically self-sufficient in those days. We had our own butcher, our own soy sauce maker, our own tofu maker . . .' His voice trailed off, as if he could scarcely believe it himself.

'But that was all a long time ago,' he said, and the gleam in his eye faded. 'The orange farmers started to come under pressure from imports from the US and Australia. They farm on a much bigger scale over there and we couldn't compete.' In the 1960s, wages for farm workers went into steep decline on the island, as they did all over Japan, and its young people moved to Hiroshima, Osaka and Tokyo in search of better paid work. 'To this day, there is no money in orange farming. The price of labour is just too high for farmers to take on more workers.'

Later that day, Tom and I were walking in the terraces of orange groves above the town when we met an old woman called Mrs Iwata who echoed what we had heard from Mr Sueoka. She was stooped and said she had some pain in her shoulder, but she looked spry in her bonnet and wellies, and was still tending her orange orchards at the age of 80. 'Old farmers like me are only making a pittance. But we are not in it for the money. We just like to stay busy, and don't know what else to do with ourselves,' she said with a good-natured cackle.

'The work ethic is still strong here. But things are harder than they used to be.' She showed us the remnants of an ingenious contraption: a little monorail that used to carry boxes of satsumas from the terraces down to the waterfront. 'They all rusted up ages ago,' she said with a dismissive wave of the hand. Like Mr Sueoka, she seemed resigned to the end of farming on the island.

Elderly farmers like Mrs Iwata would have been born in the early 1940s. When their children came of age in the early 80s, they told them to go to the city. They didn't expect them to stay in the countryside and would have been disappointed if they had. Fishing and farming were hard work, while the city promised higher wages, modern housing, education and entertainment.

However, two generations later, the city is losing its allure and more city dwellers than ever are opting to return to their grandparents' villages. Their numbers are still small – nowhere near enough to reverse the urbanization trend – but all the same they mark a welcome challenge to urban-centric modern culture.

I was keen to meet some more of these incoming migrants, so Tom took me to meet Shintaro Takeuchi, a 30-something farmer who has been farming a little orchard on a hill above Mitarai for the last five years. 'I grow lemons, limes, mandarines, bergamot, bitter summer orange, pink lemonade . . .' The last citrus fruit I found an English definition for was *amanatsu*, a sweet form of Chinese citron, like a cross between an orange and a grapefruit. The rest – *haruka*, *shiranui*, *setoka*, *gokuwase*, *nakate mikan* – weren't in the dictionary. I tried the *haruka* – it had the milky smell of sun-ripened lemons and was a delicious combination of citrus and honey.

People don't become farmers to get rich. I get by, but I'm only doing this because it allows me to be independent. I'm a loner. I started out as a *salariman*, working for a meat producing company, first in Tokyo and then in Spain. There was a time when I enjoyed being a *salariman*, but after a while, I didn't feel like working with other people any more. I got tired of having to go out drinking with my workmates after work.

When Shintaro started casting around for alternatives to the nine to five, it was only natural that he should think of Mitarai. He had grown up 40 miles away in Hiroshima, but his grandparents lived in the town, and he spent his summer holidays there. 'I'm not really a stranger here. But still, I feel like a stranger. I'm here to look for my freedom. In the morning I wake up any time I like. I don't use a clock.'

Although citrus farming offered Shintaro a precious taste of independence, he said he could not survive without the subsidies he received from the local government – they had covered half the cost of his *kei-torakku*, the tiny pick-up truck beloved of Japanese farmers. Like Yoshitada Katsuki, the budding winemaker I had met in Miyazaki, Shintaro's country lifestyle was dependent on the largesse of urban taxpayers.

The local government also paid him a fee for every wild boar he killed. 'There are lots of boar in these hills,' he said, jerking his chin up the slope with a scowl. 'Nobody likes them because they knock down the walls that hold the terraces together. They like earthworms, and root around for them. Plus, they are dangerous and smell terrible. Every January, we have an archery contest, and we always use a picture of a wild boar as a target.' Apparently, wild boar like oranges but not lemons, so perhaps it was just as well that demand for domestically grown lemons was on the rise.

Shintaro wanted to show us one of his sixteen wild boar traps, so we jumped into the back of his *kei-torakku* and he drove further up the hill, zigzagging his way along a series of narrow, paved tracks. He rummaged around in the glove compartment and handed me a mail-order catalogue advertising everything the wild boar hunter could wish for: big metal cages for trapping them in, long poles with nooses at the end for snaring them and electric prods for driving them into the cage.

When we reached the highest terrace, Shintaro parked up. 'Look at all these abandoned orchards,' he said wistfully, gesturing back down the way we had come. The vegetation was lush and green, and we got great views out over the islands of the Inland Sea. All around us, the blue sea glittered, and I could see the edge of the rocky land far beneath the surface of the crystal-clear water.

We got out of the *kei-torakku* and he led us through the trees to a metal cage. It looked sturdy enough to hold a tiger. 'As the farmers die out, the number of wild animals is increasing,' he said, casting a worried eye up the hill to the virgin land beyond the orchards. 'This cage is baited with powdered rice husks. When a boar trips the wire, the door falls down behind him.'

Since Shintaro didn't have a gun license, whenever he found a boar in one of his traps, he had to kill it with a spear. 'A boar is no pushover. Some of them weigh 100 kilograms. But if the hunter's aim is true, a single jab through the heart is enough to kill it.' He said that the previous year, he had killed 200 wild boar. 'I don't enjoy killing them, but it pays better than farming citrus fruit.'

'I make sausages with some of the meat,' Shintaro went on. In recent years, game has become a popular novelty in big-city restaurants and, if the articles I'd read in *Brutus* and *Tarzan* were to be believed, plenty of the younger generation are keen to revive the old hunting traditions that used to sustain rural communities. Back in the Edo period, when Japan was entirely self-sufficient for its food, wild boars were called 'mountain whales' because, like a whale, none of the carcass went to waste. 'Meat from boars that have been scavenging in orange orchards is particularly tasty,' Shintaro told us. However, for now at least, game remains a niche interest, and most of the sausages eaten in Japan are American-style weiner sausages, which come in a tin. As a result, Shintaro ended up burying most of the boar that he killed.

★

I left Mitarai feeling a little more hopeful about Japan's post-growth future. The people I had met really did seem to have struck a healthy balance between town and country, work and leisure, past and present. Tom, Mai and Shintaro, like the young urban migrants I'd met in Miyazaki, had all come looking for dignity at work, a better work–life balance and a sense of community with their neighbours, and, to varying degrees, they had found it. They were still struggling to find sustainable ways to make a living, but they looked to be thriving, psychologically if not financially.

Their life goals mark a sea change in attitudes. Until recently, most people's self-worth was bound up with the phenomenal success of Japan Inc. But the millennial generation can no longer take pride in the country's economic power or the dynamism of its corporations. Saddled with stagnating incomes and dwindling social networks, urban life is losing its appeal. They are realizing that there is an end point to economic growth and are looking for new measures of human progress.

As Atsushi Miura puts it in his book *The Rise of Sharing: Fourth-Stage Consumer Society in Japan*, 'We are beginning to demand that the act of living be considered sufficient unto itself.'[3] This means redefining the purpose of ambition and the meaning of success, but it also implies a need to address the isolation and loneliness that bedevils modern Japan and the importance of building more supportive communities.

One of the big draws of living in the countryside is that it makes people happy. Despite the structural problems associated with demographic decline, rural municipalities report higher rates of subjective wellbeing than urban areas, probably because they tend to have stronger social networks.[4] It might seem ironic that people should feel more sociable in the countryside than they do in the city, but perhaps this is down to evolutionary biology: feeling antisocial is a rational response to overcrowding (or at least living in overcrowded cities with strangers).

If the migrants I had met really were outliers, rather than just odd-bods, perhaps the twenty-first century will see a gradual breakdown of the division between all-powerful urban centres like Tokyo, Osaka and Nagoya and the country's long-neglected regions. The younger generation is coming to appreciate another side of Japan, one that was trampled underfoot in the rush to modernize. Perhaps they are doing penance for their parents' neglect, but plenty of them are motivated by a sense of fundamentalism. There is an amorphous sense of imminent, profound change in the air, of a country reassessing its values, struggling to return to what is familiar and in the process rediscovering what is essential about its culture.

When Takashi Tsujii, the founder of Muji, was asked about the future of Japan, he said,

> I think the challenges we are going to face in the future cannot be overcome by the centre (Tokyo). If you ask me, I think that in the future regional Japan is going to be the new centre, and we will find ourselves trying to create new communities unlike any we have seen before. Once that happens, society is going to be transformed, in all senses of the word.[5]

It's easy to dismiss the organic wine and marmalade makers of post-growth Japan as hobbyists, and their craving for community as naive. Some might say that in a highly developed consumer culture, the values of individualism are too entrenched to allow for a return to the older, pre-modern values of fraternity, connectedness and cooperation in the community. But that would be to overlook the gravity of Japan's demographic and economic problems, the human desire for connection and the opportunities created by the internet. Together, they are creating strange new forms of social life unimaginable to previous generations.

Before leaving Tokyo, I had read about a project in Gojome, a near-abandoned village in Akita prefecture, that offers city dwellers the chance to become 'virtual villagers'. The project is the brainchild of 37-year-old Masahiro Takeda, the self-appointed 'mayor' of what he calls his Share Village. It began as an attempt to restore a 134-year-old farmhouse in the village. Takeda didn't want to demolish it, but the cost of re-thatching the roof was making restoration prohibitively expensive.

With the local population in terminal decline, the municipal government was in no position to help, so he hit on the idea of crowdfunding. He set up a Facebook group with the stated aim of 'resurrecting the language and customs of a traditional village community for the internet age'. In return for paying a modest *nengu* (tribute) of ¥3,000 (£15) per year, supporters could become virtual *sonmin* ('villagers'). Takeda re-imagined the farmhouse as a shareable good and invited them to come up with new uses for it.

He keeps them updated with information about goings-on in Gojome, and, once a month, he invites them to attend a *yoriai* (village meeting) at a location in central Tokyo. Over fresh, locally grown food and a selection of some of Akita's finest sakes, the virtual villagers of Gojome mingle with one another and listen to updates from the distant country village that has become their second home.

The Share Village has proved to be a winning idea with those unwilling or unable to turn their backs on the comforts of city living. It is a classic case of *isseki nichō* – 'killing two birds with one stone'. More than a project to renovate an old farmhouse in the middle of nowhere, Takeda's virtual village has created an imagined community of strangers in the lonely megacity. Gojome has over 2,000 supporters from all forty-seven prefectures of Japan. Some are the children or grandchildren of migrants who came to Tokyo from Akita in search of work in the 1960s and 70s, but most have no family ties to the village. Whether Takeda is able to save his old farmhouse, much less his village, remains to be seen. But by building an online bridge between the growing megacity and the shrinking countryside, he has found a way to marshal twenty-first-century technology to solve twenty-first-century problems.

What I found particularly inspiring was the revival of old, near-extinct customs as an instinctive response to the cultural dead-end that the younger generation finds itself in. Every summer, Takeda encourages the villagers to 'return home' to take part in the village's annual *ikki*. The term dates back to the Edo period and is still practically taboo. More than a festival, it is synonymous with the rebellions that often broke out in poverty-stricken villages when rice harvests failed. Landowners were accustomed to exacting exorbitant taxes from the peasantry, and when starvation loomed, poor farmers often rose up in open revolt.

In whitewashing the long history of popular revolt in Japan, the modern school system has largely succeeded in confining such stories to the archives, and consequently few Japanese people know much about the *ikki*. But to young office workers with few prospects, getting drunk, letting their hair down and making friends at an annual *ikki* holds a lot of appeal. For those who have been doing what they are told for as long as they can remember, that *is* a rebellion. It is also a promise, however vague, of a return to the days when Japan was a land of thriving towns and villages, the old and the young shared meaningful connections, and the annual *matsuri* was a bacchanal.

On Mountain Roads: Hiroshima to Masuda

I had seen the first mosquitos of the year, harbingers of the rainy season, which would start at the beginning of June. There would be endless rain for a month, and when it stopped, clouds would roll in from the Pacific, trapping the air and making for oppressively hot, sultry weather. July and August must be the worst time of year to be in Japan. Only in September would the temperature drop and the sky become clear again.

My time in Mitarai had given me a welcome taste of island life, and also of what the younger generation is doing to revive the country's farming communities. Now it was time to embark on the next stage of my journey: a visit to the mountains of Hiroshima and Shimane prefectures to see the sharp end of Japan's rural depopulation crisis.

The staff at the Rural Revitalization office in Tokyo had put me in touch with Kazutaka Yamada, one of the scheme's most prominent emissaries. When the government set up the Rural Revitalization scheme, it was only natural that he be appointed its representative for Hiroshima prefecture, given the years he'd spent working for the prefectural government, trying to resuscitate the many waning villages to be found in the mountains of Hiroshima and Shimane.

A couple of months later, I met Mr Yamada in a coffee shop in Hiroshima, not far from the Atom Bomb Dome. He was 62, a physically slight, kindly and conscientious man. Although he wasn't a professional demographer, he had a near-obsessive interest in the declining population of his home region. He sat me down and guided me through a stack of papers that told the story of the ageing and shrinking of Hiroshima and Shimane prefectures in pie charts and population pyramids.

Among the reams of paper was our itinerary for the day, carefully calculated and calibrated. From Hiroshima, we would head into the mountains that divide Hiroshima prefecture from Shimane prefecture and visit a hamlet called Okamibuchi. Mr Yamada had done fieldwork there in 2008, when he was dispatched to study the depopulation process by the Shimane Research Centre for Mountainous Areas. The term *genkai shūraku* ('marginalized settlement'), defined as one in which more than half of the residents are over 65, has been used to describe thousands of communities across Japan, but it was coined by Mr Yamada to describe Okamibuchi. He had not been back for 10 years and was curious – and a little worried – to see how things had changed.

As we drove out of Hiroshima, he pointed out the new tower blocks going up in the city centre. 'In the last few years, people have been moving from the suburbs into the city centre. That's because, as suburban communities age and shrink, they are becoming less convenient places for them to live. They are looking to move closer to shops and hospitals. The city is consolidating itself, and declining land prices have made the centre affordable again.'

Leaving the city, a string of residential tower blocks emerged from the trees. This was Setouchi New Town, a small satellite town that had been built in the 1970s to house office workers and their families. 'Back then, central government was keen to support regional development projects because they wanted to stem the flow of people leaving the countryside for the cities,' Mr Yamada explained. 'But it didn't work. The children of those office workers left to find work in the city and didn't come back.' Further up the hill we passed a big new hospital and senior centre. 'Over the last 20 years, it has gradually become harder to live here, and now the remaining residents are getting old.'

Breaching the watershed in the hills overlooking Hiroshima Bay, we crossed a broad highway that was carrying goods to points east and west. Beyond it was a huge logistics centre where the deliveries companies stored their parcels. Once that was behind us, the traffic fell away, the road narrowed and soon we were winding our way through a thick forest of conifers.

Finally, we emerged above the canopy, and Mr Yamada pulled over so I could get a clear view over the mountains and valleys that run down the spine of western Japan. There was no sign of human habitation, just a thick green mantle of trees. For the previous few days, there had been warnings on the TV that the first typhoon of the season was barrelling north from the Pacific, but it had veered west towards Korea before it could do any damage in Japan. Still, gusts of warm air were roiling through the foliage and the road was strewn with broken branches.

Although I had long since finished reading the *Natural History of an Asian Archipelago*, it was remarkable how few chances I had had to enjoy nature in the raw like this. I say 'in the raw' but, in fact, few of Japan's forests are wild or natural. In the high-growth years, most of its original mixed-leaf forests were cut down to make way for vast *sugi* (Japanese cedar) plantations. The idea was that the cedars would provide timber for the construction business, but with a shrinking population, demand for new housing has stagnated, and the main purpose of these gloomy, desolate swathes of trees seems to be to give the entire country hay fever once a year.

We reached Okamibuchi. It was clear that the process of decay had advanced considerably in the time that Mr Yamada had been away: most of the fields we passed had been abandoned, and so had most of the houses. Nobody wanted to move to such an isolated community, and the property market had all but collapsed.

We came to a venerable old farmhouse, where he pulled over. It was unoccupied, but still in good condition. 'This used to be the mayor's house,' he said. An overgrown stone path led up one side of the perimeter wall, which was of cob and topped with thick silver-grey tiles. We passed through a covered porch into a yard paved with flagstones, and I spied patches of moss growing on the thatched roof. 'Maintaining these old properties is becoming more difficult as the craftspeople age and die. There are no thatchers left in Shimane prefecture,' said Mr Yamada.

We went back to the car and drove on, the road twisting and turning through a series of little basins, until we came to a man who was doing some brush cutting at the side of the road. Mr Yamada recognized Mr Okada from the last time he was there and stopped to say hello. 'Welcome to the back of the back of beyond,' Mr Okada joked. He had the ever-smiling, round face of Ebisu, the Japanese god of fishermen, good luck and prosperity. When Mr Yamada introduced me, I gave him my name card, and he said '*Sore wa sore wa*' ('My goodness'), an old-fashioned turn of phrase that I had waited a long time to hear someone use.

Mr Okada was a baby boomer. He had been born in Oka-mibuchi in 1955 and had grown up in the years of high economic growth. He had turned 18 in 1973, the year that the oil shock gave post-war Japan its first taste of recession and the fertility rate dropped below replacement level for the first time. 'When I was a boy, there were 300 people living in Okamibuchi, most of them farmers,' he told me. 'Most of the boys and girls I went to school with went on to have children of their own, but when they came of age, they moved to towns and cities in the lowlands. There are only eight people living here now, and only two of them are full-time farmers.'

Mr Okada had also moved out, in his case down the valley to Miyoshi. A market town on the Gōnokawa River, it has a popula-tion of 50,000, which has held steady as it absorbs the ageing former residents of villages in the surrounding mountains. However, he still came back to Okamibuchi regularly to tend his smallhold-ing. 'I look after several of the neighbouring plots as well,' he said good-naturedly.

Japan's mountain communities have always been less product-ive than those in the lowlands because the fields tend to be smaller and harder to consolidate into more profitable units. They are also more vulnerable to the effects of mass ageing, for the further they are from flat ground and main roads, the more quickly they waste away. A recent study by Japan's Population Strategy Council forecasts that 744 Japanese municipalities, representing over 40 per cent of the total, are at risk of vanishing due to population decline, and most of them are in the mountains.[1]

'More and more people are becoming unable to work their plots, and I can't keep up,' said Mr Okada. He put down his brush cutter and showed us around his yard. There was a little pond, where some fat carp were idly switching back and forth in the still water, and next to it the stump of a dead tree, where some pretty peach-coloured flowers were growing. He had beehives, and we listened to the sound of the bees droning in the summer heat. The plants in his rice paddy were a rich shade of green. 'I planted them in Golden Week and I'll harvest them when they turn gold at the end of October,' he said, as if talking to himself.

Just as my friend Atsushi had told me when I first got back to Japan, as the residents of country towns and villages like Okamibuchi get frailer and fewer in number, the wild animals are becoming less wary. Mr Okada was getting used to their company. His main concern was the wild boar that ventured down from the surrounding mountains, attracted by the scent of his *myōga* (Japanese ginger) plants. Among the other animals living in the surrounding hills were badgers, deer and *tanuki* (raccoon dogs), which are considered to have magical properties. '*Tanuki* are known for getting through a lot of sake and for their enormous testicles,' he said. 'At night, you can hear them drumming on their bellies with their paws.' Mr Yamada cracked up at this old folk tale – it was remarkable how he came into his own in the company of shy, modest country people.

Soon it would be Obon, the Festival of the Dead, when the spirits of the ancestors are said to return to earth. For many Japanese people, it is the most important festival of the year, a time when they leave the city behind for a weekend and return to the towns and villages where they were born. Aside from New Year, it is the only opportunity many of them get to reconnect with their extended families. They visit the family grave, make offerings to the spirits of their ancestors and invite them to return to the houses where they once lived.

Back when Okamibuchi was a flourishing village, the cemetery would be full of colourful little banners bidding the spirits back at this time of year. 'In the past, families would leave food on the graves for the spirits of their departed ancestors,' went on Mr Okada. 'But with so few people about, wild animals started venturing down to the cemetery to eat the food, so these days, they only put out tinned food.'

Most families consider the family grave to be more important than the property where they used to live. Mr Yamada explained that as villages teeter on the brink of abandonment, and the population becomes consolidated in larger towns and cities, people often move the family grave closer to the main road so they can tend it more easily. When they are no longer able to tend it themselves, they have it moved to the local temple, where, for a one-off payment, the priest will say prayers for the departed and keep the grave in good order. The money goes towards the upkeep of the temple, which in most marginalized settlements is usually the last surviving building.

As well as rice, Mr Okada also grew gentians, a dark blue flower. 'I used to sell them to visitors at Obon, when they came up from Hiroshima to tend their families' graves. But hardly anyone comes up here any more.' Even during Obon, most of the graves in the cemetery remained bare of flowers, so he sold his gentians in Hiroshima.

Mr Yamada and I left Mr Okada to his brush cutting, and walked down the road to a moss-covered *torii* gate at the foot of a steep flight of stone steps. 'They lead up to the village shrine,' said Mr Yamada. 'The villagers used to do *kagura* dances at the shrine in the autumn.' *Kagura* is a ritual Shinto dance performed in mountain villages across Japan to pray for a good harvest, and each region has its own variant. 'The dancers were usually local farmers or forestry workers. They always thought they would pass on the custom to their children, but there are no children in Okamibuchi these days.' He said that the last of the *kagura* dancers had given up when they could no longer climb the shrine steps.

It is sobering to think of all the shrines and temples that are going to be abandoned in mountain communities across Japan over the next 20 years. These places were first settled tens of thousands of years ago, when much of lowland Japan was covered in swamp. The Japanese imagination has long flowed along contours cut by its myths and legends, and most of them have their origin in the country's mountain forests. But nobody wants to live in the mountains any more. They would rather live in the lowlands, closer to the urban amenities of modern life, and Japan's upland communities are once again falling under the dominion of their original inhabitants: wild boar, raccoons, bears and monkeys.

*

Mr Yamada wanted to show me Asahichō Imaichi, the town where he was born and grew up. 'I still go back once a month to see my mother. She lives alone and runs a small shop in the town. She's 86 now.' From Okamibuchi, a one-track road wound its way down a narrow valley kept in perpetual shade by conifers. We came to some fresh asphalt. 'This part of the road was swept away by a landslide last week, but it was quickly repaired,' he said. 'Evacuation is certainly not on the table yet, but when a bridge or road collapses, it reminds people of their vulnerability. The authorities say that they will maintain the infrastructure for as long as it is being used.'

Alas, commercial operators cannot afford to be so magnanimous. In the 1990s, the government subsidized the construction of ski resorts in mountain communities as a way of generating work. 'For a time, the ski resort in Okamibuchi really flourished in the winter months. At weekends, the local train station used to be packed with people coming up to the mountains from Hiroshima,' said Mr Yamada with a wan smile. 'But Japan's "ski boom" soon passed, and before long the station's only users were local schoolchildren. With every passing year their numbers dwindled more, until, in 2018, JR

[Japan Railways] announced that it could no longer justify paying for the upkeep of the line and mothballed it.'[2]

As we came down from the mountains, the valley grew wider, and we passed more overgrown fields and abandoned farmhouses. Coming onto lower ground, the fields were full of lush, emerald-green rice plants, but looking back the way we had come, I could see rungs of neglected rice terraces climbing the steep, narrow valleys between the spurs of the mountains.

On the way into Asahichō Imaichi, Mr Yamada pulled over to show me where the steel factory that had once been the town's main employer used to stand. The site had been cleared and was now covered with banks of solar panels.

> Salaries used to be good at the factory, but they went into decline, and people moved away. There were about 4,000 people living here when I was a child. Now there are only 1,000. You see the same pattern across Japan. I left too. I liked the wealth of nature and was always interested in how to revive all these towns and villages. But there was no work here, so I went to university in Hiroshima and never came back.

After half an hour of listening to the drone of the engine and the air conditioning, it was good to open the window and let the stillness of a mountain town seep into the car. 'The modernization process all happened so quickly in Japan,' Mr Yamada went on wistfully. 'I can remember, as a child, watching the workmen putting in the town's first sewage and water pipes. In those days, the main road to Hamada was still gravel. It was only asphalted in the 1970s, but with the coming of the new expressway in the 90s, it is hardly used any more.'

Mr Yamada slowly drove down the main street. All the shops were shuttered. 'Some of the owners still live upstairs,' he said, glancing up as if hoping to see a familiar face. A little further down the road, we parked up in front of his mother's place. Mrs Yamada bowed deeply and invited us in. While she made tea, Mr Yamada and I sat on the tatami mats and looked out at the bonsai trees in her garden. 'My mother has a little shop selling fabric. The culture of make do and mend is still strong in these villages. But she plans to retire in December.'

When Mrs Yamada came back bearing tea, she explained, 'I have heart problems, and I find it too tiring to run the shop these days. Besides, I only get about five customers a day. Occasionally one of them will buy some fabric or thread to make or mend some clothes, but most of them are just friends stopping by for a chat on their way to the Co-op.'*

There were only three shops left in the town: the Co-op, where Mrs Yamada and her friends did their shopping, the post office and the local branch of the farmers' co-operative. The town's *izakaya*, ramen shop, off-licence and *ryokan* (Japanese-style inn) had all closed. 'People go to the Co-op to buy fuel, but it is no use to me, because I don't drive,' said Mrs Yamada. 'For anything I can't find in the Co-op, I have to go to Hamada, which is an hour away on the bus.' She smiled. 'As the passengers age, a lot of them are getting forgetful. Staring out of the window, they forget their stop. It's just as well the driver is a kind man and doesn't charge them for the extra distance.'

I asked Mr Yamada if many urban migrants were moving to Asahichō Imaichi.

I don't think so. All these small towns are competing with one another to attract a limited number of migrants. People who want to move to the countryside always say they want to live near the sea or in the mountains, but Asahichō Imaichi is not the sort of place that attracts urban migrants. It has no charming old customs. It has

---

* Not to be confused with the UK's Co-operative Group, the Japanese Consumers' Co-operative Union (JCCU) is a national federation of consumer co-ops. It is the largest consumers' organization in Japan, with a total of 30 million members.

been the site of no fascinating episode from history. No famous poets were born here.

He gave me another wistful smile. He had spent his entire working life trying to regenerate towns and villages like Asahichō Imaichi, but as he neared retirement, he was having to accept that he had been fighting a losing battle. Over the last seven years, he had helped over 500 jaded urbanites move to Hiroshima prefecture – all well and good, but nothing like the numbers needed to have any meaningful impact. For all the glossy brochures and upbeat talk I had met with at the Rural Revitalization office in Tokyo, as far as Mr Yamada was concerned, the depopulation of the countryside was a fait accompli. He was open to any suggestion, including inviting in foreigners, if it gave the prefecture's isolated towns and villages some hope of survival.

Before we left, I complimented Mrs Yamada on how productive her garden was looking. 'Most of the old people in the town have a little garden where they grow their own fruit and vegetables,' she said. 'We often grow more than we can eat, and since we have fewer neighbours to share things with, we have got into the habit of taking our produce up to the young people at the prison.'

Asahi Shimane prison was new, she said, having only been completed in 2008. Locals had welcomed the construction of a prison; after the steel factory closed down, the municipal government had been unable to attract any new businesses to the town. The inmates were all on short sentences and were not considered dangerous. It was built to house 2,000 inmates, but it was still only half-occupied. It was a touching thought: a prison with not enough prisoners, in a town with too many old people and too many vegetables.

★

From Asahichō Imaichi, Mr Yamada took me to Hamada, and from there I took a bus an hour and a half down the coast to Masuda, the penultimate stop on my tour of the countryside. Reclining near-horizontal on a plush upholstered seat, I found myself thinking about Asahichō Imaichi's half-empty prison. The crime rate is famously low in Japan, so I had been surprised to see signs warning against shoplifting in the convenience stores I had been into, even in the countryside. This was a novel development: I had never seen such signs the first time I lived in Japan.

Interestingly, this sudden concern with preventing crime has not come about in response to a rise in it; in 2021, the crime rate in Japan hit its lowest level in the post-war era.[3] You would never suppose so watching the evening news, which keeps the public fed on a diet of gory murder stories, but the younger generation is simply not large, idle or delinquent enough to turn to crime. But this is one of the oddities of post-growth Japan: while it consistently ranks among the world's safest nations, its citizens are more fearful of crime than their counterparts in other OECD countries.

One indication of this fearfulness is the startling number of crime prevention groups. Between 2003 and 2008, this increased from 3,056 to 37,774, and the number of volunteers rose tenfold. By one account, as many as 3 million Japanese citizens are volunteers in a crime prevention group.[4] These volunteers, usually led by the elderly men of the neighbourhood, conduct patrols and plaster neighbourhoods with crime prevention posters. They organize community events, such as 'crime prevention rice-cake making day' and visit schools to give the kids lessons in crime prevention.

In the name of improved surveillance, brick walls are replaced with wire-netting fences, shrubs in front of windows are cut back and the number of utility poles on the streets is reduced. Even jogging or taking your dog for a walk can become a 'crime prevention initiative' if it increases the number of 'watchful eyes' on the street. 'Patorun', for example, is a volunteer organization that combines jogging and neighbourhood patrolling to create a 'new style of crime prevention.' According to one Patorun volunteer, there was a surge of interest when the organization was first launched, but members' motivation dwindled when they realized that 'nothing ever happens'. The only observable outcome of their patrols was the time one of them found a missing dog.

But the fact that crime prevention volunteers hardly ever encounter crimes while out on patrol needn't matter, because their vigilance is driven, not by crime per se, but by the pervasive anxiety borne of Japan's uncertain future. Government officials see 'community' as both the source of and solution to the 'crime crisis', linking crime to deteriorating community ties and emphasizing the importance of restoring them.

In an ageing, deeply conservative country like Japan, 'crime prevention' is akin to an early warning system for the nation's healthcare workers and undertakers. Japan's biggest newspaper, the *Yomiuri Shimbun*, instructs its delivery staff to maintain a watchful attitude while doing their rounds and report any abnormalities to the police. In a list of their achievements, published to celebrate the tenth anniversary of the Yomiuri Crime Prevention Association, almost none were related to actual crimes. The majority involved delivery staff discovering elderly citizens who had collapsed in their homes.

Crime prevention groups provide their mostly elderly volunteers with a rare opportunity to get to know their neighbours and feel like valued members of the community. According to a National Police Agency survey, volunteers see being thanked and widening their social circle as the most beneficial parts of volunteering.[5]

I have to say, I have my doubts. Crime prevention campaigns certainly demonstrate Japanese people's willingness to be dragooned into service for a good cause, but they also heighten the pervasive atmosphere of anxiety in post-growth Japan. Constant warnings of imaginary threats and the so-called risks of everyday life make children of citizens, while encouraging a general wariness towards strangers, and this only strengthens the exclusionary, isolating tendencies in Japanese society.

Fear of crime has become self-perpetuating, a feedback loop

that, though it has little basis in fact, is the creator of a never-ending melodrama in which everyone is expected to play their part. It also functions as a fig leaf for the mainstream media, most of which is too acquiescent to challenge popular delusions and too timid to hold politicians to account. The media is part of the conservative fantasizing and gleeful escapism that allow the bigger story – Japan's stagnant economy, declining standards of living and growing social isolation – to go unquestioned.

Of course, none of this is to say that crime doesn't happen. While Japan's reputation for having a low crime rate is well deserved, when it comes to offences like fraud and cyber-crime, it is something of a villains' playground. While I was in Shikoku, I had seen signs warning elderly people not to fall for the scams of con men, who are often members of organized crime groups. But even the *yakuza* have been suffering labour shortages in recent years, partly in response to legislation designed to starve them of revenue, and partly because their members are ageing fast.

Ironically, in the topsy-turvy world of mass ageing, the elderly are more likely to be perpetrators of crime than its victims. Between 1988 and 2007, the number of over-65-year-olds in Japan doubled, but the number of crimes they committed increased fivefold.[6] Such is the boom in geriatric crime that, in some correctional facilities, being a prison officer is little different from working in an old people's home.

Like the young inmates of Asahi Shimane prison, most elderly prisoners are serving short sentences for minor crimes; nine out of ten of them have been convicted for shoplifting.[7] Some say that they stole because they were homeless and hungry; others to draw attention to themselves. But the golden thread linking the vast majority of crimes committed by the elderly is the breakdown of the extended family. A survey by the Tokyo metropolitan government found that more than half of seniors caught shoplifting lived alone, and 40 per cent of them either had no family or rarely spoke to them.[8] In court, many elderly defendants say that they only stole because they had no friends and thought that prison would be a good place to find some company.

★

I was on my way to Masuda to find out more about bear attacks. Shortly before returning to Japan, I had read an article that described how gunshots had rung out at a large shopping mall in Kaga, a small city in Ishikawa prefecture, on the coast of the Sea of Japan. Shortly afterwards, the body of a large adult bear was carried out of the building. It had wandered in 13 hours earlier, causing panic among shoppers.[9]

Across Japan, prefectural authorities reported 219 casualties, including six deaths, from bear attacks in the 12 months to March 2024.[10] The story of the bear in the supermarket – another instance of wild nature returning to fill the vacuum created by a hollowed-out rural settlement – seemed connected to everything I had been learning about on my travels. To find out more, I had arranged to meet Hiroaki Myōjō, a warden in the Forestry Department of the Western Shimane Agriculture, Forestry and Fisheries Promotion Centre, which is based in Masuda.

We met outside the town's station. Hiroaki was 29, but he had a disarmingly boyish manner. He wanted to introduce me to a bear hunter in Hikimi, a depopulated village in the mountains. We jumped into his 4x4, and he followed the Takatsugawa River into the mountains. I noticed that he had some birds' feathers under the sun visor in his car: some were from the *yamadori* (copper pheasant), which is one of Japan's national birds.[11] His favourite was from a *kumataka* (mountain hawk eagle), a rare bird with a wingspan of up to 175 centimetres.

Hiroaki was the first person I had met who knew all of Japan's native species. He had come across many of them in the course of his work; he had seen salamanders in the upper reaches of mountain rivers, glimpsed *serow* (wild goat) on distant mountain slopes and occasionally disturbed a civet cat while walking in the woods.

He told me that Japan is home to two species of bear – the brown bear, a giant that only lives on the northern island of Hokkaido, and the smaller Asian black bear, which is found in the rest of the country. 'The sharp increase in the number of bear attacks is bound up with rural depopulation. Many of the elderly residents of Japan's depopulating mountains live in neighbour-less communities, which often means they can't maintain their own safety and security.'

With mountain villages inhabited by fewer residents, and residents getting older and frailer, bears that have grown up near populated areas are losing their fear of humans. The last residents are at increased risk of attacks from bears, their homes are raided and ransacked by monkeys, and their plots are torn apart by wild boar and deer. Experts believe a steady fall in the number of children, whose noisy behaviour once helped keep bears at bay, is another factor behind the rise in bear attacks.

It was a beautiful day for a drive. Often called Japan's prettiest river, the Takatsugawa is one of only a handful of rivers that have not been dammed or canalized. Its banks were still in their natural state and the densely forested valley rose up steeply on either side. Under the bright sun of midsummer, the foliage had a near-silver sheen. Fishermen were wading in the river, fishing for little *ayu* sweet fish with poles and nets. Like eel, *ayu* are synonymous with summer. They are said to taste of cucumber or melon, and can only live in extremely clean water, earning them the elegant nickname *seiryū no jōō* – 'the queen of clear rivers'.

'Over the past 20 years, a lot of farms in mountain communities have been abandoned,' Hiroaki went on. 'The price of rice went down, and that made it harder for farmers to make a living. When they left, they left lots of persimmon and plum orchards behind.' These are the traditional fruit of Japan, popular among old people but less so among younger generations, who prefer imported fruit. 'Bears love persimmon and plums. They are a lot tastier than acorns, which is what they live on most of the time, and there has been a shortage of acorns recently.'

Japan's bear population is growing, with one estimate from 2024 putting the number of black bears at 44,000 – quite a leap from the 15,000-strong estimate made in 2012.[12] In recent years, bear sightings have become so common in mountainous areas that the government has issued guidelines to schoolchildren, telling them what to do if they come across one on their way home from school. 'Warnings about the presence of bears have become a regular occurrence,' Hiroaki told me. 'We alert residents and conduct awareness-raising activities about bears. We also go into schools and give the children bells to put on their backpacks.'

And what did he do when bears ignored his warnings, and decided to help themselves to a farmer's precious persimmons? 'When bears show up on farms, or in villages, we drive them away. If they have caused any damage, for example by eating a farmer's chestnuts, or destroying the walls of a storehouse, we give the farmer advice on how best to deal with them. Generally, that means putting up electric fences.'

After an hour or so, we came to Hikimi, a village surrounded on all sides by steep, conifer-covered mountains. It was so quiet I could hear the dragonflies switching back and forth in the warm, still air of late afternoon. We headed to the community centre, where we met Masafumi Murakami, a retired forestry worker who has been immersed in the ancestral culture of *matagi* (bear hunting) all his life.

Were there a lot of bears in the area? I asked him. 'Oh yes. In the winter months we used to make charcoal, and when we had time on our hands, we would go hunting for bears in the mountains.' In the course of hunting bears, Mr Murakami had grown to like and respect them, but as he got older, he was becoming scared of them. 'They are getting bigger. These days, it is common for them to grow to be 1.5 metres long. Perhaps it's because they are eating the wild boar,' he speculated.

Like Okamibuchi and Asahichō-Imaichi, Hikimi was in its death throes. In 1950, it had been a thriving town of 8,000. 'Even after the war, this place did alright because it supplied timber,' said Mr

Murakami. 'Timber was very important in those days because most of the houses in Japan were made out of wood. But these days, they're not building like they used to, and they import what timber they need from abroad. That means there's no work for our young people, so they leave for the lowlands.'

The community centre had once been the village elementary school, but it had closed down as the population shrank. When I visited, the population of Hikimi stood at 900. Seventy per cent of its residents were over 65 and many of them lived alone. 'Just yesterday, they found the body of an old man,' said Mr Murakami. 'The water wasn't working at his house. It looked like he had gone round the back to see what the problem was and had had a stroke.'

As well as getting bigger, the bears were getting more numerous and less wary of humans.

There used to be worries that bears would become extinct, and hunting was banned. But now there are lots of bears in Shimane pre-fecture. In the past, they did their best to avoid contact with people and you'd only see them early in the morning or at dusk. But they are getting bolder, knowing they have no reason to fear humans any more, and now I often see them in broad daylight.

Mr Murakami's eyes widened in astonishment. He was not an aggressive man; he wasn't even an assertive one, and I found it hard to square his gentleness and consideration for others with his being a lifelong hunter.

'In the next ten years, many of the residents of these mountain villages are going to die. Once they are gone, the bears will have free run of the place.' Mr Murakami had an unsettling habit of laughing at bad news. 'There is nothing to be done about it.'

With dusk drawing in, Hiroaki was keen to get back to Masuda. Mr Murakami suggested we take the back way; when he was a boy, he had come over the mountain every day to go to school in the village. Although the road was little used, it was still paved. Hiroaki and I set off up the steep and narrow road, following the luxuriant strip of bright-green grass running down its middle.

I wasn't expecting to see anyone living in the mountains above Hikimi, but when we passed a little group of houses, I caught sight of a hardy old woman tending her vegetable plot. Seeing her, I thought again about the disarming prospect of human life waning, while the bear and boar populations explode. She was the polar opposite of a pioneer; she was a remnant, one of the last residents of the soon-to-be-no-more village of Hikimi, stubbornly resisting the appeals of those beating an orderly retreat.

The time I had spent cycling around Shikoku, visiting farmers in Miyazaki, wandering the orange groves above Mitarai, and now exploring the mountains of Hiroshima and Shimane, had given me an opportunity to see the depopulation of the countryside up close. In my own inexpert way, I had learned to see Japan as a demographer does, looking thirty years ahead. When the tally of this year's births is published, demographers will calculate how much all those future taxpayers are going to contribute to the Treasury in the course of their working lives, and whether their contribution will cover the cost of looking after them, first as children, and, 50 or so years later, as pensioners.

Knowing what these contemporary seers know, I think it very likely that over the next 10–20 years, many of the farms I had visited will be abandoned for want of successors. The same process of ageing and shrinking is playing out across much of the European countryside as well, and over the next couple of generations the pace of decline is only going to pick up.

In an ideal world, the process of withdrawal will be an orderly one, planned well in advance. Teams of deconstruction workers from the Department for an Orderly Withdrawal will be sent in to take houses to pieces, and re-assemble them in Zones of Consolidation, with whatever cannot be re-used being broken down into its component pieces and recycled. They will take down the cables that have carried electricity to villages in the hinterland for the last century and pull up the telegraph poles. They will take up the railway tracks and prise the sleepers from the compacted ground, and then bulldozers will clear the gravel and level the ground.

In practice, however, it probably won't pan out like that. By 2070, Japan is unlikely to have the money to clear things up in an orderly way. Two more generations of 'lowest-low' fertility rates, and its people will be tired. They will need to save their energy for more important tasks, so the country's smaller towns and villages will fall into neglect, and when the last of their residents has died, they will be abandoned. The rust and the rot will gradually start to eat into the ruins, and one warm night in the typhoon season, the last of their timbers will be blown to the ground. In time, the last of those who remembered the last of the villagers will die, and by the time the rain and the sun have leached the last nutrients from the timbers, everyone will have been long forgotten.

★

On the way back to Masuda, Hiroaki told me that, although he had grown up in the city, he had always wanted to live in the countryside. That made him an 'I-turn' migrant. I asked him if he knew of any other city folk that had settled in the area. 'A few,' he said. 'Some have come with Rural Revitalization, but once their three-year term is up, they usually up and leave.' Like Asahichō Imaichi, it seemed that Masuda just wasn't the kind of place that lured in jaded city dwellers.

Many migrants have problems adjusting to country life. They complain about the lack of privacy. In farming communities, people tend not to lock their doors, which means that anyone can walk in at any time. Often, it is a well-meaning neighbour wanting to share his vegetable crop, but some people find it a bit intrusive.

Rural people, in turn, are having to come to terms with these migrants from the cities. The country's rural communities are humble places because they have been neglected, but also because of a loss of rural pride which I keenly felt as I travelled. In the post-war years, the best the regions could aspire to was to become clones of Tokyo. They have internalized the idea that city life is better than village life, and that they are in a hopeless situation.

That evening, Hiroaki took me to a restaurant in Masuda, where we ate an array of local game from the grill: wild boar, deer and bear. Figures issued by the Ministry of Environment show that, as part of pest-control efforts by municipal governments, around 5,500 bears were culled in Japan in 2020, approaching a record set in 2019. Little of this meat is eaten, but that could be changing.

'Tasty meat, if rather smelly,' said Hiroaki, chewing on a slice of badger bacon. I had first heard the word *jibie* (from the French *gibier*, meaning 'game') when I was with Shintaro Takeuchi, the orange farmer, in Mitarai. He told me that game hunting had been enjoying a boom, as part of the rustic, self-sufficient lifestyle promoted in men's magazines, but it was only now that I was getting to try some. With the number of young hunters on the rise, I wondered if Hiroaki had ever tried his hand. He said he liked the idea and had a gun licence but was still wary of picking one up for the first time.

We washed down our meal with an array of sake from all over Japan. Until then, my experience of rice wine hadn't extended beyond One Cup, the cheap brew available in every *konbini*. For the first time, I was able to appreciate the huge variety of flavours of sake, depending on when the rice is harvested, the quality of the mountain water used, and the soil and stone it flows through.

Reflecting on the time I had spent travelling in the margins, I had to admit that, despite the pleasures of cycling country roads and meeting country people, the sight of so many emaciated towns and villages had only dispirited me further. In Mitarai, I had seen the first tentative stirrings of revitalization, but the time I had spent in Hiroshima and Shimane was a reminder of its limits.

Despite everyone's best efforts, Japanese society seems to be at an impasse. In the cities, women are struggling to square the circle of having careers and children, and men are struggling to find partners at all. Meanwhile, in the countryside, young people are leaving their hometowns and villages, never to return, while their ageing relatives have to fend off marauding bears. Where can Japan go from here? After my time in the countryside, it was time to come in from the margins and return to the big city.

The Future

Osaka: Museum of Fecundity

In early 2023, Prime Minister Fumio Kishida warned that Japan's low birth rate posed 'an urgent risk to society'. The country, he said, was 'standing on the verge of whether we can continue to function as a society'.[1] His grave pronouncement garnered headlines around the world. Finally, the Japanese government was going to grasp the nettle and take meaningful action to address the country's demographic crisis.

Except this was not the first time the Japanese government had sounded the alarm about the long-term consequences of failing to reproduce. Government officials first declared sexless marriages a 'national problem' back in 1994. A public debate ensued, and years of earnest tinkering followed, with self-appointed experts offering counselling to sexless couples.[2]

In 1999, the government agreed on a Basic Plan for the Promotion of Measures for the Declining Birth Rate, with improved child benefit payments and tax breaks for young families. It acknowledged that, at the dawn of the twenty-first century, family structures were changing, and women could no longer be expected to raise children unsupported. Child-rearing had to be recognized as a public good that the government had a duty to facilitate.

However, none of the policies the government introduced had any lasting impact on the birth rate, which continued to decline. In 2003, another LDP government came up with a Plan to Urgently Implement Support for the Upbringing of the Next Generation. It reiterated that supporting families was the responsibility of society as a whole and vowed to tackle the obstacles households faced in raising enough children to keep the population steady. In 2005, the government established a Minister of State for the Declining Birth Rate and Gender Equality, and the Diet passed a Law to Promote Support Structures for the Upbringing of the Next Generation, which encouraged companies and local governments to create support systems for families.[3]

While welcoming these initiatives, critics pointed out that nothing would change until women felt able to combine motherhood with having a career. This is something the government had acknowledged in 1996, when it made the realization of a gender-equal society an objective, and the Diet had approved in 1999, when it passed the Basic Law for a Gender-Equal Society. The following year, the government brought in a Plan for Gender Equality, which created a host of new quangos, including a Headquarters for the Promotion of Gender Equality, a Council for Gender Equality and a Gender Equality Bureau. Still the birth rate refused to budge. It looked as if the inert power of Japanese social norms was capable of resisting any policy designed to make baby-making easier.

Critics of government policy are outnumbered by those urging gradual adjustments. The way the gradualists see things, the alarmists are over-egging the pudding. Demographic change is a gradual, predictable process, they argue, and it is only right that the Japanese government make gradual, predictable adjustments in response. Over the last four decades, it has introduced a welter of family-friendly policies to help working women balance their careers with their lives as carers, mothers and wives. It has increased the financial support it offers to the parents of newborns and created financial incentives to encourage couples to have children.

In the gradualists' defence, it is fair to say that government policies probably have helped women who already have a partner and have decided to have children. The fertility rate of married couples in Japan has declined over the last 50 years, but only from 2.2 in 1971 to 1.9 in 2021.[4] Given the rising cost of having children, it would doubtless have declined more dramatically had the government *not* intervened. However, the primary cause of Japan's falling fertility rate is the dwindling number of people getting married in the first place, and when it comes to tackling that obstacle, successive governments have shown themselves to be stumped.

The inconvenient truth is that there is only so much that governments *can* do to boost birth rates. After the fertility rate fell to a record low of 1.13 children per woman in 2006, the South Korean government began pouring money into efforts to reverse the decline. Over the next 16 years, it spent 280 trillion won (£148 billion) on measures designed to encourage women to have more children.[5] It gave parents of newborns 29.6 million won (over £15,000) over eight years in cash payments.[6] It offered couples everything from IVF to free housing and subsidized taxis if they would only agree to have a child. But cash handouts and subsidies have been to no avail: in 2022, South Korea's fertility rate fell to 0.78, the lowest in the world.[7]

Pronatalists like to point to France, where government-led improvements do seem to have had a positive impact. At 1.66, France has one of the highest fertility rates in the EU, a fact that its policymakers attribute to well-funded childcare services, generous family benefits and tax breaks for parents. There are many successful working women in France, they point out, and many of them have not just two but three, or even four children.

Birth-rate optimists also like to highlight the Hungarian government's success in encouraging people to have more children. It offers married couples who commit to having three children a £23,200 allowance towards the cost of buying a house. When a woman has her first child, her income-tax liability is reduced by 25 per cent for the rest of her life, and this rises to 100 per cent once she has had four children. As a result of these and other pronatalist policies, in the last ten years the Hungarian government has managed to raise the country's fertility rate from 1.3 to 1.6.[8]

Such 'baby bonus' programmes don't come cheap; Hungary is estimated to spend 5 per cent of its GDP on pronatalist policies.[9] And, while they make for newsworthy headlines, their long-term effects are questionable. There is significant evidence to suggest they just encourage those who would have had kids at some point in their lives to have them sooner – once they have had them, the fertility rate tends to revert to what it was before the bonus was introduced. This phenomenon, which is also prevalent in Sweden, is known as the Swedish Rollercoaster. Sweden enjoys one of the highest fertility rates in the developed world, which it attributes to its enlightened family policy. Yet Denmark has the same relatively buoyant fertility rate without Sweden's liberal family policies.[10]

There is also a question of ethics to consider: is the prospect of a handout from the government a good reason to bring a new life into the world? One would hope that there are more laudable reasons. But if there are, why give couples money to have children – or any other inducement, come to that? Unsurprisingly, most people don't like being told to have kids by the government, as the Danish government discovered after it launched a campaign to encourage more people to procreate. So far, the 'Do it for Denmark' campaign has had little effect on the country's fertility rate, with a survey finding that many Danes found the campaign 'insulting and embarrassing'.

Public mistrust of state pronatalist campaigns may change as awareness of the demographic crisis grows in the developed world. If nothing else, they let people know that the government values parenthood and is prepared to support families who choose to have children. But for now, awareness of the problems associated with low fertility rates, though growing, is still not widespread.

*

There aren't many examples from history of declining fertility, let alone of governments successfully reversing it. There was a time when no one in Ancient Rome wanted to get married or have children. Concerned about the decline of the native population, in 18 BCE the Emperor Augustus introduced measures to encourage citizens to get married and have children. Given that they included a law that made adultery a criminal offence, they can't have been popular, and it is not clear if they were effective.[11]

There have certainly been times when the Japanese government has urged the nation's women to have more children. In the Meiji period (1868–1912), for example, competition with the West prompted the government to introduce policies to increase the population. Abortion was criminalized and the virtues of motherhood were celebrated. Pronatalist propaganda made a comeback in the 1930s, when Japan turned militarist and competition with the West degenerated into open conflict. During World War Two, the Ministry of Health and Welfare came up with the slogan 'Give birth and multiply for the nation.'[12]

With the rise of the feminist movement around the world from the fifties onwards, such explicit state intervention in women's reproductive choices has been discredited, but that is not to say that future governments won't become more overtly pronatalist. Where does this leave women? This is the question that Margaret Atwood tries to answer in her 1985 dystopian novel *The Handmaid's Tale*, in which she imagines a near future in which the United States government has been overthrown by a patriarchal, totalitarian state. Set in New England, it posits a return to the days when the country's rulers believed themselves to be fulfilling a divinely inspired mandate. Women become the lowest-ranking class and are not allowed to read or write, own property or handle money.

They are also deprived of control over their reproductive functions. The handmaids of the title are women who have been forcibly assigned to bear the children of the government's high-ranking men. Reproduction takes place during 'the Ceremony', a ritual conducted in the presence of the men's wives. Atwood has said that she wrote *The Handmaid's Tale* in response to those who say that the kind of oppressive, religiously inspired government that has taken hold in countries like Iran 'can't happen here'.[13]

Even today, forcing women to have children is not beyond the realms of possibility, as the overturning of Roe v. Wade in the United States in 2022 illustrates all too well. The lead author of a study led by the University of Washington and published in the *Lancet* in 2020 speculated that in the future, as governments become more aware of the terrible impact of mass ageing on state finances, they may well introduce draconian measures designed to raise fertility rates. One such measure would be to reduce access to birth control, effectively forcing women to either have children or stop having sex with men.[14]

Is there really no solution to this conundrum, apart from co-ercing women into having children? To understand why govern-ments have found it so hard to boost the fertility rate, we have to understand why so many women are not having children. It is strik-ing that Germany, Japan and Italy all began to see dramatic falls in fertility rates in the early 1970s. Commentators came up with differing explanations. In Japan, they put it down to changes in the work–life balance. In Germany, they blamed it on the longstanding expectation that mothers of newborns should not go back to work straight after giving birth, which hurt their careers. In Italy, they blamed high unemployment, declining incomes and the rising cost of raising children.

All of these explanations hinge on economics, but cash is just one of several possible explanations for why women in three of the wealthi-est countries in the world opted to 'vote with their wombs', and have fewer, or no, children. It may be no coincidence that the former Axis powers (Japan, Italy and Germany) have some of the lowest fertility rates in the world. According to Italian feminist Mariarosa Dalla Costa, the low rate in her country is a subconscious birth strike by women against machismo.[15] Other countries with a history of authoritarian rule, like Greece, Portugal and Spain, also have very low fertility rates. Traditionalist men tend to have fixed ideas about who should do what in the home; when women have more independence, financial and intellectual, they are more willing to challenge those ideas and the men who hold them. One thing is clear: this is a story about the free-dom, empowerment and respect afforded to women.

This certainly rings true when it comes to Japan. Some aspects of the lived experiences of women in the post-war years – in their families and intimate relationships, in the workplace and in politics – have clearly changed for the better. But as Akiko told me when I met her in the beerhall in Otemachi, others have stood still.

Gender roles that were defined during the boom years of the late 1950s and early 60s have ossified. The LDP is still run by men of a certain age, and they have a limited appetite for change.

Yoshiro Mori, a former prime minister, demonstrated as much in 2003, when he angrily insisted that unmarried women should lose their entitlement to a pension. 'It is truly strange to say we have to use tax money to take care of women who don't even give birth once, who grow old living their lives selfishly and singing the praises of freedom,' he said.[16] It is hard to imagine the former prime minister of any other developed nation insisting on a woman's duty to bear children in the twenty-first century.

The Japanese government is encouraging more women to enter the workforce and, on the face of it, is committed to helping them to strike a better balance between work and family life. But its efforts to create a gender-equal society are hampered by the traditionalism of the old men who run the LDP and their unrelenting focus on promoting nuclear families, urging single people to find spouses and married couples to have children. The growing number of divorced working mothers doesn't come into the picture, perhaps because they challenge the LDP's outdated notions of the ideal family and the model worker. It is hardly surprising that, when Japanese women see how little support they are likely to get from the state in the event of a divorce, they feel that they either have to make their marriages work or not get married at all.

The same pattern can be seen across East Asia. As the *Economist* put it in an article published in 2023, 'the region as a whole is stuck between modernity and tradition, suffering some of the worst effects of both. East Asians are free to disdain traditional family roles, but not to redefine them. That is why millions resort to childlessness and solitude.'[17]

What is to be done? One solution would be to encourage women to have children out of wedlock, but this is a tactic fraught with risk. In the 1980s, the Singaporean government launched a pronatalist campaign that included a proposal to 'encourage unmarried mothers'. Unfortunately, traditionalists – among them many women – didn't like the idea. When Prime Minister Lee Kuan Yew encouraged single women to have children with married men, outside wedlock, women's organizations protested, declaring the government's campaign 'an enemy of marriage and the family'.[18]

Given the enduring appeal of traditionalist ideals, it may well be that, in the years to come, science is going to do more to raise birth rates than changing social norms. Indeed, once you stop moralizing and start embracing the possibilities opened up by medical technology, any number of new parents come into view. Katsuhiko Hayashi, an internationally renowned pioneer in the field of lab-grown eggs and sperm, is leading a team at Kyushu University that has been working on a technique to treat severe forms of infertility. By generating eggs from male cells, he has created mice with two biological fathers, a development that opens up radical new possibilities for human reproduction. Hayashi believes that within the next decade it will become possible to create a viable human egg from a male skin cell, an advance that raises the tantalizing prospect of same-sex couples being able to have biological children together.[19]

*

Leaving the countryside behind felt sad but inevitable. As its rural towns and villages age and die, Japan is becoming a land of mega-cities. It is already among the most urbanized countries in the world, and the tendency to cluster in ever-larger cities is only going to become more marked in the years to come. Perhaps, I thought, the shrinking is as unstoppable as the urbanizing.

On the way to Osaka, I spent a night in Matsue, the prefectural capital of Shimane, which was only an hour up the coast from Masuda on the train. While I was there, I got an unexpected insight into how people are responding to the loneliness of life in post-growth Japan. I stayed at another rather dour, if spotlessly clean, guest house. It had hardboard walls and no windows, and was in one of the timber-framed, corrugated iron-roofed houses that proliferated in the post-war years. The spartan lack of adornment put me in mind of a barracks.

When I had called ahead to book a room, the owner had asked me if I was allergic to cats, and on arriving I could see why: the entire place had been fitted with childproof safety bars to accommodate the master of the house, a large male cat with a white-and-dun coat. She gave me an English-language tour when I arrived, issuing clear instructions in a sing-song voice on how to sort the rubbish from the recycling, when I was allowed to use the living room and the importance of keeping the baby-doors closed so the cats didn't get out. There were two other, rather less visible, cats in the house: one was curious but scared, and the other I heard meowing plaintively but never saw, for she kept him in the little office at the front of the house. 'It's for his own good,' she said to me.

'And please take a shit,' she said when we came to the toilet. She explained that if I peed standing up, I was liable to cause splashes on the floor, so I should 'shit down' to pee, and if any drops should fall when I stood up again, I was to wipe them up and spray the area with the sanitizing fluid provided.

There was a TV in the living room, so when the tour was over I turned it on and did my best to be inconspicuous. Under the gaze of the oversized male cat, I watched a programme about the heirlooms unearthed by a middle-aged man while sorting through his late father's empty house.

Over the course of the next hour, a succession of other guests arrived, and I overheard each of them being given the same tour, with the same long list of instructions and warnings, delivered in the same ostensibly kindly, but faintly menacing tone of voice. One of the guests came into the living room and gave me a friendly wave, and the cat a good rub, which he accepted begrudgingly.

Given the dearth of children and the love of all things *kawaii*, it should come as no surprise to find that Japan is the only country in the world in which pets outnumber children. In 2021, 886,000 new furry family members came into the world, surpassing the number of babies born for the first time.[20] The human birth rate hit a record low that year, but there were 7 million dogs and almost 9 million cats living in Japanese homes – both record highs.[21]

Back when I lived in Tokyo, I had made a trip to a pet shop in Komazawa, a neighbourhood that has become a go-to destination for all kind of pet services, and it only confirmed my suspicion that a lot of pampered pets are child substitutes. It was dotted with dog-oriented restaurants, hotels and spas offering an array of specialty dog foods, dog/baby carriages and dog attire from boots to sunglasses. Of course, owning a pet and having a child are not mutually exclusive; plenty of pet owners are also parents. But it is telling that in Japan there are more pet owners in the 20–29 age group – the very demographic that would have been having kids a generation or two ago – than there are in any other.

That evening in Matsue, I went out for my customary dinner of miso ramen, gyoza and a cold beer. Coming back from the ramen shop, I saw the owner of the guest house taking the master cat for a walk on a lead in the largely empty car park outside. Like neighbourhoods I had stayed in in Tokushima, Kōchi, Uwajima and other provincial towns, this one had no shortage of freshly tarmacked little car parks, built on plots where houses had stood until recently. Her guest house stood in what was left of Matsue's entertainment district, so I suppose the parking spaces had once been bars, eateries and little knocking shops. With their flimsy walls, rusting corrugated-iron roofs and rattling window frames of frosted glass, most of the remaining houses looked like they would soon be going the same way.

Had the owner's family once run such a place? I wondered. Ordinarily I would have asked her, but I couldn't face it. I got the sense that she, too, would rather spend the evening with her cat than talk to a guest. While he dithered over whether or not he wanted to have a pee, she warbled away to him about what a hot day it had been and the second typhoon of the season, which was bowling towards us from the Pacific Ocean.

Anthropologist Paul Hansen has studied Japan's pet boom. In the course of his research, he made a study of the photographs that pet owners have on display in their homes and found that pets featured more often than partners, family members or friends. When he asked the study participants why they had decided to get an animal companion, the most common reason they gave was the breakdown or end of a human relationship. 'I got divorced and the dog is my new partner,' said one. 'Our children moved away so, being lonely, we bought a dog,' said another. 'When my father passed away, the house became a quiet and sad place, so we needed to buy a dog,' said a third.[22]

Much like *moe* – the intense feeling of attachment that obsessive manga and anime fans develop for their favourite characters – Japan's pet boom is underpinned by isolation. Indeed, the love that some people feel for their pets may be stronger than any love they ever had for their fellow humans. It's strange to think that while the countryside struggles not to be overrun by wild animals, in the cities, domestic animals are displacing infants in the nation's affections.

This is having interesting consequences. As more people come to regard their pet as a member of the family, growing numbers of Buddhist temples are receiving requests from bereaved people wanting to bury their dead pet in the family grave. One of them is Kannō-ji in Setagaya, west Tokyo, which has earned the affectionate moniker of 'the cat temple'. The head priest started to provide funeral services for pets around 13 years ago, and today almost half of the funerals that Junkyō Narita conducts are for cats or dogs. His temple even has a special pet crematorium, and Mr Narita allows pet owners to be buried with their pets' ashes.

The blurring of the boundary between humans and animals has generated debate among Buddhist scholars. Can animals be born again in the Pure Land after death, they wonder? Toshihide Adachi, a member of a Buddhist research institute in Kyoto, thinks not. 'Hōnen believed it was impossible for animals to experience rebirth in the Pure Land without first being reborn in another form,' he told a reporter from Nippon.com in 2019.* In order to be reborn in

---

* Pure Land Buddhism is the most common school of Buddhist thought in Japan. It is based on the teachings of the twelfth-century monk Hōnen, who believed

the Pure Land, you have to chant the sutras, and since dogs and cats cannot chant, they would first have to accumulate good karma in the realm of animals. They could then be reborn as humans, which would give them the opportunity to recite the sutras.

However, Kōjun Hayashida of Taishō University has argued that this is a misinterpretation of what Hōnen said about reincarnation. 'Hōnen taught that animals can achieve rebirth in the Pure Land through *ekō*,' he says. The concept of *ekō*, a 'transfer of merit', arose in response to complaints that conventional Buddhist thought leaves no room for people who are unable – through mental or physical disability – to chant sutras. Mr Hayashida believes that if, following the death of a pet, their owner chants the sutras for 49 days, the merit they earn will be transferred to their pet's soul, thereby allowing it to be reborn in the Pure Land.

However, this take on the meaning of *ekō* is far from conventional and, for now at least, most Buddhist priests maintain that humans cannot be reunited with their pets in paradise after death. Distraught at the refusal to bury or say prayers for their pet, some owners have even severed ties with their family temple over the matter. They say that, far from being New Age mumbo-jumbo, the practice of saying prayers for dead animals stretches back as far as the Jōmon period (14,000–1,000 BCE).

While true, this rather misses the point. In the past, people prayed for the spirits of dead dogs because they were frightened of dogs. The intense sense of attachment that many pet owners feel for their animal companions is a recent phenomenon, a result of the renewed interest in all things spiritual that sprang up in late twentieth-century Japan. Commentators like Haruki Murakami have attributed this 'rush hour of the gods' to the vapid materialism at the heart of Japan's post-war economic 'miracle'. Be that as it may, it has only been amplified by the wasting away of the family, the dearth of children and the chronic loneliness that many Japanese people feel today.[23]

---

that a person could be reborn in the Pure Land after death simply by reciting the words '*Namu Amida Butsu*' ('I take refuge in the Amida Buddha').

Before turning in for the day, I took a shower, and when I got back to the dorm and lay down on my mattress on the floor, I could hear the cat's wife spraying her sanitizing gun after me. She was clearly a stickler for cleanliness. Is this how the human story ends, I asked myself? Not with a bang but the whimper of a childless centenarian, heard only by a tom cat in a sailor suit wondering who's going to feed him now that his owner has given up the ghost?

*

I was a little disappointed to find that the train from Matsue to Osaka didn't have a smoking booth or any vending machines, facilities I had grown accustomed to seeing on long-distance trains. All the same, it was beautifully maintained, with the seats handsomely trimmed in shades of cherry, and the carriages suffused with the scent of furniture polish.

The carriage I was riding in was full of the chatter of foreign tongues, which came as some surprise after a few weeks in the sticks. The tourists – mainly Chinese or South-East Asians, with a smattering of Europeans and Americans – were back after the pandemic, enjoying the cheap yen. The Japanese passengers looked perturbed. Tourism – foreign, not domestic – is destined to become a mainstay of Japan's post-growth economy, a turn of events they appeared to be in two minds about. Who could have foreseen in the early 1990s that Japan would have to become a living museum to pay its way in the twenty-first century?

I arrived in Osaka later that morning and went straight to a guest house in the Korean part of town. It was quite lively near the metro station, but the crowds soon tailed off as I made my way down the covered shopping street, and I soon found myself in a typically quiet, near-deserted neighbourhood of densely packed timber-framed houses.

The guest house was only 40 years old but it felt older. Everything had been given a thick coat of paint, as if in an attempt to hold it all together. The owner was a good-natured and surprisingly gregarious woman whom everyone called Nami-san. Breakfast was included, so every morning her front room was full of young European backpackers eating the Japanese equivalent of Mother's Pride bread and jam.

When the last of them had gone out sightseeing for the day, I asked Nami-san how she came to be running a guest house for foreign tourists. She was 73, she told me, and had been running the place for the last 20 years. 'I worked out how much money I needed to pay for a nursing home and started saving up. I don't want to end up on *ubasuteyama*. The term, which might be translated as 'granny dump', refers to a village custom in the Edo period whereby the elderly would be taken up the nearest mountain and abandoned there when they were no longer able to work. It was a grim reminder of a time when few Japanese got to enjoy their retirement.

When I told Nami-san about my interest in her shrinking country, she suggested that I talk to one of her tenants, who worked in a local care home for the elderly. I was accustomed to seeing old people living in these rickety post-war houses, and foreign backpackers found them interesting, but I was surprised that Nami-san's guest house also functioned as a share house for low-paid workers.

She gave Mariko a shout, and she came and joined us for a coffee. Although she said she was 31, she looked prematurely middle-aged in her dress, as though she were half-child, half-spinster. I mentioned how few old people's homes I had seen on my travels. This was surprising, given how many elderly people lived in them, as if they were deliberately being hidden away. 'Yes, and some of them look like prisons, don't they?' said Mariko. 'I look after elderly and disabled people in a group home. It is like a share house for the aged. We have room for nine people.'

She admitted that she was as surprised to be working there as the residents were to be there. Until recently, it was generally assumed that the husband would be the first to become ill or bedridden and would be nursed by his wife. But with people living longer than ever, a growing number of men are having to nurse their sick wives or geriatric parents. For many of them, doing unpaid social work is a rude awakening. Most men born during the post-war baby boom have no experience of household affairs and find it hard to cope when their wives become bedridden or die before them.

This dependency is strained because the extended family all but collapsed in Japan a generation ago. 'In the past, old people used to live in the family home, and one of their kids would look after them,' Mariko told me. Back in 1980, 70 per cent of elderly people lived with one of their children; by 2006, this had fallen to 44 per cent, still a higher proportion than in most Western countries, but all the same a startling change in the eyes of most elderly Japanese.[24] Many of those who are not cared for by a child or spouse can't or won't turn to their extended family when they need help and, consequently, growing numbers of them end up living alone.

'And a lot of them die alone too,' said Mariko with a nervous laugh. 'It's very sad. People don't have time for their ageing parents any more. They get frazzled looking after them, so they put them in a care facility.' Paying strangers to care for elderly family members is still a novel, and not always welcome, idea in Japan, but long working hours and the rising number of working women mean that care in the family is no longer feasible.

Kaigo tsukare or 'care-giving fatigue' is the label given to an increasing number of crimes reported in the press. I remembered reading about an 89-year-old man from Asahikawa in Hokkaido who had killed his wife. She had been suffering from dementia and, in his defence, he maintained that he had only killed her because she had asked him to. Such cases are rare, but they inevitably make headlines, which give the impression that the neglect and mistreatment of ageing relatives are becoming more widespread. They are all the more compelling because they run counter to who the Japanese believe themselves to be: caring, patient and forgiving.[25]

'Some of the staff where I work bully the old people, especially the ones suffering from dementia,' Mariko told me. 'They can be quite violent.' In Japan, one in five people over the age of 65 has dementia.[26] How did the elderly people that Mariko looked after feel about ending their days in a nursing home, I asked her. 'Some of the ones with severe dementia don't understand why they are there. They forget things all the time, so it's not easy to communicate with them. Sometimes they get violent too.'

While families are struggling to cope with their ageing relatives, Japan's social welfare system, once a model of cost-effective universal care, is no longer able to provide adequate support. This isn't for lack of government funding; rather, there just aren't enough people of working age to look after so many retirees. Japan currently faces a shortage of around 380,000 care workers, and this is expected to rise to 700,000 by 2040.[27] This puts the existing workforce under great strain. 'It is hard work,' Mariko told me. 'I have to help the old people get up from the toilet and help them put on their nappies and some of them are heavier than me.'

Proposed fixes include raising care workers' salaries to make the profession more appealing and recruiting more retirees and volunteers. Allowing in more foreign workers is still regarded as a last resort. I asked Mariko if there were any immigrants working in her nursing home. 'None at the place where I work, but I have heard that there are Vietnamese and Filipinas working in other nursing homes in Osaka,' she said. 'They have problems learning the language.' The government insists that non-Japanese nurses sit a language exam after three years. Given that it has a pass rate of only 10 per cent, it's easy see why many foreign staff believe it is designed to be nigh-on impossible to pass.

With the shortage of care workers only growing more acute, and immigration still a 'third-rail' issue for the traditionalists who make up the bulk of the LDP's members, it's no mystery why public and private investment is pouring into the development of care robots. In 2020, Japan's health ministry launched eight 'living labs' dedicated to developing 'carebots'. Their inventors say they can provide physical therapy, assist with bathing, lifting and mobility, and monitor the whereabouts of their charges through sensors. The hope is that, as carebots acquire AI capabilities, they will function as live-in carers for Japan's elderly population, thereby obviating the need for old people's homes and the young immigrants who would staff them.

It is striking how readily Japan's care industry is turning to technology to provide stand-ins for the country's absent humans. At Yume Paratiis, a nursing home in Amagasaki, a city near Osaka, a robot called the Hug carefully lifts patients out of their wheelchairs and transfers them to their beds. Staff at the 116-resident home say the Hug enables them to do lifting and lowering tasks by themselves instead of in pairs.[28] Meanwhile, a short-staffed nursing home in Natori, Miyagi prefecture, is using a toddler-sized humanoid known as the Telenoid to interact with residents. It can capture the voice and movements of a family member hundreds of miles away using a microphone and camera, which it then replicates for the stranded relative. Staff say that residents, especially those with dementia, become more positive and active when communicating with the in-house Telenoid.[29]

Carebots may well be able to imitate social interaction, provide physical assistance and deliver therapies, but how much actual care work can we realistically expect machines to do? Do a Google search for 'Japan + robots' and you can see how English-language media tends to uncritically buy into the Japanese government's utopian vision of seamless interaction between humans and robots. But like the Gatebox promising users access to a 'virtual girlfriend', the pathos of trying to get a machine to love or care for a human seems lost on the invariably male engineers charged with plugging Japan's demographic gaps.

Interviews with robotics researchers suggest that, like Japan's politicians, journalists may have allowed themselves to get a bit carried away by the potential of robots to come to humanity's rescue. The Robobear, for example, was developed to carry frail people to and from the bath and bed. It can certainly lift a human, but by all accounts it is an extremely uncomfortable ride. Like a real-life bear, the Robobear is more than capable of breaking an elderly person's arm. Unsurprisingly, in trials, it is always supervised by a team of anxious researchers.

Ultimately, many robotics researchers are finding that their reach is longer than their grasp. They are having to restrain their technophilic imaginings and take a sober look at the practical tasks that a robot can realistically accomplish. Although most of what a human carer does in the course of a day's work is beyond the abilities of a carebot, they can take on a lot of the mundane tasks that human carers don't enjoy. For example, there is a carebot that will happily spend an entire day ironing, folding and putting away clothes, and another that will make as many omelettes as you can eat.

And many care recipients like having an unobtrusive, unquestioning machine around. Old people who live alone sometimes feel lonely, but they are also prone to feeling irritated when younger people tell them what to do and what is good for them. They want to preserve their autonomy for as long as possible, and don't always appreciate having an intrusive stranger in their homes. If hell is other people, having a robot of one's own might appear heaven-sent. There is no need to feel embarrassed about getting naked in front of a robot, and devices like Amazon's Alexa, which vocalizes all the information available on the internet, are already helping elderly people to feel less isolated. AI can remind them when to take their medication and dispense pills, but it can also give them mental agility tasks and play games with them, which makes robots especially useful for people living with dementia.[30]

And yet there is a paradox at the heart of the matter: Japan's politicians, bureaucrats and business leaders want robots to fill labour shortages in the very professions to which they are least suited. Most jobs in healthcare and social work require levels of emotional sensitivity, nuanced judgement and fine-motor dexterity that are beyond the powers of even the most sophisticated robot. Advances in robotics might look exciting, but many researchers admit that they are 50–100 years away from developing a robot with the intelligence and sensitivity required to be called 'caring'.

Quite aside from their technical limitations, 'carebots' are incredibly expensive to buy, and require additional human labour to develop, build, and maintain. The idea that care for the elderly can ever be fully automated is a chimera, not least because Japan cannot afford to roll out carebots to all those in need of care. We all like to see a scientist rise to the challenge posed by a social problem, but all the *Tomorrow's World*–style pieces in the press can be misleading. In 2019, a survey of over 9,000 institutions providing care for the elderly in Japan found that only about 10 per cent used care robots, and those that did used them primarily for monitoring residents rather than lifting, bathing or interacting with them.[31]

When I asked Mariko if there were any robots or AI in the facility where she worked, she looked at me as if I were a simpleton. So what will happen in the next couple of decades, as more elderly people become residents in Japan's care facilities, and labour shortages put the workforce under ever-increasing strain? She was not optimistic. 'With the rise in the consumption tax, it has become a lot harder to make a living. Care workers might get paid more than convenience store workers, but that's because our work is much harder than theirs. I've seen a lot of care workers quit.'

★

Later that morning, I sent a message to Yusuke, the young *salariman* I had interviewed at the Café Paulista in Ginza. He was based in Osaka, and I wondered if he might be up for a drink. We arranged to meet in an *izakaya* in the basement of a huge office block near the city's main station that evening. That left me with an afternoon to kill, so I went to have a look at Ohatsu Tenjin shrine, which was just a short walk away.

The shrine was founded more than 1,300 years ago, when Osaka was just a village on an island in the mouth of the River Yodo. It is named after a woman called Ohatsu, who was driven to commit suicide with her lover Tokubei in the grounds of the shrine in 1703. Their story was made famous by the playwright Chikamatsu Monzaemon, who turned it into a *bunraku* (traditional puppet theatre) play called *Sonezakishinjū* (*The Love Suicides at Sonezaki*, that being the name of the village).

Walking into the grounds of the shrine, I remembered the long tradition of doomed love that the young Austro-Japanese sociologist Alice Pacher had talked about when I met her in Tokyo. True love was rare and rarely ended well, for in a society governed by the norms of Confucianism, the obligation to do one's duty always trumped personal feelings. Marriages were arranged by one's parents with property and status in mind, and the passion of romantic love was an afterthought. Chikamatsu's play aroused such strong feelings of pity in theatregoers that many of them visited the shrine to pray for the spirits of Ohatsu and Tokubei. Ever since, Ohatsu Tenjin has been a place where singletons go to pray that they will find true love, and couples go to pray for a happy relationship.

The modern-day shrine would be unrecognisable to the tragic couple. The marshes that once surrounded Ohatsu Tenjin have long since been drained and the land reclaimed, and these days the shrine is hemmed in by skyscrapers. Walking down a narrow, winding corridor of *torii* gates, I came to a bronze statue of the ill-fated lovers. They were sitting side by side, Ohatsu resting her hands on Tokubei's leg. They were demure, middle-aged figures, with hands worn smooth by the touch of sympathetic visitors.

I doubled back to the other end of the corridor, where there was a wooden kiosk with a copper-tiled roof and a gentle old woman selling slips of paper printed with fortunes, known as *omikuji*. This was the secondary *enmusubi* shrine (that is, one dedicated to the blessing of relationships), and it was clearly aimed at a younger audience. It was festooned with fluttering banners, the largest of which depicted Ohatsu and Tokubei in manga style. Unlike the middle-aged statues, they looked like painfully earnest school-leavers, with dewy, milk chocolate-coloured eyes that occupied a fifth of their faces. Designed to endear, they betrayed no trace of the tragedy that had so moved past generations of visitors.

I had seen this twin-track approach to marketing at many of the historical sites I had visited on my travels: one was aimed at the older generation and rested on a staid, comforting interpretation of the past; the other, designed to appeal to the younger generation, channelled the Edo period through a *kawaii* kaleidoscope that turned everyone into a cartoon character. Seen through the rose-tinted glasses of the manga fan, samurai warriors became playful midgets, Shinto gods were depicted as baby birds and mythical heroes were reimagined as puppies or kittens.

The banks of *ema* lining the path that led from the kiosk back to the main shrine also veered towards the fantastical. *Ema* are little wooden votive boards, originally offered upon fulfilment of a vow. These days, shrinegoers are more likely to use them to express their wishes for the future or to give thanks for divine favours received. There must have been over a hundred *ema* at Ohatsu Tenjin, each framed by a pink love heart on which a young woman had written her most cherished wish in tiny, neat handwriting.

One wished for everlasting love, while another asked to be 'blessed with a good connection' so that she could get married that year. What struck me most, however, was how many of the messages were addressed to members of boy bands. 'I want to be chosen in the lottery for tickets to see 7Men live,' read one. 'Please let me see 5Now Man,' wished another. These fangirl fantasies outnumbered hopes for a real relationship by a factor of five.

Not for the first time, I couldn't help thinking that there had to be a connection between these candy-coloured dreams and Japan's plummeting fertility rate. Young women who have grown up immersed in a *kawaii* universe of fluffy pink ponies are destined to idealize themselves as perennial children. This makes it hard for them to imagine themselves as adults, much less parents. They follow adult rules, dutifully attending school, university and then work, because they believe that they have no choice in the matter. But getting married and having kids are matters of personal choice, and they are choosing not to surrender their precious autonomy.

At the end of the banks of *ema* was a series of blank slates: on each board was a faceless version of Ohatsu that visitors could fill in with their ideal facial features. Among the wide-eyed, long-lashed ideals, I was heartened to see a couple of Japanese nails that insisted on sticking up.* One face looked to have been driven mad by keen-

---

* Japanese people often say that 'a nail that sticks up will be hammered down' to explain the importance of conforming to social norms.

ness to please. Another depicted a bloodshot, gap-toothed pig bleeding from its nose and hairline. They were a timely reminder that not all manga conforms to the rules of *kawaii*, with its saccharine fantasies, and that plenty of young women want nothing to do with the demure maiden who has come to define the feminine archetype in Japan.

*

The *izakaya* where I was due to meet Yusuke was one of many in a subterranean warren of hostelries catering to Osaka's *salarimen*. Come six o'clock, they were crowded with office workers relaxing over beers at the end of another working week. Yusuke had suggested we meet at this particular *izakaya* because the owner was famous for his progeny. He had twelve children, several of whom worked in his establishment.

The interior was a dayglo celebration of sex and fecundity, illuminated by florescent lights and garlanded with masses of coloured tinsel, with a variety of dildos displayed in cases. The owner, a short, stocky man in a Hawaiian shirt and a pork-pie hat, sat on a stool at the door, enjoying the attention. When I asked him why he had so many kids, he solemnly sketched the shape of an outsized phallus with his hands and gave me a knowing wink.

Yusuke, who turned out to be a regular, introduced me to one of the great offspring-maker's sons, a sweet, earnest young man who was big on karate, like everyone in the family. 'He is ranked third in the country,' said Yusuke admiringly. Did he plan to get married and have kids, I asked him. 'Oh yes,' he answered sincerely. 'My dad has made it clear it is expected of me.'

Over drinks, I told Yusuke about my travels in the Japanese countryside: the empty houses I had seen on my travels in Shikoku, the urban migrants and budding entrepreneurs I had met in Miyazaki, and the villages of stoical OAPs I had passed through in Hiroshima and Shimane prefectures. I asked him if he was worried about the consequences of a declining population. 'Not really. I enjoy rock climbing, so I go into the mountains a lot and I've grown to appreciate the natural world. I think it is good that a lot of the houses on the islands and in the mountains are disappearing.'

This urban-centric way of thinking is what is killing the countryside, I thought to myself. Wasn't he concerned about the disappearance of the rural way of life? 'Well, there is a green belt around London, and when I travelled from Oxford to Cambridge, I saw loads of countryside. We don't have that kind of scenery in Japan.' Point taken. It was only to be expected that Yusuke, who had grown up in the sprawling suburbs of Saitama, appreciated the peace and quiet of the countryside, just as those who have grown up in the sticks often itch to leave.

But surely, he wouldn't wish the decrepitude I had witnessed in the countryside on the suburbs as well? 'Personally, I don't think it's a problem if the population of Japan goes down. In fact, I think it *should* go down. The population density is really high in Japan compared to other countries.' All those mornings spent stuffed into commuter trains had clearly taken their toll.

'From young people's point of view, Japan's biggest problem is not population decline per se, but the ageing society. We have lots of people aged between 65 and 85. Maybe 30 years from now, once the baby boomers have died, the problem will come to an end. By then, the population will be smaller, but so will the proportion of old people.'

But Japan is likely to be a very different country by then, isn't it? Spending so much money on pensions and healthcare is already eating into government spending on education and training for young people. Yusuke had a young daughter; wasn't he concerned that her generation was going to come of age in a country with fewer high-tech industries, shrinking exports and a declining standard of living?

'Yes, I am,' he admitted with a sigh. 'It's tricky. A shrinking population means that GDP is going to decline. But the government can't reduce the number of pensioners, so it has to increase the budget for pensions and long-term care. Some old people live to the age of 90 or 100. Young people can't just say, "Please die." Euthanasia is illegal in Japan.'

I was reminded of the film *Plan 75*, which imagines a future Japan in which euthanasia has been legalized. 'A state-sanctioned solution like *Plan 75* is far from impossible in a country that is growing ever more intolerant of socially weak people – the elderly, the disabled and people who have no money,' the film's director, Chie Hayakawa, told journalists when the film came out in 2022. 'It means that we have to take care of ourselves instead of relying on the government or being a burden to society.'

Hayakawa believes that the idea of taking responsibility for oneself, and not causing *meiwaku* ('trouble' or 'bother') for others, has become an obsession in Japan over the past decade. The definition of *meiwaku* is very much in the eye of the beholder: for some, even asking for a hand in getting up the stairs constitutes an intolerable intrusion. The pressure not to impose on others, she says, comes from the government and the media. 'They create shame among those who need welfare, meaning those who need it don't apply for it – which makes their lives even more desperate. But it also infects the younger generations, building up a huge resentment towards all older people.'[32]

The idea of taking responsibility for oneself taps into a long tradition of family-based 'self-reliance'. The state expects families to look after their own in times of hardship, and when it comes to carers and single mothers, the welfare state doesn't really exist. But with millions of single, unmarried women looking after ageing relatives, it is unclear how much longer this can be expected to last. So, who should bear the labour costs involved at the beginning and end of life – the so-called labour of love?

Before taking my leave of Yusuke, I asked him what he thought should be done to raise the fertility rate. 'Maybe compulsory education should be shortened by three years,' he volunteered. 'Let young people leave school at 15, so that they can become adults sooner. That would allow them to start earning money sooner. Or make university courses two years long instead of four.'

Yusuke was thinking along the same lines as Stephen Shaw, director of the documentary *Birthgap*, who believes that when it comes to explaining low birth rates, the job market in highly developed economies has a lot to answer for. Companies often demand that new entrants have post-graduate qualifications, and expect them to put in long working hours for little pay, on the understanding that they will be on a good salary by the time they hit middle age. In the process, employers are inadvertently forcing young people to defer parenthood.

Shaw emphasizes the importance of lifelong learning, so young people don't feel so compelled to get a higher education before they settle down and have kids of their own. He argues that companies should allow younger workers to take time out in their careers so that they can both go back into the education system and focus on finding a partner and raising children. He even suggests that certain occupations come with a health warning, making it clear to prospective employees that they are associated with an increased risk of unplanned childlessness.

13.

Robots in the Showroom, Immigrants in the Back Room

I had a surprise when I went to Osaka station the following morning to catch a bullet train back to Tokyo. After watching the locomotive at the front of the train glide into the station, I was astonished to see that the driver who stepped down onto the platform looked to be about 14. I watched in disbelief as he handed over to the next driver, before slipping off his pristine white gloves, putting them into his briefcase and melting away into the crowd of passengers waiting to board the train.

The *shinkansen* train too was a wonder to behold, with its extraordinarily elongated snout painted a beautiful shade of metallic green. For people of my generation, the bullet train is still the most impressive Japanese invention of the second half of the twentieth century. I had never travelled on one before. The windows were smaller than I expected, which made me feel as if I were on a plane. However, once we had reached top speed, it was like being in a racing car: while the carriage was comfortable, the abiding impression was of sheer power.

The *shinkansen* still evokes great pride in Japan. However, with plans underway to build a mostly underground, 310-miles-per-hour maglev line between Tokyo and Osaka, its speed is not as awe-inspiring as it was when I first lived in Japan. Daydreaming about the enormously expensive Chūō Shinkansen project, I soon became distracted by the little imperfections on the train I found myself riding – the scuff marks, signs of use and age. Naively, when I think of the future, I expect perfection.

The purpose of building a high-speed rail network was always to breathe new life into Japan's regions. The beauty of the *shinkansen* is that it allows people to make long journeys in a single day, uniting the country by bringing everywhere within reach. By strengthening connections between the urban hubs and the rest of the country, it has changed the fortunes of many towns, and, to this day, every rural municipality in the land dreams of becoming a stop on a *shinkansen* route.

The Tōkaidō *shinkansen* between Osaka and Tokyo is named after the old highway that used to run along the Pacific coast between the imperial court in Kyoto and the seat of military power, which was originally in Kamakura before moving to Edo. For 800 years, the Tōkaidō was the spinal cord of the country, carrying messages between the emperor and the generals, the former the embodiment of peace-loving refinement, the latter of hard-headed pragmatism. Commerce flowed along the highway, towns and cities grew up around it, and it was celebrated by generations of artists and painters.

There is rather less to celebrate these days, as the Pacific coastline between Japan's two largest cities has been ravaged by industrial sprawl and a seemingly endless belt of cities and suburbs. At the eastern end of the Tōkaido, Yokohama runs into Kawasaki, which runs into Tokyo and Chiba, forming the largest megacity in the world. At its western end, Osaka has expanded to the city limits of Kobe, and before long it will likely merge with Kyoto, forming another vast metropolis.

If the next generation of maglev trains makes it off the drawing board, they will run almost entirely underground. From a deep subterranean terminal, passengers will pass through an air lock – designed to shield them from electromagnetic forces – before embarking on a journey that will cut the travel time between the country's two biggest cities in half. Zooming under central Japan at twice the speed of the current generation of *shinkansen*, there will be no scenery to look at and nothing to give them a sensation of having travelled at all.[1]

★

A few days after returning to Tokyo, I was waiting for a latte at the Dawn Avatar Robot Café in Nihonbashi. I'd heard that owners of humanoid robots often brought them to the café for meetups, rather like dog owners who take their dogs to the park to meet other dogs. However, on the day I visited, the customers were all foreign tourists, keen to get a glimpse into the future. They were in for a disappointment, as a sign in the window explained that the 'robots' were not really robots at all, but 'avatar robots'. The contraption that greeted them when they came into the café was effectively just a big plastic toy that could move its arms up and down.

The Dawn Avatar Robot Café is innovative, in fact, not for its use of robots but for the employment opportunities it offers to disabled people. The voice of the 'robot' that served me belonged to a woman in another part of Japan, who was keen to keep working but unable to leave the house. Armed with an internet connection and a remote control, she was able to play the part of a robot for the benefit of the tourists, who were intent on getting a photo of one while they were in Japan. After days of monosyllabic interactions with strangers, I found the volubility of my 'robot' server quite disarming. She seemed all the more animated for being invisible.

I was not the only one feeling disconcerted at interacting with such a chatty, keen-to-please 'robot'. The other tourists placed their orders with bewildered looks on their faces. Not that the robots behind the counter actually made the coffee. I was given the option of having my coffee brought to my table by a robot, but that would have been part of the café's 'robot experience' package, which cost an additional ¥1,000, so I opted to be served by a regular human.

While I was waiting for my order, I eavesdropped on the foreigner being served in the 'robot experience space'. He politely asked the robot if he could take his photo, and the disabled man controlling the robot politely obliged. 'Where are you from?' he asked the tourist. 'Near Oxford, in the UK,' he replied with an embarrassed smile. The robot said he had heard of it, but he spoke English with a strong Japanese accent, and it was not a good line, so the tourist had to ask him to repeat himself a few times. There was an awkward pause. 'I'm afraid I must be boring you,' said the tourist. 'Oh no, not at all,' said the robot. 'Would you mind if I take a photo of you?'

A Japanese customer came in, and lunged towards the first human server she saw to escape the embarrassment of having to talk to a robot. In a lull before the next customer arrived, the two robots behind the counter turned to face one another and started chatting about their pets. I was touched, but their voices were both high-pitched and amplified, and I wanted to tell them to turn the volume down a bit. The future wasn't supposed to be like this, I told myself.

Of course, there are plenty of proper robots in Japan, and its robotics engineers can still make science fiction come true. Consider Philip K. Dick's 1955 short story 'Autofac', in which he describes an automated factory of the future that has no need for human staff. This fantasy has become a reality in Amaga-saki, where use of industrial robots allows Panasonic to run a factory that produces 2 million television sets a month, mostly high-end plasma LCD screens, with a human workforce of just twenty-five.

Other automated factories have no human staff at all. The world's largest maker of industrial robots is a Japanese company called FANUC. The robots in its factory near Mount Fuji build other robots at a rate of about fifty a day, and can run unsupervised for as many as 30 days at a time. Since 2001, the factory has been operating as a 'lights-out' factory, so called because, having no human staff, it doesn't need lights. 'Not only is it lights-out, we turn off the heating and air conditioning too,' says FANUC vice-president Gary Zywiol.[2]

For decades, robots have been playing an ever more important role in Japan. In 2014, the government created a Robot Revolution Realization Council, as part of its Council on Investments in the Future. The government has committed tens of millions of dollars to an industry whose revenues are expected to surge to nearly $70 billion by 2025. 'Robotics is to be for the Japanese economy in the 21st century what automobiles were in the 20th,' says

Jennifer Robertson, a professor of anthropology at the University of Michigan.[3]

As I'd witnessed throughout my time in Japan, technology is the mantra invoked to solve all manner of social problems. Former prime minister Shinzo Abe promoted a speculative policy platform called Society 5.0, which mapped out Japan's high-tech hopes for the twenty-first century. The promotional ad for Society 5.0 was mightily impressive, with drones delivering parcels to isolated mountain communities, doctors offering online medical consultations to ageing patients, and households packed with devices hooked up to the Internet of Things.

Even more ambitious than Abe's Society 5.0 are the Moonshot goals, an R&D programme inspired by a utopian vision of humanity overcoming its most intractable problems by 2050. The scientists behind Moonshot are confident that they can create 'a society in which human beings can be free from limitations of body, brain, space, and time'.[4]

There's a lot of money riding on this techno-utopianism. Japan's consumer-electronics companies, which made their money supplying the world with household goods for 50 or so years, might have been priced out of the market by their Korean and Chinese rivals, but they are cash-rich and on the lookout for profitable ventures in which to invest. Japan's car companies are in a similar position. Toyota may no longer be one of the world's top 500 multinationals, but Mr Toyota says that, by 2030, the company will no longer be a car company. By then, it will have evolved into a 'mobility company', providing a variety of transportation services, including ferrying people about in flying cars, and developing the infrastructure for the 'smart cities' of the future.

Talking to Mariko in Osaka had given me a sense of the limitations of robots in addressing the fundamental challenges facing Japan's burgeoning geriatric care sector. But Japan's love of robots is strong, in marked contrast to attitudes in the United States, where people worry about the impact that robots and AI are going to have on jobs. Sam Altman, the CEO of Open AI, the company that created ChatGPT, has given testimony at a Congressional hearing in which he admitted that AI will probably lead to job losses.[5] Goldman Sachs says that job losses around the world could run as high as 300 million.

The British are worried too. In 2016, the Bank of England's chief economist warned that 15 million of the country's jobs might be taken over by robots. According to Andy Haldane, automation poses a risk to almost half those employed in the UK.[6] 'The Future of Employment', an oft-cited study by academics at Oxford University, examined over 700 occupations and found that some jobs are at more risk of being automated than others. Unsurprisingly, those most at risk tend to be routine and repetitive. Fast-food cooks, for example, face an 81 per cent probability of being replaced by robots like Flippy, an AI-powered kitchen assistant.

Jobs least at risk are those that require some degree of creativity, such as being an artist or a scientist, or developing new business strategies. Intrinsically unpredictable jobs – plumbers, for example, who have to respond to emergencies in different locations – are also safe, as are most supervisory roles.

Those who say that robots and AI are destined to put half of us out of a job may well be proven wrong in time. After all, in the last 60 years, the only job that automation has definitely done away with is lift operator. As an article in the *Guardian* put it, 'Very few of us are working the 15-hour work week that, in 1930, the economist John Maynard Keynes predicted would be the norm for his grandkids. If anything, we're working 15-hour days.'[7]

Nomura Research Institute, a data analysis firm, says that about half of all jobs in Japan could be done by robots or AI by 2030.[8] But if there is one thing that ageing, shrinking Japan is not worried about, it is unemployment: as Japan's population dwindles, there are far more situations vacant than workers available to fill them. Labour shortages are growing all the time, so it's easy to see why the government is banking on robots becoming stand-ins for the non-existent workers of the future.

★

AI can teach us a great deal about medicine, psychiatry and dentistry, but that doesn't mean that robots make good doctors, psychiatrists or dentists, let alone advisors, counsellors or therapists. Many scientists in Japan, however, do not seem to be deterred by the inherent limitations of robots. Among those involved in the Moonshot programme is Hiroshi Ishiguro, a professor at Osaka University known as the Godfather of Humanoids. Professor Ishiguro envisions a day when robots are considered members of the family. He sees it as only a matter of time until the typical family unit comprises two parents and 1.3 kids, plus a dog and a robot.

SoftBank also had high hopes that its four-foot-high humanoid robot would come to be seen as a member of the family. When it was released in 2015, Pepper was marketed as the world's first commercially available robot able to communicate with humans. 'People describe others as being robots because they have no emotions, no heart,' Masayoshi Son, chief executive of Softbank, said at a press conference. 'For the first time in human history, we're giving a robot a heart, emotions.'[9]

Plenty of credulous customers were won over by the promise of having a robot for a friend, among them a woman called Tomomi Ota, who told an American journalist that she had quickly grown attached to her robot. 'Obviously there are hundreds of Peppers just like this one and I suppose they all have similar characters. But there's a personality that exists only in this Pepper and I feel this Pepper's personality is somehow connected to me.'[10]

Pepper attracted a great deal of attention from the press and certainly aroused people's curiosity. Between 2015 and 2016 alone, the number of 'communication robots' in Japan doubled, and it is now common to see them in big cities like Tokyo, Osaka and Nagoya, where they are often deployed as sales gimmicks in retail outlets. But is AI really able to develop affective relationships with humans, as early converts to the faith like Tomomi Ota maintain? If it can, will robots be able to step into the shoes of Japan's missing babies, lovers and care workers?

Call me a technophobe, but I have my doubts. One day, not long after my visit to the Dawn Avatar Robot Café, I was walking in Roppongi when I saw a plump, baby-like robot in a shop window. It was called a Lovot, and had clearly been designed to fill the gap once occupied by Japan's babies. 'Technology that was made to be loved. Let's activate a new life,' ran the sales blurb. It was shaped like a kettle on caster wheels, and claimed to have an internal heating element, which mimicked the warmth emanating from a living creature. If you could ignore the camera sticking out of the top of its head, which made it look like a Google Maps surveillance car, it made a convincing cartoon baby, but you had to suspend a lot of disbelief.

The pathos inspired by the Lovot's outsized, tropical-sea-coloured eyes was only heightened by the fact that it had a slight squint. It looked to be pleading – for what I do not know, as it had no mouth, which only made it look more pitiful. Unwittingly hooked, I went into the shop and read some tips on 'how to become emotionally attached to your Lovot'. 'Like a new kitten, it may be disorientated when it arrives at your home for the first time, but over the next three months, it will learn to relax,' ran the blurb.

Through the accompanying app, users can give their Lovot a name, so that it responds when called. As it settles into its new home, it learns how to recognize the face of its 'parent' and gradually finds its own voice (box recorder). This is where things start to get really creepy. 'The Lovot recognizes those it loves and rushes towards them on its little wheels, following them around the room, and looking up expectantly. It spins its little arms when it wants a hug, and if you pick it up and swaddle it in your arms, it will close its eyes and fall asleep.'

What kind of human could love a machine pretending to be a baby? Or am I being old-fashioned in insisting on a clear boundary between humans and machines? After all, we invest all kinds of objects, animate and inanimate, with characteristics that, as far as we know, are unique to humans – the Tamagotchi craze that swept the world in the 1990s provides ample proof of that. Perhaps the Lovot's makers are to be applauded for filling a gap in the market for love objects?[11]

Robots are being drafted in to do all kinds of potentially fraught tasks that Japanese people find awkward, most of which involve love, sex or death. Funeral services, for example, which don't come cheap in Japan, there being all kinds of costs to factor in, including the hire of a Buddhist priest, whose services usually run to around ¥240,000 (£1,206). In 2017, plastic-mould manufacturer Nissei Eco came up with an economical alternative: for ¥50,000 (£251), it will provide bereaved families with an automated funeral service. It is conducted by one of SoftBank's Pepper robots, which is specially programmed to chant the sutras of any one of four Buddhist sects while tapping on a drum.

The introduction of robot priests is a matter of necessity. With so many of Japan's rural communities on their last legs, the traditional *danka* system, by which parishioners make donations to support their local temple, is no longer able to sustain the country's priests, many of whom are having to find part-time jobs in the temporal world to make ends meet. Pepper functions as a stand-in while they are away from the temple.

As prototypes, communication robots make for interesting test studies, and can be relied upon to garner headlines around the world, but many of them have struggled to find practical roles in the real world. In 2018, Honda stopped producing the Asimo, an advanced humanoid robot that it launched in 2000, after its creators admitted that it did not have enough practical uses to be marketable as anything but a gimmick. It is now in the Miraikan, Japan's Museum of Emerging Science and Innovation, where it awaits visitors keen to go 'back to the future' for a day.

Robots like Pepper have their uses, but they have a long way to go before they become the human-like entities seen in science fiction films. While AI programmes can now respond spontaneously to situations and questions in ways similar to humans, my hunch is that robots will never come close to human consciousness, which is shaped by a sense of self and mortality that no machine will ever know.

*

Popular culture in the Anglophone world often casts robots as forces of evil. Think of Mary Shelley's *Frankenstein* and Charlie Chaplin's *Modern Times*, or *The Matrix* and *The Terminator*. For as long as robots have existed, Westerners have feared being enslaved by them. They are a modern rendition of the zombie, physically human – or at least humanoid – but devoid of conscience.

So why the stubborn faith in humanoid robots in Japan? Even Pepper's most enthusiastic early adopters admit that their value is more symbolic than real. Humanoid robots have become vessels for their owners' faith in technology's ability to make a brighter human future. Lose that faith, and the future looks a lot less shiny.

There is another reason for the Japanese faith in humanoid robots: they are safer and more predictable than humans, doing their makers' bidding without complaint. This makes them attractive to those who live by numbers: the country's systems' engineers, data analysts, bureaucrats and statisticians. Even for the average person – the young woman looking for a lover, or the old man needing round-the-clock care – they are, perhaps, easier to get along with than other people. Like the country's booming population of cats and dogs, robots are prized as loyal friends, credited with an innocence that humans have lost.

This anthropomorphic bent is leading people to invest their emotional energy in creatures that are incapable of returning it in kind. They give life stories to cats and dogs and, when they die, they remember them through photos. Meanwhile, their neighbours live and die as ghosts, barely tethered to the real world at all. It's tragic, really. Other people have become the enemy within, it seems; they are the guilty parties, continually threatening contamination. This old fear was given new impetus by the coronavirus pandemic, when everyone covered their mouths and noses, and were told to refrain from talking.

Japan's embrace of robotics has affected Western impressions of the Japanese. As David Morley and Kevin Robins argue in their book *Spaces of Identity*, there was always a racialized element to this, and it rested on a conflation of the Japanese with robotics technology. 'Western stereotypes of the Japanese hold them to be sub-human, as if they have no feeling, no emotion, no humanity,' they write. These stereotypes took shape in the 1980s in response to the perceived threat of the rapidly expanding Japanese economy. Combine this with longstanding fears of the dehumanising potential of technology, and you end up with what Morley and Robins call 'techno-orientalism'.

Now that we are into the third decade of the much-heralded twenty-first century, Western fears of techno-capitalist Japan look decidedly quaint. Westerners still like to think of Japan as a techno-logical paradise, where robots have become integrated into everyday life, but most of Japan's robots are industrial, and only used in fac-tories. Humanoid robots still have the power to instil fear in us, but for the most part they are pretty trivial and disappointing, little more than props in the dayglo theme park that is Cool Japan.

The curious thing is that, despite its innovative industries, Japan lags behind many Western countries in adapting to globalization and contemporary work culture. Japan's high-tech star has waned. It has fallen in the international rankings of R&D budgets, and the government's vaunted My Number national ID card scheme has consistently run into problems.

The Moonshot goals, and the high-tech schemes devised to make them a reality, are hugely impressive. But look beyond the glitzy offerings of Japan's big-name multinational corporations and venture out into the declining provincial towns and cities where most Japanese people live and work, and the picture is considerably less inspiring. Indeed, Japan is often described as a 'digital dinosaur'.

This makes Japan a good country in which to be a semi-skilled or unskilled worker, especially in the small- and medium-sized enter-prises (SMEs) that employ 70 per cent of the workforce. Many SMEs are stuck in the 1980s and would benefit from some AI, as working practices are outdated and inefficient. But Japan lags behind in equip-ping its people to be able to work with AI, so while it might offer a 'lucky moment' to those with the right skills, it is likely to be bad news for those without them.

*

The idea that robots and AI can solve Japan's chronic labour shortages is a fantasy. Throughout Japan, every sector that employs unskilled or semi-skilled workers – manufacturing, hospitality, agriculture, retail, care for the elderly, transport, logistics and construction – is crying out for more workers. There are also labour shortages in more skilled occupations like IT, nursing, sheet metal processing, welding and shipbuilding.

Foreign observers say that, by failing to embrace mass immigration, the Japanese government has brought its demographic crisis upon itself. In 2020, a *Guardian* editorial restated conventional Western thinking on how best to address population decline in the rich world, positing that 'planned and humane population movement could benefit both growing and shrinking countries'.[12] By this reckoning, immigration is a critical component of the demographic transition that all developed economies have to make in the twenty-first century, bringing in young adults to help rich countries cope with labour shortages while redistributing capital to poorer countries.

In just about every OECD country apart from Japan, the proportion of the population that was born in a foreign country stands at 10–20 per cent. It has increased rapidly since 2000 – by about a third in the UK, and by more than double in Spain, Italy, Norway, Iceland and Austria.[13] Even in Japan, where the government is famously reluctant to allow foreigners to live in large numbers, the number of immigrants is higher than ever. As of 2024, there were 3.7 million resident foreigners, comprising just over 3 per cent of the total population – small potatoes in the eyes of most Europeans, but a game-changer in a country where the population is shrinking by upwards of 800,000 people every year.[14]

To find out more about the multicultural society taking shape in Japan, I joined another press tour with the Foreign Press Centre.

On a typically sultry midsummer day, we took a train an hour north of Tokyo to visit Ōizumi, an industrial town in the north of the Kanto Plain. Ōizumi is the future of Japan in miniature: of its 42,000 residents, 8,000 are foreigners.

The man from the Gunma prefectural government gave us all the data a journalist could wish for. Masao Nakajima's introduction, like Ōizumi itself, was very tidy. He presented a slide show with photos of the town's main attractions and the neat flowerbeds lining its litter-free streets. The major employers, he told us, are the carmaker Subaru; Ajinomoto, a food-processing company; and Panasonic, which has two factories in the town, one making computer chips and another display cabinets for shops. There are also many SMEs, which would have gone bankrupt had they not been able to recruit workers from abroad.

Across Japan, integrating foreign-born residents into local communities is proving to be a challenge for both the authorities and Japanese residents. Whatever their reservations about mass immigration, everyone wants to defuse tensions and avoid the formation of a parallel society. In 2021, Gunma became the first prefecture in Japan to introduce an ordinance for 'the promotion of intercultural co-creation', urging Japanese and foreign residents to 'respect each other's differences' and use their diversity 'to create new values'. Ōizumi has become a test bed for an inclusive, multicultural society.

As of 2018, there were more than 180,000 Brazilians living in Japan. The majority of them are of Japanese descent, their forebears having moved to Brazil in the first half of the twentieth century. In response to labour shortages in the 1980s, many opted to move to Japan and more of them live in Ōizumi than in any other town or city. Mr Nakajima showed us a slide of the sign outside Nishi Ōizumi station, which had been decorated in green and yellow to make the Brazilian community feel welcome. He also showed us the town's mascot: a cat with a feathered headdress and ostrich-like feather skirt, a nod to Ōizumi's annual carnival.

Kayoko Kakuta is a third-generation Japanese-Brazilian and one of the town's official 'cultural interpreters'. She was keen to impress

upon us that the authorities were doing all they could to make foreigners feel welcome, including establishing a one-stop information
hub for immigrants. 'It is a place to learn Japanese, volunteer to take
part in the town's litter-picking programme and learn about disaster prevention,' she said. It was also a place to pick up a copy of the
town's multilingual newsletter, which provided practical advice on
how to use an Asian-style squat toilet and where to find an *ikebana*
(flower-arranging) class, and was full of kindly admonishments
about the importance of taking your shoes off before walking on
tatami mats.

'Most of the older migrants had language problems when
they first arrived in Japan,' Ms Kakuta told us. 'Many of them
still do,' she added bashfully. This restricts their chances of marrying a local, and many *nikkeijin* (second-generation immigrants)
have married among themselves. But the local schools provided
Japanese-language classes for their kids, and they seemed to be integrating well. 'Brazilians like living in Ōizumi. Our only worry is the
threat of earthquakes,' she said with a nervous smile. Fortunately
for them, the town's earthquake drill had been translated into mul-
tiple languages, as had the medical terminology used in its clinics
and hospitals.

We left the town hall and piled into a minibus for a tour of the
town. The team of officials pointed out the supermarkets and restaurants on the main street with Portuguese-language signs, and
we visited the Supermercado Takara and the Paulista Restaurante e
Churrascaria, where we had a tasty lunch. It was good to eat bean
soup – I'd missed both beans and soup, neither of which crop up on
menus in Japan very often.

After lunch, we visited the Japan Settlement Museum, where
Paolo Hirano Isamu, another third-generation Brazilian-Japanese,
showed us around. He and his family had left Brazil for Japan when
he was ten and had settled in Ōizumi. As an adult, he had married
a fellow Japanese-Brazilian, and had gone on to have kids of his
own. Despite having spent most of his life in Japan, he still spent a
lot of time thinking about his identity, he told us. He had concluded

that he didn't feel entirely Brazilian or Japanese, a realization that he was still struggling to come to terms with.

'Many of the older Brazilians in the town are retiring now, and pensions and nursing care have been surfacing as issues,' he said. The profile of Ōizumi's foreign-born community is changing. Until recently, over half of the foreigners in the town were Brazilian, most of them of Japanese descent. However, by 2023, just 19 per cent came from Brazil, with the rest hailing from a plethora of Asian countries, including China, Vietnam, the Philippines, Nepal, Indonesia, Myanmar and Bangladesh. The municipal government, which had nicknamed Ōizumi 'Brazil Town' a generation ago to make the newcomers feel welcome, had recently rebranded it 'International Town'.

A journalist from the largest daily newspaper in Bangladesh wanted to know about the Japanese government's Technical Intern Training Programme. He had heard that some Bangladeshis on trainee visas were struggling to make enough to live on. 'There are limits to how many hours they are allowed to work,' he said. 'It is supposed to train them, after all, rather than employ them.' There had been reports that some trainees had had their passports confiscated by their employers to stop them looking for work elsewhere.

After consulting his colleagues from the prefectural government, Mr Nakajima said that none of them had ever heard of such things happening in Ōizumi, but the man from *Prothom Alo* wasn't satisfied. 'The trainee visa programme is a bogus scheme,' he said indignantly. 'It allows Japanese lawmakers to pretend that they are sharing skills with developing countries, but the real beneficiaries are Japanese companies, which would go under without cheap foreign workers.' Mr Nakajima looked down at his notes and smiled faintly, but said nothing more.

Japan's Technical Intern Training Programme was originally set up to provide manpower to agriculture and factories, two sectors that face particularly severe labour shortages. Ostensibly, the idea was not just to plug these gaps, but to pass on skills that trainees could use when they returned to their home countries. But the scheme has been massively abused by employers, and there have been allegations that many 'trainees' have been working illegally.

The underlying cause of this exploitation is the reluctance of LDP politicians to admit that Japan needs immigrant workers. Despite the amendments to its immigration laws, Japan still has no official immigration policy, and as a result only 18 per cent of foreign workers have a work visa. Of the rest, 35 per cent qualify for a visa through their family or spouse, 20 per cent are on the Technical Intern Training Programme and 20 per cent are on student visas. With labour shortages becoming more acute by the day, Keidanren, the employers' association, is putting pressure on the government to both clean up and expand the trainee worker scheme. It would like to see more Asian immigrants coming to Japan on three-year, non-renewable work visas.

In 2019, the government relented and revised the Immigration Control Law again, a move that employers heralded as 'the first year of immigration'.[15] However, while the government has begun making more work permits available to migrants from Asia, most are only given short-stay visas and not all local authorities make an effort to help them integrate. Most Asians have only a rudimentary understanding of Japanese, which leaves them unable to do better-paid, white-collar jobs. Discrimination against foreigners is rife (as well as perfectly legal) in the housing market, and in many prefectures their children get little help to learn the language. Since most Asian immigrants don't have the money to put their kids through cram school, many of them fall behind. The message is clear: 'Come and work in Japan, but don't think you're welcome to stay.'

Clearly, the LDP has yet to make up its mind on the issue of immigration, and its ambivalence is reflected in opinion polls. In Soja, a town in Okayama prefecture where foreign residents make up 1 per cent of the population, pollsters asked residents if they thought an increase in the number of immigrants was a good thing. Twenty per cent said they were in favour, and 10 per cent were opposed, but the majority said they were 'not sure'. Another poll, this one conducted in Shinjuku ward, central Tokyo, where one in nine residents is a foreigner, came back with similarly non-committal results.[16]

From the Japan Settlement Museum, we piled back onto the minibus and drove back to Ōizumi station. On the way, an Italian journalist asked Mr Nakajima if there had been a rise in crime since the arrival of foreigners in the town. 'We used to have quite a high crime rate,' the man from the prefectural government admitted. 'Nothing serious – no murder, mugging, rape or burglary. Most offences involved the theft of bicycles from outside the station, usually by foreigners, who assumed that an unlocked bike was theirs for the taking. When they were told that they belonged to someone, they stopped taking them, and the crime rate went down.'

It is still too early to say how the Japanese public will react to mass immigration, but it is safe to say that the younger generation and people in cities tend to be less hostile than the older generation and country dwellers, who often share the concerns of LDP members. These concerns sometimes tip over into outright racism: hostility towards Japan's resident Chinese and Korean communities is longstanding and has only been amplified by territorial disputes with China and North Korea.

Under Shinzo Abe's right-wing government, this hostility gave the LDP reason to oppose extending voting rights to the country's Special Permanent Residents (Koreans, some with Chinese nationality, whose roots in Japan date back to the period of Japanese colonial rule over Korea). Many LDP representatives in the Diet are not keen to offer residency, let alone citizenship, to more recent arrivals either. They worry about what mass immigration can do to a country. Reports of rioting in France in response to the police killing of a young French-born Arab man were headline news in Japan in 2023. The demand for labour can be offset by robots and AI, they say. Self-driving vehicles will obviate the need for truck drivers, and fully automated supermarkets and convenience stores will do away with the need for foreign workers to staff the tills.

For the time being, there is no consensus on mass immigration, and therefore no real change. The country pretends that it can get by without immigrants, because it has become politically impossible to welcome them. The result is that more and more jobs simply stay vacant, not just in industry and agriculture but in care for the elderly. It's a bright red warning sign of demographic meltdown, and an indictment of a society that has chosen homogeneity over diversity, and blinkered nostalgia over a pragmatic commitment to the here and now.

Whatever the misgivings of older voters and traditionalist politicians, it is widely accepted that the proportion of foreigners is only going to increase in the future. The NIPSSR estimates that by 2070 11 per cent of the Japanese population will be foreign nationals.[17] The government hopes that, as Asia develops, growing numbers of these immigrants will be highly educated. In recent years, it has made it easier for IT professionals to come and work in the country, and among more progressive bureaucrats there is talk of introducing an American-style green-card scheme.

However, immigration is more complicated than either its opponents or its advocates like to admit. Even those campaigning for the government to allow in more foreigners prefer not to talk about blue-collar immigration, which would have a dramatic impact on small-town Japan. And whatever the government does, it is unlikely to allow in enough foreign workers to fully plug the gaps in the workforce, which by some estimates would require the entry of 600,000 immigrants a year.[18]

Japan receives a low number of immigrants compared to other G7 countries, not just because it doesn't have an official immigration policy, but because few migrants want to go there. Worldwide, the number of potential migrants who say that they would like to move to Japan is 12 times less than the number who want to go to the US.[19] Most migrants would rather work in a country where they don't have to learn a notoriously difficult new language, are not expected to work all hours and don't feel like they're being held at arm's length all the time.

Unfortunately, another of the burdens Japan is carrying into the twenty-first century is an exaggerated sense of its own importance on the world stage. The country has yet to accept that, just as the weak yen makes it more appealing to Asian tourists, it also makes it less appealing to Asian workers. Would-be migrants are hungry not just for higher salaries, but also for more education and training than Japan is prepared to offer them. With Japan's financial clout in long-term decline and competition for skilled workers growing stiffer across the developed world, tackling discrimination and creating an inclusive, multicultural society is becoming an urgent issue for the Japanese government.

If Japan's multinationals are serious about attracting more foreign workers, its corporate culture will need to change too. Most large Japanese companies have too many generalists and not enough specialists. If they want to recruit people from abroad, they have to create a more fluid labour market, in which foreign-born specialists can change jobs easily, accrue experience working for various companies and be paid competitively for their expertise.[20]

Across the developed world, citizens are arguing amongst themselves over the pros and cons of immigration. What they all too often overlook is that immigration can only offer a medium-term fix. The developing world cannot keep supplying them with fresh blood, for the simple reason that, like the developed world, its fertility rates are declining.

For example, the US economy has long been dependent on cheap labour from Mexico, but Mexico is a rising economic power, and the decline in its fertility rate – from 6.8 in 1970 to 1.8 in 2021 – is unprecedented.[21] The United States is already having to turn to Central American countries for its young workers, and a generation from now, rising numbers of these workers may well opt to work in Mexico rather than the US. By then, America's baby boomers will be in their dotage and in more need of help from foreign workers than ever. With fewer foreign workers to mow their lawns and flip their burgers, the price of labour is likely to rise just as the price of property starts to fall, since the millions of suburban houses built for baby boomers don't appeal to America's growing population of singletons, who prefer to live in cities. With no one to buy their houses, the value of most boomers' single most valuable possession is likely to go into free fall, putting an unprecedented squeeze on living standards just as they are going into advanced old age.

Europe's gerontocrats might comfort themselves with the thought that they will always have sub-Saharan Africa as a source of young workers, but change is afoot there too. The average woman in sub-Saharan Africa has four children, but this number is falling by one child every 15 years.[22] This is down to fewer women dying in child-birth and fewer children dying in infancy. Once the probability that a child will die before it reaches adulthood starts to fall, families stop having kids 'just in case' and start thinking about how many they actually want. As we have seen, the increasing importance conferred on education and its rising cost are also key drivers of falling fertility rates, whether in Tokyo or Togo.

The upshot is that, in the future, there are going to be fewer immigrants for the rich world to choose from.[23] This is going to make migrants more valuable. Immigration controls have become stricter in recent years, but a century that is unfolding badly for the world's migrants may yet belong to them. As Japan continues to age and work opportunities at home dry up, its young people may get a taste of this peripatetic existence for themselves, as they too find themselves with no choice but to leave their home country and look for work overseas.

14.

Mount Fear: A Last Trip to Aomori and Akita

About 1,200 years ago, a Japanese priest called Jikaku En'nin was studying Buddhism in China. One night he had a mysterious dream in which a monk told him about a sacred mountain, 30 days' walk from Kyoto. He told him to return to Japan and look for the mountain. When he found it, he was to build a temple and dedicate it to the deity Jizō, the Buddhist guardian of travellers, pregnant women and children.

Following the monk's instructions, Jikaku En'nin returned to Kyoto, and began walking. It must have taken him a lot more than 30 days to reach the volcanic crater on the Shimokita peninsula in the far north of Honshu, but the landscape he found there was as the monk had described it in his dream. In the centre of the crater was a beautiful lake with a white-sand beach. Around it were eight wooded peaks, representing the petals of a lotus flower, the symbol of the world of Buddha. He named it Osore-zan, meaning 'Mount Fear', and in time it became one of the three most sacred mountains in Japan.*

According to the leaflet I picked up at the entrance to Osorezan Bodaiji, the temple that Jikaku En'nin founded on the shores of the lake, the surrounding landscape is thought to be the closest likeness of Buddhist purgatory on earth. While the lake in the crater of the dormant volcano suggests the beauty of paradise, close by are 108 ponds of boiling water and mud, each of which corresponds to one of the 108 hells that await sinners in the afterlife.

On the day I visited Mount Fear, the clouds were hanging low

* Japan's two other sacred mountains are Koyasan and Hieizan.

266

over the lake. Due to its high sulphur content, the water is highly toxic, which made its beautiful shade of electric blue all the more sinister. The vibrant blue of the water and the lushness of the greenery on the surrounding hills contrasted with the gnarled and jagged rocks around the lake, which were ash-coloured or black.

I walked down to the water's edge, the wind tearing at my umbrella, where the black rock gave way to white sand and, beyond it, aquamarine water. The shore on the other side of the lake was lost in dense, pewter-coloured cloud, and a strong smell of sulphur permeated the sultry air. The ground around me was pocked with vents that steamed and bubbled. One of them was rimmed with solidified sulphur, which made it look like a mouth; the water gushing out of it was bright yellow, like a buttercup. Another vent was charred black, as if a fire was burning under the ground, and I could hear the sound of boiling water.

People have been coming to Mount Osore since ancient times to pray for the peaceful repose of their ancestors' souls, and in hope of being reunited with them in the afterlife. It is said that the small brook that flows into the lake represents the River Sanzu, which all souls must cross on their way to purgatory.

Among those trying to cross the river are the souls of dead children and unborn babies, who must build piles of pebbles along the riverbed in order to reach the other side. They are supported in their struggle by Jizō, who protects their piles of pebbles from evil demons intent on knocking them down. The bereaved parents of these children come to make offerings of pebbles to the deity, in the hope that he will use them to help their children gain access to paradise. There were little stone statues of Jizō everywhere, his impassive features weathered by centuries of wind and rain, and countless piles of little stones stacked on rocks like cairns.

In these times of 'lowest-low' fertility rates, it's easy to forget that, well into the twentieth century, infanticide was a common practice in rural Japan. It was called 'thinning out', and was done whenever a woman became pregnant and the patriarch of the family judged that there were too many mouths to feed. Peasants could not always afford to feed their dependents – infants and the elderly – particularly in times of famine. During the Edo era, children were given chores to do as soon as they were able, and at the other end of the life cycle, when the elderly and the infirm were no longer able to work, they were carried into the mountains and left to die. This was the practice of *ubasuteyama* that Nami-san had told me about when I stayed at her guest house in Osaka.

I followed a path that led up to one of the wooded peaks, watching out for snakes, until I reached a bronze statue of Fudō Myōō, the fierce Buddhist deity whose head is depicted ringed with flames. Visitors to Mount Osore had left offerings for him: jars of One Cup sake, energy drinks, packets of rice crackers. Perhaps they were left by *itako*, I thought to myself. These are mediums – blind women trained to commune with the dead – who follow Fudō Myōō. The practice has been on the decline for a long time, and there are now only twenty living *itako* in Japan, but several of them are associated with Osorezan Bodaiji.

In the Edo period, everyone was expected to contribute to family wages, but blind people had limited opportunities to support themselves or their families. Blind women were believed to have special spiritual powers, and the parents of blind girls often sought training for them as *itako*. Initiation began between the ages of 11 and 13, and consisted of three months of purification rituals, incorporating sleep deprivation, semi-starvation and intense cold. Hundreds of buckets of ice-cold water were poured over the girl's body until she lost consciousness, which was considered a sign that Fudō Myōō had taken possession of her spirit. At the end of this training, the *itako* was married to her patron deity and thereafter she was deemed able to communicate with the spirits of the dead.

*

I found a perch with a good view of the lake and considered the end of my time in Japan. After eight months of travelling around the country, I would soon be going back to London. I had cycled along the southern coast of Shikoku and visited farmers in

Miyazaki prefecture. I had crossed the Inland Sea from Imabari to Mitarai and then on to Hiroshima. I had ventured over the back of the main island and travelled east along the Sea of Japan coast to Osaka. Lastly, I had been up to Gunma, where the conurbation of Tokyo reaches the edge of the Kanto Plain, and gives up to the mountains.

Before heading home, I had decided to make one last trip, this time to Akita and Aomori, the two northernmost prefectures of mainland Japan. This time, I had allowed myself the extravagance of hiring a car. This was my last chance to see nature in the wild, and a car would allow me to access the depopulated mountain communities in the two prefectures where the ageing and shrinking process is most advanced.

I had stopped at Osore-zan on my way to Akita, which is where you can really see the shape of things to come. It has the lowest birth rate and the highest death rate in the country, and almost 40 per cent of the population is over 65, a higher proportion than in any other prefecture. For every child born in Akita, three people die.[1] With two people disappearing every hour, the prefecture has the fastest rate of population decline in the country. The NIPSSR expects its population to fall by 41 per cent by 2045, and some observers have speculated that over the course of the next hundred years the entire population could die out.[2]

In 2015, Akita's prefectural government came up with a plan to put the brakes on the plummeting population, with steps such as expanding medical subsidies for schoolchildren and providing extra day-care support for mothers. It also offers workers help to repay their student loans, in the hope that this will encourage them not to leave for Tokyo, and free them up to think about starting families of their own.

So far, however, these measures have had little effect, and most stakeholders seem resigned to living with decline. 'As Japan's total population will likely fall by 30 or 40 million by 2060, it is unlikely that every municipality will stage a sharp rebound,' Yutaka Okada, a senior economist at the Mizuho Research Institute says diplomatically. 'The population in Akita will need to be consolidated as much as possible to one or two places.'[3]

In the course of my travels, I'd met plenty of urban migrants, and individuals who were trying to find their way to a sustainable future for themselves. I had spoken to local government officials who were all too aware that depopulation poses an existential threat. But I had yet to meet anyone with the will or the means to think at scale, so when a friend told me about a bold serial entrepreneur by the name of Hiroyuki Sato, I decided to visit him at his office in Akita City. I hoped that his vision for the prefecture's future would help me end my travels around rural Japan on a more positive note.

On the first two days of my trip to Aomori and Akita, there had been unseasonably heavy downpours. The nightly news showed the centre of Akita City to be under several feet of water, so rather than drive, I decided to check into a hotel in a nearby upland town called Takanosu and take a train down to the prefectural capital. The train had a faint smell of damp and a stronger smell of urine. Everyone was doing what they do in the city: either sleeping or looking at their phones.

From the station, I walked to Hiroyuki Sato's office in the outskirts of Akita City. It was hot for the first time since I had arrived in the north, and I passed through a familiar landscape of hastily assembled retail boxes, fast food outlets and car showrooms. The only thing that caught my eye was a Museum of Modern Life, but it had closed down.

Hiroyuki Sato was surprised when I said I had come by train, and even more surprised that I had walked to his office from the station. 'It's hard to get around without a car,' he said. Mr Sato was a brisk, busy man, but not unfriendly, with a positive spirit that I warmed to. He was a native son, born in Akita City in 1961. 'The population of the city peaked in 1978, when I was a high school student. The place was full of people back then.' After graduating, he had worked as a stockbroker for an American company in Tokyo, only returning to the city in 1996, when he took over the running of his father's construction equipment business.

By then, Akita City was well on the way to long-term stagnation. 'When I came back, the shops were all shuttered, and the place was empty. There was nowhere for young people to work, and most of them had left.' He took me through a familiarly gloomy Power-Point presentation. He started with some statistics from the Japan Policy Council's Subcommittee on Population Decline Issues, which, in 2014, had warned that Akita prefecture was 'in danger of extinction'.

Having got the bad news out of the way, Mr Sato was keen to move on to the good. 'The mass media is pessimistic and if you just look at the data, it might make you pessimistic too. But the media doesn't study the future. You have to look ahead, and you have to exercise some willpower. I am optimistic.'

In 2012, he had established Wenti Japan, the first local company to enter the wind power business. 'If there is one thing that we have plenty of in Akita, it's wind. Nationwide, this prefecture is number one in wind power generation.' Backed by Hokuto Bank, which shared his determination to revitalize the local economy, Wenti had its first wind farm up and running by 2020. When I met him three years later, he was developing thirty-seven wind farms in eight locations, both inside and outside Akita prefecture. 'We already generate more power than we can use,' he said gleefully.

Mr Sato was also chairman of a consortium that sought to reinvigorate the local economy by creating industries around wind power generation and expanding employment. 'Our mission is to revive Akita's economy. In order to revitalize the weakened regions that have been sucked up by the capital, we want to set up dynamic movements with the spirit of "Let's counterattack outside."' It was a curious turn of phrase, one I assume he'd picked up while playing Go.

If local people are not actively involved, the benefits derived from Akita's windfarms will be taken to Tokyo. We want to stop the colonization of Akita by turning wind power generation into a local industry. We don't need Tokyo any more. It is hard to live there. Summers are so hot there – it's hard on the body.

People are going to stop moving to Tokyo. Telework allows them to leave the cities. Unless they do, Japan is going to lose power. I think young people are finally starting to realize this. Of course, the politicians don't believe in the regions, but they don't count for much around here.[4]

He introduced me to one of his team, Kaori Yomogida, who was sitting in on our meeting. 'Japanese people aren't very interested in politics, are they?' he asked her. 'No, not really,' she said with an embarrassed laugh.

'What you have to realise is that the LDP is not one party,' Mr Sato went on.

People vote for individuals because they like them, or because they are locals. I don't expect much from the government. People are going to have to rise to this challenge by themselves, through private enterprise.

Young entrepreneurs can see that the way of life that Japan has been striving for ever since the Meiji Restoration – the idea that 'bigger is better' – is dying out. We are in an era in which diversification and miniaturization are what matter – energy risk diversification, social infrastructure risk diversification.

We have to cultivate the idea that the regions can be cool. The regions need to develop new industries – not heavy industries, but IT. Like Silicon Valley, we can have a laid-back way of working, offices where people wear T-shirts to work. A global company may emerge from Akita.

I put it to him that most young people aren't interested in living in the countryside. 'Well, they don't want to live in the middle of nowhere, but Japan's small cities are becoming more popular. A lot of Japanese people still think of Akita as small and dark, but that's not the case. This prefecture has a lot of potential – delicious food, great sake, a more relaxed way of life.

'Let me introduce you to some of the people who are fighting the pessimism,' he said. He told me about a woman called Junko Hatakeyama, whose organization was helping Akita's ageing, shrinking communities. He gave her a call, and Ms Yomogida kindly offered to give me a lift to her office in her car.

On the way, she told me that Mr Sato was quite unusual in spending so much time thinking about the shrinking population and what it meant for the future. 'Most people are not as active or as interested in politics as he is.'

She asked me with some surprise why I was so interested in the subject. I said that I was surprised that she was surprised. Maybe she was past caring about the future of Japan. Not that she gave any indication of cynicism; in my experience, few Japanese people do. If she was resigned, it was because she was pragmatic and realistic about the future.

'I like children, but I don't want any of my own. If a nice partner comes along, all well and good, but I'm not interested in getting married just to have kids.' Her tone of voice suggested she was quite clear about that, and I didn't detect any hint of remorse.

Why was that?

Kids cost a lot of money. And besides, living with someone else means compromising, right? That means sacrificing yourself, and these days, people can't see the point. People are not getting married like they used to. They don't think it's important and are happier spending time alone. I am happy to go the cinema by myself or go to Starbucks and read a book on my own.

*

Unfortunately, for every individual happy with the autonomous self-sufficiency modern life affords them, there is another person struggling with loneliness and isolation. Junko Hatakeyama is head of a coalition of local NGOs called Akita Partnership. 'We are an NGO that supports other NGOs. We only established this place 20 years ago, but we have a lot of social problems in Akita these days, and we have a lot of welfare organizations.'

Junko showed me around the building, a barn conversion on the outskirts of Akita City. It was easy to overlook, being on a ring road and surrounded by apartment blocks and out-of-town retail parks, but it was a wonderful sight to behold. She said that restoring the building had given some of the region's ageing craftspeople an opportunity to pass on their skills to the younger generation.

Junko had a lovely, supportive manner about her. Or maybe I just warmed to her because, after seeing so many examples of isolated people, I had finally met someone who was trying to change things for them.

People turn to the NGOs because there are more and more things that they can't do by themselves. Couples have to do everything by themselves, and if they are both going out to work, it puts a lot of pressure on the woman. Going out to work every day and then having to get a meal on the table when they get home, a lot of them get stressed. Women argue with their husbands more than they used to.

The biggest problem we have is young women moving to the cities. That means there are more men than women in Akita. They can't get married, so they spend their lives living with their parents. There is no work for them here, and a lot of them have mental problems. We have young *hikikomori* who can't find jobs and just retreat into their shells – they don't want to leave the house. We also have more people relying on food banks, especially young people – that too has only become a problem in the last ten years.

How did Junko account for the sudden rise in the number of people who can't cope with other people? 'I don't know. Maybe it has something to do with more people living alone. I grew up in a small town in the mountains of southern Akita. There was no privacy at home, but you had help and support, people to talk to.'

'It's sad. The population is shrinking, and the communities are dying out.' I asked her if any of the villages had been abandoned yet. 'I can't think of a community that has actually died out, but you can see that over the next ten years, a lot of them are going to.'

And what about the older residents, the ones who cannot leave? 'Most of them are resigned to what's happening. They don't see what they can do about it and are happy to die up there. They help their neighbours, they drive one another to the clinic or to the shops. Nothing is particularly inconvenient for them.'

I had come across this sense of resignation everywhere I had been on my travels. Most Japanese people seem to take population decline as inevitable. Their fatalism has deep roots. Consider the virtues and vices that informed polite good taste in pre-modern Japan: the love of *wabizumai* ('the quiet life'); the insistence on *enryo* ('restraint'); the taste for the plain and the understated expressed in the aesthetic of *wabi* and *sabi*. The inward search for peace so characteristic of Japan is centuries old. Atomization has come from the turn towards individualism and the breakdown of the workplace and family, but it also draws from a well of loneliness built long ago.

This is what makes Junko's Akita Partnership, and other examples of problem-solving in the community so inspiring. Local government is often seen as complicit in managing the decline of provincial Japan. Combined with the scepticism engendered by the official response to the disasters in Kobe in 1994 and at Fukushima in 2011, you can see why plenty of local residents have decided to take matters into their own hands.

*

Junko gave me a ride back to Akita station, where I caught a train back to Takanosu, where I'd left the hire car. There were only two carriages, and they were crowded with elementary-school kids on their way home from school and middle-school athletes heading to baseball practice. It was a beautiful summer evening: the sky cobalt blue overhead, fading to white at the horizon, with just a hint of gold in the sunlight. For the first time since coming north, the air was perfectly clear, giving me an unblemished view over a plain of paddy fields planted with emerald-green rice to a range of low mountains in the distance.

I felt sorry for the town of Takanosu. The name, which means

'Hawk's Nest', had put me in mind of tough-minded northerners, but when I arrived the place was as dead as a doornail. Come the evening, I went out to find some dinner. There were covered arcades leading down from the station for 200 metres on both sides of the road, but practically all the shops were shut. A musty smell of damp buildings, reminiscent of a church, hung in the air on the main street and three times I found myself wiping cobwebs from my face. I walked the length of both arcades and saw just one woman on the street and one customer in the only coffee shop. It was so quiet I could hear what he was saying to the owner from outside.

As in most of the shrinking towns I had visited, people were doing their best to keep up appearances. There was no trace of sourness, and everyone was as dutiful as ever. Relatives of the deceased still tended their abandoned houses, and someone from the neighbourhood came by from time to time to cut the grass and sweep the street outside. A sign in a shop window promised, in French, to 'continue research into perfecting the art of cake making'.

I found some dinner in the only place open, and ordered my usual miso ramen and gyoza. Two customers were watching the TV news in silence. The newsreader informed them that a famous baseball player had visited his old school to encourage the youngsters, and the emperor had watched some traditional Latin American dancing (I should point out that this was the national, not the local, news).

After dinner, for want of anything better to do, I decided to peruse the racks of magazines in the town's only convenience store. There was a lovely smell of temple incense in the air outside, and the man behind the counter welcomed me with a heartfelt '*Irasshaimase*'. The selection of magazines on offer told me a lot about the hopes and fears of the people of Takanosu. One was a Japanese version of *How to Win Friends and Influence People* in manga form, which promised to teach readers how to 'read the air', and thereby improve their social lives. It promised to show the reader 'where to sit when invited to a restaurant by your boss' and 'how to show a woman that you are interested in her without appearing rude'.

Another magazine promised to teach readers how to 'prevent the ageing of the brain'. 'What did you have for dinner last night? Who won the World Cup in 2022? Whose face appears on the ¥1,000 note? If you can't answer all three questions, you need to read this book!' it exclaimed. A third magazine explained all you needed to know about the government's nursing-care insurance scheme, including what to do about an ageing parent living alone with senility and how to find a good care worker.

Walking back to the hotel, I picked up the easy-going vibe of an overlooked town with a stoical attitude to its fate. Two teenagers, one on a bike, the other jogging, went by listening to hip-hop on a portable stereo; the sound of some smooth 80s soul music drifted from a passing car. These were firsts for me: everywhere else I had been in Japan, people had been too worried about causing offence to play their music loud enough for anyone else to hear it. The exception was commercial establishments, which played what they liked – usually ersatz pop – as loud as they liked.

Sure enough, when I got back to the Hotel Yagi, the sound of 'How Green Was My Valley' was still oozing from the worn-out speakers in the lobby, just as it had been when I arrived. The receptionist was immaculately dressed in a freshly laundered white shirt and cufflinks, waiting expectantly for the last of his guests to arrive. Paying no heed to the wallpaper peeling overhead, he handed me my room key as if it were a precious object and stood with his hands folded in front of him, a look of utmost solicitude etched on his face, until I turned and went upstairs to my room.

★

The following morning, I drove to Fujisato and from there took the road that led up to the Tsurubeotoshi Pass. I was planning to drive from the pass down to Miyama Lake, a journey of 50 kilometres that would take me through the untouched beech forests for which Aomori prefecture is famous. There were no villages up there, just mountains and natural-growth woodland. I was looking forward to doing some 'forest bathing', which I hoped would be a good antidote to the claustrophobia induced by spending so much time in the lowlands.

The road, fat and yellow on the map, turned skinny and white, the buildings on either side thinned out, and I was soon in a farming landscape of lush rice paddies, bordered by steep, forest-covered slopes. It was beautiful country, reminiscent of Switzerland. The summer had finally reached northern Japan, the cicadas were whirring, and the rain was falling in fits and starts. I passed a short old woman in a bonnet pushing a little four-wheeled cart and, further on, an old man making slow sweeps of the grass in front of his house with a cheap brush cutter. There was a rusting tractor, and the first traditional farm building I had seen in a long time: a little wooden hut with a rotten thatched roof that had sprouted bright green grass.

As the road narrowed, the valley closed in on me from either side, and I left the last of the fields behind. I climbed towards the treeline and soon came to a metal barrier over the road. Beyond, I could see what I had been looking for: an untouched landscape of steep mountain slopes thickly covered with trees, and a river churning white water. Notwithstanding the bears, boars and snakes, I needed to spend some time communing with nature.

But it was not to be: a sign on the barrier told me that the road ahead was closed due to the danger of landslides. I was being denied entry, for my own good. I had often felt deflated, on my travels, by what seemed to me to be an excess of caution on the part of the authorities. This time, however, it wasn't without foundation: Japan's rivers might be short, but there are lots of them and they grow fat with rainwater as they course down from the mountains.

I had no choice but to turn the car around and head back down the valley to Takanosu. On the way, I noticed that the river was indeed swollen with milky brown water. Huge trees had been tossed up onto the banks at crazy angles, their trunks stripped of bark on the way downriver. The land had absorbed so much water that it had given way in places, sending trees sliding down the mountainside before coming to rest at the point where the forest met the rice paddies. One of the trees had crushed the outbuildings next to a farmer's house. I'd reached the end of the road: it was time to go home.

Conclusion: No Sex, No Kids, No Future

On the *shinkansen* heading back to Tokyo from Akita, I saw a poster advertising the 50th anniversary of a well-known recruitment agency. 'An era with no future in sight,' it read. 'The road ahead hasn't been decided yet, so let's change ourselves and change the future together.' The strapline read, 'Building a world with a future you can see.' The message was clear: for Japan, there is no longer a well-signposted road leading into the future, or a clearly marked frontier to breach.

The bullet train ran on an elevated track, giving magisterial views over a wide valley of rice fields. Given everything I'd seen of rural decline, barrelling along like this should have given me a chance to get an overview of the problem. What did I see? Not ranks of abandoned homes or crumbling infrastructure – far from it. Here, at least, there were no signs of decrepitude; money was still coursing through the landscape. We passed prosperous farmhouses with beautiful glazed roof tiles in black and orange that glittered in the sun. The houses were all new, the roads and bridges were well maintained, and the fields, each only a few acres in size, had all been put to good use, with not an inch of ground wasted.

The view from the window was like watching jump cuts in a film, with the passengers as the audience, sitting stock still, dazzled by the spectacle. One moment we were watching an old farmer in a straw hat chug along the edge of a field in a little tractor, the next we were plunging into some woods, and then the pitch darkness of a tunnel. Seconds later we were back in the trees, and then we were passing through another isolated upland plain. The view only lasted a few seconds before the trees closed in again, but it was long enough to see that here, too, everything was in perfect order: new houses, neat fields of green-eared rice, a little road running along the edge of a bamboo grove.

If demographic stagnation is ultimately a consequence of higher living standards, better education and the new ways of thinking that come with modern life, then Japan has certainly outdone most of Europe and North America. It is as if, in the rush to develop and grow, it has become more 'Western' than the West; as if it has built up such a head of steam that it is being carried over the edge of a precipice. This points to something both sides find hard to admit: that, in several senses of the word, Japan has always been more developed than the West. Modern Japan is a plan that was realized: its rulers succeeded in perfecting modern life, at least in material terms, and now it is reaping the rewards.

Japan is the oldest country in the world in terms of life expectancy and median age, and the first non-Western country to make the demographic transition from high mortality and high fertility to low mortality and low fertility. By most measures, these changes are irrefutable evidence of an extremely successful society. Indeed, were it not for the unusually long life expectancy of its people, Japan's population would have fallen further and faster.

Long life plays a key role in masking the inability to reproduce, and Japan is also the country that has advanced furthest down the road to demographic collapse. By 2067, the number of Japanese people aged 100 or over is expected to have risen to 565,000, surpassing the annual number of births for the first time.[1] Such a steep decline in the birth rate and such a dramatic rise in the elderly population are unprecedented in world history.

What would happen if Japan's fertility rate were to fall to just one child per woman? In a land of a million people, if everyone coupled up and each couple produced just one child, the population would be down to just 976 – the size of a village – within ten generations. Fast forward another ten generations, and there would only be one person left. This is the downward spiral that Japan finds itself in today. Given that the average Japanese mother has her first child at the age of 31, twenty generations is 620 years. That means that, if the current fertility rate continues, the last Japanese person will die sometime around the year 2643.

*

I drifted off to sleep, and by the time I woke up the train had discreetly glided into Utsunomiya station. Soon we would be back in Tokyo, where I would have to adjust my internal clock to the capital's tightly wound tempo. Out of the window I watched *salarimen* rushing to and fro. Sitting all by herself on a seat on the platform was an old woman. She was dressed in anonymous suburban style: everything new and clean, comfortable trainers and a neat grey bob. She didn't see me, or anything else for that matter, for her eyes were cast down and she appeared to be lost in thought.

Unless you stopped to consider her for a moment, there was nothing remarkable about her appearance, but I couldn't help but notice the way she twitched her shoulders, as if trying to shrug off something sitting there. She was in such pain, yet so caught up in her thoughts and so oblivious to her surroundings that, for a moment, I wondered if she was asleep and having a nightmare.

No one else saw her. It is considered impolite to look at other people, at least up close, so the other passengers just dashed past her on their way to their trains. Politeness and discretion are much appreciated when you want to be alone, but they also serve to trap people in their solitude. People say they don't want to be nosy, or that they are too busy, but seen through the eyes of the lonely, their good manners are just a mask for their indifference. The upshot was the same: no one wondered about the old woman, and she was left alone with the malevolent little creature sitting on her shoulder.

Many of the people I had met on my travels seemed resigned to living without intimate relationships. They had boundless energy for observing social obligations, be it to colleagues at work, neighbours or society at large, but were all at sea when it came to forming friendships or romantic attachments. Some of them had been so distracted by social obligations and the possibility of causing offence that their speech had become a performance, and they seemed incapable of talking with any spontaneity. I don't know how much they suffered as a result of turning their backs on the possibilities of friendship. Lots of people appeared depressed: lacking in motivation, uncommunicative, distracted. They seemed content to have a vivid inner life. Could it be that they had simply run out of desire – whether for happiness, love or children?

*

But perhaps I was mistaken in interpreting Japanese people's lack of communication as indifference. Discussing their responses to the World Values Survey, an executive from adverting giant Dentsu noted, 'Despite high levels of interest in "politics," political matters are not discussed. Many Japanese respondents replied, "don't know" when asked to choose between "protecting the environment" and "economic growth".' The results showed, he said, 'numerous cases where responses appear at first glance contradictory or respondents tended to avoid clear choices when asked'.[2]

Moving between Japan and the UK over the course of 25 years has given me a singular perspective on how my own country has changed too. The waning authority of all kinds of hierarchical organizations, be they churches, trade unions, political parties or the press. The growing importance of work and, with it, performance. The rising power of individualism, convincing us that we no longer need other people, at least not as family members. The rise of mental health problems like anxiety and depression; and the growing number of people who feel unable to have children, or simply don't want to – these have all become features of modern life in the UK, just as they have in Japan.

Still, in some ways, Japan's low birth rate is down to its own, very particular failure to move on from the attitudes formed when everyone lived in patriarchal extended families. They were tenable for as long as women stayed at home and raised children, but as soon as women started to go out to work, they earned a measure of independence that allowed them to challenge traditional attitudes.

Japan Inc. was built on a specific kind of family, with clear roles for men and women. Men served the company, and women looked after the home and raised the children. There were clear masculine and feminine ideals that people were expected to follow. The boys were supposed to become can-do, team-playing businessmen, while the girls were expected to be sweet-natured, practical and cheerful.

These ideals have come under pressure as the way men and women negotiate work, intimate relationships and family responsibilities changes. At the root of Japan's demographic problems is a collective failure to grasp the radical implications of gender equality. The fragility of identity has combined with a growing number of women in the workplace and declining incomes for men to sow confusion about gender roles.

My own feeling is that this move towards defining life on one's own terms is to be welcomed, but I am wary of the self-absorption that it can lead to. I say that not because I want to see a return to patriarchy, or traditional roles per se, but because a sense of purpose, and identity within a social framework, helps to maintain connections between people, including sexual connections, in the face of the forces that conspire to isolate us from one another – work, very often, being the worst culprit.

Japan is not blessed with many natural resources; it has no iron ore, gas or oil, no vast wheatfields or cattle pastures. What it does have is people. The country only became a global behemoth because its corporations and society at large were united in their commitment to economic growth. At the heart of the problem is the huge personal sacrifice that the post-war generation made in the name of work. Japan's bubble economy may have deflated, but millions of workers still give their all to the office. They have allowed their relationships with family members, friends and the wider community to wither on the vine. In the name of becoming ideal workers, neighbours and citizens, they have neglected their own humanity.

As far as the Treasury is concerned, it is in the state's interests to encourage people to stay healthy and form families that can look after them when they are no longer able to look after themselves. But people are tired. Remaining single and childless appear, in this context, to be acts of rebellion against an all-pervading system that sacrifices people's emotional life to the demands of a work-obsessed society.

Japan's prosperity has been undermined by the transition away from manufacturing, but demography poses a bigger threat. The extremely good health of its people and their collective reluctance to reproduce have combined to make the life of the nation unusually long and thin.

Elon Musk has tweeted that he is going to miss Japan when it is gone.[3] But to quote the title of a well-known book, 'Such a lovely country will never die.' Japan might not have globally sought-after natural resources, but its rich volcanic soils are a blessing for farmers. It is never going to starve and doesn't need the outside world to survive. If it wanted to, it could turn its back on the world, and embark on a crazy journey to autarky. It wouldn't be the first time: indeed, until modern times, this was all the country knew, and the oldest generation still remembers how to do it.

The more introspective, less energetic younger generation is wondering if it can afford to forget how to go it alone. Certainly, the country is fully enmeshed in interdependency. For every old biddy growing leeks in the country's wonderfully fertile soil, there are five grandsons who have to call a handyman every time they want to change a lightbulb. But, amongst other things, the internet is very good at showing people how to change lightbulbs.

Sooner or later, something significant will have to be done. Those advocating piecemeal adjustments say that European countries are going through the same shrinking pains, but, to my mind, this only shows that Japan's traditionalists are not concerned by numbers per se, but by their country's weight relative to others in the rich world. The reasoning goes that since the population of the entire developed world is shrinking, Japan will not decline relative to the United States and Europe, and that is what matters.

But this way of thinking is grounded in twentieth-century

assumptions: that the rest of the world is going to get numerically bigger without getting any richer. Like the UK, the US and other rich nations, Japan is still struggling to imagine a world in which it no longer has a monopoly over money, power and authority. We are clinging to the past. It's time we opened our eyes to the future.

Acknowledgements

I would like to thank all those who agreed to be interviewed for this book. In addition, I would like to thank the following for their help in researching and writing it:

Takeshi Hayakawa; Graham Meredith; Giles Murray and Naoko Ito; Tim Hornyak; Chris Kirkland of Tokyo Cheapo; William Andrews; David H. Slater, Professor of Cultural Anthropology at Sophia University; Shunichi Ito, who works in community revitalization in Iwamiginzan, Omoricho, Oda-shi in Shimane prefecture; Sam Holden, who runs Tokyo Little House in Akasaka and gave me lots of tips for who to talk to about renovation activism; Hidetoshi Ōno, Professor of Architecture and Urban Planning at the University of Tokyo, who was a good source of speculation about what is likely to happen to Tokyo over next 50 years; Jeff Kingston, Professor of History & Asian Studies at Temple University; Barbara Holthus, Deputy Director of the German Institute for Japanese Studies (DIJ) and Nora Kottmann, Principal Researcher at the DIJ; Susanne Klien, Associate Professor of Modern Japanese Studies at Hokkaido University.

Annette Schad-Seifert, Professor at Heinrich Heine University in Dusseldorf and also Ochanomizu University; Patrick W. Galbraith, author of *The Moe Manifesto: An Insider's Look at the Worlds of Manga, Anime and Gaming* and lecturer at Senshu University in Tokyo.

All the staff at the Foreign Press Centre Japan.

Sharon Kinsella; Sam Low; Satoru Yoshida; Tatsuya Goke; Debbie Warrener; Yumiko Kageura and Hide Enomoto in Fujino; Leah Fahy; Scott Murray, Hiroko Murray and Shigeru Okamura of the Ojima Fishermen's Cooperative in Omihachiman; Anna Nakamura and her brother Mario Nakamura.

Stephen Shaw, director of *Birthgap*; Reiko Hayashi, Deputy Director-General of the National Institute of Population and Social

Security Research; Akiko Hatano; Asa Quesenberry, founder and president of SkyScape in Osaka.

Peter Ueda; Hisatada Kono, chairman of the Fussa *seinen shien sentaa*, and Ryo Kuwahara.

Satomi Abe and Miki Hirata at the Rural Revitalization Centre in Tokyo; Aomori representative Chie Sawa, who went to great lengths to put me in touch with migrants to Aomori prefecture; Haruki and Tomoko Kimura in Tago/Takko, Aomori prefecture; Ryota Kawaragi and Hideo Suzuki in Kita-Akita; Ayaka Tsuchiya in Kuriyama, Hokkaido.

Adam Fulford, who put me in touch with Tom Miyagawa Coulton and his wife Mai in Mitarai on Osaki-Shimozima, and Remco Vrolijk in Hirado, Nagasaki prefecture; Shinsuke Koike, Associate Professor of Ecology at the Tokyo University of Agriculture and Technology, who put me in touch with Hiroaki Myōjō at the Masuda Office of the Western Shimane Agriculture, Forestry and Fisheries Promotion Centre; Teruyoshi Yamane.

Dr Megha Wadhwa at Free University Berlin, author of *Indian Migrants in Tokyo: A Study of Socio-Cultural, Religious and Working Worlds*; Yogendra Puranik, who runs the Edogawa Indian Cultural Centre; Prasad Bakre and Supriti Sethi; Le Phuong Anh of the Waseda Institute of Asia-Pacific Studies, who arranged for me to talk to her friends Ms Dinh Tran Nam Chi, Mr Pham Ba Loc and Mr Nguyen Tuan Phong.

The Great Britain Sasakawa Foundation, for the financial support they gave me while I was travelling in Japan. My agent, Matthew Hamilton at the Hamilton Agency; my editor at Allen Lane, Chloe Currens; Miko Yamanouchi, President of Japan UNI Agency, and her colleague Takeshi Oyama. And last, but not least, IZ, thanks to whom I was never really alone in Japan.

Notes

Introduction

1 One of the indicators of a growing economy is rising prices. After its economy stalled in the early 1990s, Japan experienced practically no inflation for a quarter of a century. The value of ¥1,000 in 1998 was just ¥1,021 in 2022, meaning that prices had risen by only 2.1 per cent. They did rise, however, in 2023, driven by the rising cost of commodities on the world market. See: < https://www.worlddata.info/asia/japan/inflation-rates>.

2 'Japan's Marriage Market Needs to Break from Tradition', East Asia Forum, 11 November 2022.

3 David Pilling, *Bending Adversity: Japan and the Art of Survival*, Penguin Press 2014, p.160.

4 '10% of Japan's 2070 Population Expected to be Foreign Nationals', *Asahi Shinbun*, 27 April 2023.

5 'Japan's Annual Births Fall to Record Low as Population Emergency Deepens', CNN World, 5 June 2025.

6 Miho Iwasawa, cited in '10% of Japan's 2070 Population', *Asahi Shinbun*.

7 Fertility Rate (Births Per Woman) – Japan, World Bank, <https://data.worldbank.org/indicator/SP.DYN.TFRT.IN?locations=JP>.

8 Sarah Lubman, 'Japan Confronts a Stark Reality: A Nation of Old People', *National Geographic*, 12 January 2023.

9 'Will Japan's Population Shrink or Swim?' East Asia Forum, 26 October 2022; Nate Berg, 'Raze, Rebuild, Repeat: Why Japan Knocks Down its Houses After 30 Years', *Guardian*, 16 November 2017; Toshihiro Menju, 'Population Decline and Immigration Policy – Making Japan a Popular Destination for Immigration', video Report for Foreign Press Centre Japan, <https://fpcj.jp/en/worldnews-en/briefings-en/p=99078/>; 'Japan's Population Declines Again: Seniors 75 and Over Top 20 Million for First Time', nippon.com, 24 April 2024.

10 '10% of Japan's 2070 Population', *Asahi Shinbun*.

11 The most moderate of the NIPSSR's three forecasts suggests that by 2100 the population will have fallen to 75 million. See Samuel Holden, *The Vacant City: An Ethnography of Alternative Spatial Cultures in Post-growth Tokyo* [unpublished master's thesis], University of Tokyo, 2017.

12 Data provided by demographer Paul Morland, cited in Andrew Anthony, 'The Global Fertility Crisis: Are Fewer Babies a Good or a Bad Thing? Experts Are Divided', *Guardian*, 2 November 2024.

13 In 2022, Musk warned that 'Population collapse due to low birth rates is a much bigger risk to civilisation than global warming. (And I do think global warming is a major risk).' Cited in Jenny Kleeman, 'America's Premier Pronatalists on Having "Tons of Kids" to Save the World: "There Are Going to be Countries of Old People Starving to Death."', *Guardian*, 25 May 2024.

14 *Demographic Winter* Part One [documentary], dir. Rick Stout, <https://www.youtube.com/watch?v=L8XQjfG2wYc>.

15 George Thomas, 'Japan Is Dying', CBN News, 12 December 2016.

16 Drew Ambrose, *Ageing Japan: The Burden of a Graying Planet* [TV news segment], Al-Jazeera English, 101 East, November 2012.

17 Lubman, 'Japan Confronts a Stark Reality'.

18 'The Guardian View on Population Growth: A Small Planet Needs Big Solutions', *Guardian*, 23 July 2020.

19 The developed countries with the highest fertility rates are France, the United States, Ireland, New Zealand and Australia, which have fertility rates of between 1.65 and 1.60. See: List of Countries by Total Fertility Rate, Wikipedia, <https://en.wikipedia.org/wiki/List_of_sovereign_states_and_dependencies_by_total_fertility_rate>.

20 Stephen J. Shaw, director of the documentary *Birthgap*, mentions these figures in his discussion with Jordan Peterson, 'The Epidemic that Dare Not Speak Its Name', Jordan B. Peterson, YouTube, <https://www.youtube.com/watch?v=Qrg8t34yXRs>; also in notes taken from Q&A with Shaw following a screening of *Birthgap* at Temple University, Tokyo, 29 March 2023.

21 '"I Can't Give Up on Hope": As the World's Population Passes 8bn, New Parents from Italy to India Look to the Future', *Guardian*, 15 November 2022.

22 P. Matanle, 'Achieving the "Depopulation Dividend": Japan as the World's Research Laboratory for a More Sustainable Future', Open-pop.org, 4 May 2014. Available at: <https://www.researchgate.net/publication/316017867_Achieving_the_21st_Century_'Depopulation_Dividend'_Japan_as_the_World's_Research_Laboratory_for_a_More_Sustainable_Future>.

23 'Why a Nation of 1.45 Billion Wants More Children', BBC News, 16 December 2024.

24 'The Guardian View on Population Growth' *Guardian*. See also: Tory Shepherd, 'Birthrates Are Plummeting Worldwide. Can Governments Turn the Tide?' *Guardian*, 10 August 2024; Lucy Lamble, 'With 250 Babies Born Each Minute, How Many People Can the Earth Sustain?', *Guardian*, 23 April 2018.

25 Shepherd, 'Birthrates are Plummeting Worldwide'.

26 Kawai Masashi, *Mirai no nenpyo* (*Chronology of the Future*), Kodansha Gendai Shinsho, 2017.

Chapter 1

1 Florian Coulmas, 'The Quest for Happiness in Japan', Working Paper 09/1, German Institute for Japanese Studies Tokyo, 2008.

2 Lubman, 'Japan Confronts a Stark Reality'.

3 '1.8% of 365.8m² of Tokyo's Residential Space Is in Buildings Built Before 1959' [blog post], 5000 Cities, <https://5000cities.wordpress.com/2023/12/29/1-8-of-365-8m-m2-of-tokyos-residential-space-is-in-buildings-built-before-1959-almost-40-built-in-2000s-2010s/>.

4 The urban sprawl across the Kanto Plain, which includes the cities of Tokyo and Yokohama, has a population of 37 million, making it far and away the largest urban conglomeration in the world. See: List of Largest Cities, Wikipedia, <https://en.wikipedia.org/wiki/List_of_metropolitan_areas_by_population>.

5 Allan Richarz, 'In Japan's Vanishing Rural Towns, Newcomers Are Wanted', Bloomberg UK, 15 November 2019.

6 For the time being, Tokyo is still growing, but it is also ageing – the first sign of shrinking. By 2055, people aged 65 or older will account for 33 per cent of the city's population, up from 23 per cent in 2015. Tokyo's city government expects its population to peak in 2025 before going into steady decline. By 2035, the only one of the city's twenty-three wards that will still be growing will be Minato-ku – the central ward that hosts its glitziest developments. The rest of the city, along with the rest of the country, will be shrinking. See: Junko Fujita, 'Tokyo Office Boom Fades with More Space, Fewer Workers', *Japan Times*, 17 January 2017.

7 Holden, *The Vacant City*.

8 'Aging Japan: Akita Prefecture May be Glimpse of Country's Graying Future', *Asahi Shinbun*, 4 July 2018.

9 'Japan Keeps Building Suburbs Even as Population Shrinks', Nikkei Asia, 27 December 2019, <https://asia.nikkei.com/Economy/Japan-keeps-building-suburbs-even-as-population-shrinks>. Data from 2018.

10 Pilling, *Bending Adversity*, p.79.

11 Richard Katz, 'Xi Jinping Seeks to Ban "Socialism with Japanese and Singaporean Characteristics," Part One: What Deng Xiaoping Learned from Japanese and Singaporean Advisors' [blog post], Substack, 20 September 2023.

12 Pilling, *Bending Adversity*, p.84.

13 Pilling, *Bending Adversity*, p.82.

14 Pilling, *Bending Adversity*, p.93.

15 Cited in Pilling, *Bending Adversity*, p.91.

16 David Chiavacci, 'From Class Struggle to General Middle-Class Society to Divided Society: Societal Models of Inequality in Post-war Japan', *Social Science Japan Journal* Vol. 11, No. 1, pp. 5–27, 2008.

17 Chiavacci, 'From Class Struggle to General Middle-Class Society'.

18 Cited in Chiavacci, 'From Class Struggle to General Middle-Class Society', p.16.

19 Among young Japanese men who entered the job market between 1946 and 1955, only 18 per cent joined a large corporation or the state bureaucracy. However, this rose to over 30 per cent among those who

entered the job market between 1976 and 1985, and in the 1986–1995 cohort it was over 40 per cent. See: Chiavacci, 'From Class Struggle to General Middle-Class Society'.

20 'The Curse of the Fire-Horse: How Superstition Impacted Fertility Rates in Japan' [blog post], World Bank Blogs, 22 January 2019.

21 Johan Galtung, 'Social Structure, Education Structure and Lifelong Education: The Case of Japan' in *Reviews of National Policies for Education: Japan*, ed. OECD. Paris: OECD: 131–52, 1971. Cited in Chiavacci, 'From Class Struggle to General Middle-Class Society'.

22 According to the OECD, average salaries went from $40,379 in 1991 to $41,509 in 2022. See: John Power, 'Japan's Workers Get Rare Pay Bump After Decades Without a Raise', Al Jazeera, 18 July 2023.

23 Barbara Holthus, Isaac Gagne, Wolfram Manzenreiter and Franz Waldenberger, 'Understanding Japan through the lens of Tokyo 2020', a chapter in Barbara Holthus, Isaac Gagne, Wolfram Manzenreiter and Franz Waldenberger, *Japan through the lens of Tokyo 2020*, Routledge 2020, p.4.

24 Yoshio Sugimoto, *Introduction to Japanese Society*, Cambridge University Press 2014, p.105. See, too: Kojima et al., 'Abe Shinzō's Campaign to Reform the Japanese Way of Work'.

25 Pilling, *Bending Adversity*, p.155.

26 Yamada's essay appears in *Reimagining Japan: The Quest for a Future That Works*, eds. Clay Chandler, Heang Chhor and Brian Salsberg, VIZ Media 2011. Cited in Pilling, *Bending Adversity*, p.192.

27 Sugimoto, *Introduction to Japanese Society*, p.106.

28 Atsushi Miura describes these people in his book *Karyu Shakai (The Lower Society)*, Kobunsha, 2005.

Chapter 2

1 Virtually unlimited overtime is made possible via something called an Article 36 agreement, which needs to be signed by both management and labour representatives. See: Kojima et al., 'Abe Shinzō's Campaign to Reform the Japanese Way of Work'.

2 Parissa Haghirian (ed.), *Japanese Business Concepts You Should Know*, Sophia University 2019.

3 Not counting 1967, the year after the Year of the Fire Horse, which was considered an inauspicious year to give birth to a daughter. The fertility rate temporarily dropped by 25 per cent in 1967, from 2.1 to 1.6. See: 'The Curse of the Fire-Horse', World Bank Blogs.

4 To clarify, by 2020, the proportion of employees working for more than 60 hours a week had dropped to 11 per cent of male full-time employees and 4.7 per cent of female full-time employees. The earlier data is from Annette Schad-Seifert, 'Coping with Low Fertility? Japan's Government Measures for a Gender Equal Society', DIJ working paper, April 2006. The latter is from: Share of Full-Time Employees Working 60 Hours or More per Week in Japan 2023, By Age and Gender, Statista. com, <https://www.statista.com/statistics/858359/japan-percentage-people-working-60-hours-or-more-per-week-by-age-gender/>.

5 Haghirian (ed.), *Japanese Business Concepts You Should Know*.

6 Kojima et al., 'Abe Shinzō's Campaign to Reform the Japanese Way of Work'.

7 'Japan's Marriage Market', East Asia Forum.

8 Bricker and Ibbitson, 'What Goes Up'.

9 Peter Matanle, 'Towards an Asia-Pacific "Depopulation Dividend" in the 21st Century: Regional Growth and Shrinkage in Japan and New Zealand', *Asia Pacific Journal* Volume 15, Issue 6, Number 5, 15 March 2017.

10 Number of Registered Marriages per 1,000 inhabitants in Japan from 1960 to 2023, Statista.com, <https://www.statista.com/statistics/1249856/japan-marriage-rate/>.

11 According to an NHK poll conducted in 2018 and cited in Toru Suzuki, 'Fertility Decline and Policy Development in Japan', *Japanese Journal of Population* Vol.4, No.1, March 2006.

12 'Women in Japanese Society', NHK World, 6 January 2019.

13 Chizuko Ueno, 'The Declining Birthrate: Whose Problem?' *Review of Population and Social Policy*, No. 7, 1998, pp.103–28.

14 Mean Age of Marriage Japan 1955–2023, By Gender, Statista.com, <https://www.statista.com/statistics/611957/japan-mean-age-marriage-by-gender/>.

15 The same point, citing the same statistic, is made by Jordan Peterson in his discussion with Steven J. Shaw, 'The Epidemic that Dare Not Speak Its Name'.

16 'Women in Japanese Society', NHK World. NHK Broadcasting Culture Research, who conducted this survey, has been taking opinion polls every five years since 1973 to learn about people's views on family, life and work. It surveyed 2,751 people in 2018. Respondents were all above the age of 16, chosen at random nationwide.

17 Chizuko Ueno, 'The Position of Japanese Women Reconsidered', *Current Anthropology*, Vol. 28, No. 4, *Supplement: An Anthropological Profile of Japan* Aug.–Oct. 1987, pp.S75–S84.

18 Ueno, 'The Position of Japanese Women Reconsidered'.

19 Steven Vogel, *Whatever Happened to Japanese Electronics? A World Economy Perspective*. Cited in Paul Murphy, *True Crime Japan: Thieves, Rascals, Killers and Dope Heads: True Stories from a Japanese Courtroom*, Tuttle Publishing 2016, p.55.

20 Justin McCurry, ' "A Free-for-All": Japan Divided as Return of Tourists Brings Instagrammers and Litter', *Guardian*, 3 February 2024.

21 From Anne Allison, 'The Cool Brand and Affective Activism of Japanese Youth', *Theory, Culture & Society*, 2009, Vol. 26(2–3): 89–111.

Chapter 3

1 'Case of Childcare Worker Chided for Getting Pregnant before Her "Turn" Not Uncommon', *Mainichi*, 2 April 2018.

2 David McNeill, 'Sayaka Murata: "I Acted How I Thought a Cute Woman Should Act – It Was Horrible" ', *Guardian*, 9 October 2020.

3 Schad-Seifert, 'Coping with Low Fertility?'.

4 Data is from 2016. See: Thomas, 'Japan is Dying'.

5 Alana Semuels, 'Japan is No Place for Single Mothers', *The Atlantic*, 7 September 2017.

6 Kumiko Nemoto, 'Postponed Marriage: Exploring Women's Views of Matrimony and Work in Japan', *Gender and Society* Volume 22, Issue 2, 2008.

7 See: Richard Katz, 'Mr. Kishida: To Get 30% Female Executives, Enforce the Law' [blog post], Substack, 2 May 2023.

8 Ueno, 'The Position of Japanese Women Reconsidered'.

9 The number of dual-income households surpassed the number of households in which only the man worked for the first time in 1991. By 2017, 74 per cent of women between the ages of 15 and 64 were in employment. See: 'Women in Japanese Society', NHK World.

10 'Women in Japanese Society', NHK World.

11 Ekaterina Hertog and Miho Iwasawa, 'Marriage, Abortion, or Unwed Motherhood? How Women Evaluate Alternative Solutions to Premarital Pregnancies in Japan and the United States', *Journal of Family Issues* Volume 32, Issue 12. First published online 5 June 2011.

12 Abigail Haworth, 'Why Have Young People in Japan Stopped Having Sex?', *Guardian*, 20 October 2013.

13 Kazuhisa Arakawa's talk about solo living at the Foreign Correspondents Club Japan (FCCJ), <http://fpcj.jp/en/worldnews-en/briefings-en/p=55978/>.

14 'Japan's Marriage Market', East Asia Forum.

15 Nemoto, 'Postponed Marriage'.

16 Nemoto, 'Postponed Marriage'.

17 Data from Japan's National Tax Agency and the Ministry of Health, Labour and Welfare suggest that, in 2025, the average salary in Japan was ¥4.60 million (£23,115). However, the median was likely closer to ¥3.96 million (£19,899). See: 'What is the Average Salary in Japan?' [blog post], Gaijinpot, 23 January 2025. Based on an exchange rate of £1=¥199, correct as of 22 September 2025.

18 'Japan's Marriage Market', East Asia Forum.

19 Ueno, 'The Declining Birthrate: Whose Problem?'.

20 It was in 1990 that the proportion of arranged marriages and workplace marriages first fell below 50 per cent of all marriages. See: Kazuhisa Arakawa's FCCJ talk about solo living.

21 Ueno, 'The Declining Birthrate: Whose Problem?'.

22 See: Erika Alpert, ' Stoicism or Shyness? Japanese Professional Matchmakers and New Masculine Conversational Ideals', *Journal of Language and Sexuality* Volume 3, Issue 2, January 2014, pp.191–218 (pp.199, 207).

23 The UK might have been going through the same kind of birth strike as Japan were it not for the loosening of social mores surrounding marriage and childbirth. Marriage has long been in decline in England and Wales: in 2019, 213,000 heterosexual couples got married, half as many as in 1972. But the fertility rate has held up comparatively well, partly because prospective parents no longer feel obliged to get married. In 2021, more babies were born to unmarried mothers in England and Wales than to those in a marriage or civil partnership, for the first time since records began in 1845. See: Number of Live Births in England and Wales in 1938–2022, By Marital Status, Statista.com, <https://www.statista.com/statistics/294571/live-births-in-england-wales-uk-by-age-and-marital-status-of-mother>.

24 Hertog and Iwasawa, 'Marriage, Abortion, or Unwed Motherhood?'. See too: 'Are More Babies Born Inside or Outside Marriage?', Eurostat, 16 April 2018.

25 'Japan's Marriage Market', East Asia Forum.

26 Hertog and Iwasawa, 'Marriage, Abortion, or Unwed Motherhood?'.

27 Ueno, 'The Declining Birthrate: Whose Problem?'. I have used the fertility rate in Sweden for 2025, which has changed since Chizuko Ueno's article was published.

28 McNeill, 'Sayaka Murata'.

29 According to Stephen J. Shaw, director of the documentary *Birthgap*. He cited these statistics in the Q&A session that followed a screening of his documentary at Temple University in Tokyo on 29 March 2023.

30 Coulmas, 'The Quest for Happiness in Japan'.

31 In the words of David Pilling. Pilling, *Bending Adversity*, p.107.

32 Pilling, *Bending Adversity*, p.109.

33 Note that the ellipses indicate where I have spliced together two separate quotes from Pilling's interview with Murakami. Pilling, *Bending Adversity*, pp.110, 184.

34 Miura, *The Rise of Sharing*, p.283.

Chapter 4

1 Cited in Colin Marshall, 'Ways of Seeing Japan: Roland Barthes's Tokyo, 50 Years Later', *Los Angeles Review of Books*, 31 December 2016.

2 Data from the 2020 census, cited in Justin McCurry, 'Life at the Heart of Japan's Lonely Deaths Epidemic: "I Would Be Lying if I Said I Wasn't Worried"', *Guardian*, 1 July 2024.

3 Kazuhisa Arakawa, 'A Community of Connections: Looking Forward to the Solo Society', nippon.com, 13 January 2020.

4 *Kirawareru Yūki (the courage to be disliked)* is by Ichiro Kishimi and Fumi-take Koga. *Gokujō no Kodoku (supreme solitude)* is by Akiko Shimoju.

5 Leo Lewis, 'Japan's literature of loneliness depicts solitude as a noble state', *Financial Times*, 7 June 2018.

6 'Where in the World Do People Live Alone?', *Psychology Today*, 5 October 2022.

7 Klinenberg alludes to this study in his talk, 'Eric Klinenberg: Living Single', Poptech, YouTube, <https://www.youtube.com/watch?v=YHPBYLFA_vQ>. He mentions that the study was made at the University of Michigan, but doesn't give a date.

8 Daniel de Visé, 'A Record Share of Americans is Living Alone', The Hill, 10 July 2023.

9 Arakawa, 'A Community of Connections'. Arakawa is an advertising man turned sociologist, like many of the people I came across in my research who are writing about Japan's demographic changes.

10 Zygmunt Bauman, *Liquid Modernity*, Polity Press 2000.

11 Population ages 0–14, percent of total, 2023, TheGlobalEconomy.com, <https://www.theglobaleconomy.com/rankings/percent_children/>. Children means people aged 0–14. The country in which children make up the largest proportion of the population is Niger, where 49 per cent of people are under the age of 14. The article uses data from the United Nations Population Division.

12 'Japan's Population Projected to Fall to 87 Million in 2070', nippon.com, 12 May 2023.

13 Haghirian (ed.), *Japanese Business Concepts You Should Know*.

14 Except where indicated, all statistics about convenience stores are taken from 'Konbini Morphology' and 'Itadakimasu', both by Gavin H. Whitelaw, in *Tokyo Totem: A Guide to Tokyo*, eds. Christian Fruneaux and Edwin Gardner, Monnik 2015, pp.128–31, 160–63. See, too: George Lloyd, 'Tokyo: A Wonder of the Modern World Fed by Its *Konbini*', Grape Japan, 29 October 2020.

15 See: Campaign to End Loneliness, <https://www.campaigntoend-loneliness.org/facts-and-statistics>.

16 Quoted in Gaynor Parkin and Erika Clarry, 'You Don't Have to Be Alone to Experience Loneliness – and More Friends Isn't the Answer', *Guardian*, 28 May 2023.

17 Justin McCurry, 'Isolation Nation: Japan Tries to Draw its Citizens Out of Post-Covid Seclusion', *Guardian*, 12 May 2023.

18 'Social Isolation in Japan, Hikikomori Are Now Opening Up' [TV news segment], NBC Left Field/On the Fringe, NBC News, <https://www.youtube.com/watch?v=imR1-CaSxZE&list=LLp_Wqvns3UP dJh3cja-fjWw&index=2774>.

19 Allison, 'The Cool Brand and Affective Activism of Japanese Youth', pp.15–16.

20 Annette Schad-Seifert and Shingo Shimada (eds.), *Demographic Change in Japan and the EU: Comparative Perspectives*, 2010, p.33.

21 In 2022, 21,584 people killed themselves in Japan. This is considerably more than in the UK, which has about half the population, where 6,588 people died by suicide in the same year. See: *Saving 10,000: Winning a War on Suicide in Japan* [documentary film], dir. Rene Duignan, <https://www.youtube.com/watch?v=oooSHLxc2do>.

22 Suicide in Japan, Wikipedia, <https://en.wikipedia.org/wiki/Suicide_in_Japan>.

23 Allison, 'The Cool Brand and Affective Activism of Japanese Youth', p.20.

24 Susanne Klein, 'Japan's Younger Generations Look for a New Way of Living', *Current History*, September 2021.

25 Officially, the biggest city in the world in 1700 was Ayutthaya in Thailand. However, given that it, too, had a population of 1 million, there wasn't much in it. See: Max Galka, 'From Jericho to Tokyo:

The World's Largest Cities Through History – Mapped', *Guardian*, 6 December 2016.

26 The numbers of men and women in Edo only reached something close to parity in the middle of the nineteenth century. Paul Waley, *Tokyo: City of Stories*, Weatherhill 1991, p.144.

27 Material related to single men's culture in Edo is from Kazuhisa Arakawa's talk about solo living at the FCCJ.

28 In *The Happy Youth of a Desperate Country*, Noritoshi Furuichi argues that, despite the economic and demographic challenges Japan faces, its young people are largely satisfied with their lives. He highlights the disconnect between the perception, common among their parents' generation, that all young people are on the verge of a nervous breakdown, with surveys that show that Japanese millennials score higher on scales of life satisfaction than previous generations.

Chapter 5

1 Maki Hirayama, 'Sex in the Village', Chapter 26 in *Japan Through the Lens of the Tokyo Olympics*, eds. Barbara Holthus, Isaac Gagné, Wolfram Manzenreiter, Franz Waldenberger, Taylor & Francis 2020.

2 Hirayama, 'Sex in the Village'.

3 'Japanese University Students Less Sexually Active', nippon.com, 17 December 2018.

4 'Growing Indifference to Relationships and Sex in Japan', nippon.com, 28 September 2022.

5 Alan Booth, *The Roads to Sata: A 2,000 Mile Walk Through Japan*, originally published by John Weatherhill in 1985; republished by Penguin in 2020, p.253.

6 'The Japanese Sex Drought: Why Are Married Women So Uninterested in Making Love?', *Guardian*, 20 March 2024.

7 'Survey Finds Record Number of "Sexless" Married Couples in Japan', nippon.com, 23 February 2017.

8 Interestingly, it would appear that Japanese people are indeed more self-contained than Americans or Britons. This is borne out by a study

conducted by the *Economist*, which found that while 22 per cent of adults in the US and 23 per cent in Britain 'always or often feel lonely, or lack companionship, or else feel left out or isolated', just 9 per cent of Japanese people feel that way. See: 'Loneliness Is a Serious Public-health Problem', *Economist*, 1 September 2018.

9 Abigail Haworth, 'Why Have Young People in Japan Stopped Having Sex?', *Observer*, 20 October 2013.

10 Cyrus Ghaznavi, Haruka Sakamoto, Kenji Shibuya and Peter Ueda, 'Let's Talk About (No) Sex: A Closer Look at Japan's "Virginity Crisis"', *Diplomat*, 8 April 2019.

11 Kathleen Benoza, 'Japan Ranks Last in Romance Satisfaction for Second Straight Year', *Japan Times*, 20 November 2024.

12 In 2023, Japan's fertility rate hit a new low of 1.2, with the rate for Tokyo falling to 0.99 for the first time. See 'Japan's Fertility Rate Drops to New Record Low', nippon.com, 12 June 2024. In Greece, the fertility rate is 1.3. See: 'Greece's Shrinking Population Could Leave Some Islands Barren', *National Herald*, 10 October 2024.

13 Barbara Ellen, 'If Robbie Williams Has Given Up on Sex in Marriage, What Hope Do Any of Us Have?', *Observer*, 29 April 2023.

14 According to the Center for Disease Control and Prevention's Youth Risk Behaviour Survey. 'Over the last thirty years' refers to the period between 1991 and 2017. See: Kate Julian, 'Why Are Young People Having So Little Sex?', *Atlantic*, December 2018.

15 'Are We Really in the Middle of a Global Sex Recession?', *Guardian*, 14 November 2018.

16 Data is from 2014. Julian, 'Why Are Young People Having So Little Sex?'.

17 Julian, 'Why Are Young People Having So Little Sex?'.

18 Sonia Sodha, 'It's Time to Ditch the Stereotypes and Look at the Realities Behind Singledom', *Guardian*, 8 September 2018.

19 Kitty Drake, 'I Spent Months Interviewing People about Their Sex Lives. This Is What I Learned', *Guardian*, 29 June 2024.

Chapter 6

1 Ho Swee Lin, 'Private Love in Public Space: Love Hotels and the Transformation of Intimacy in Contemporary Japan', *Asian Studies Review* Volume 32, Issue 1, 2008, p.31.

2 This statistic dates from 2006. 'Love for Sale', *Forbes*, 6 May 2006.

3 'No Room for Romance? Japan's Love Hotels Court New Clientele', *Nikkei Asia*, 19 July 2017, <https://asia.nikkei.com/Editor-s-Picks/Japan-Update/No-room-for-romance-Japan-s-love-hotels-court-new-clientele>.

4 Gaijinpot, 'Understanding Valentine's Day (and White Day) in Japan', *Japan Today*, 11 February 2022.

5 Ghaznavi et al., 'Let's Talk About (No) Sex'.

6 Ueno was named one of *Time* magazine's Most Influential People of 2024. In China, where the state stigmatizes single women older than 27 as 'leftover women' (*sheng nu*), Ueno, who has no children, has become especially popular, and a role model for millions of Chinese women quietly rebelling against the pressure to marry and have babies.

7 Cited in Alpert, 'Stoicism or Shyness?'. *Sōshoku-kei danshi no ren'ai-gaku* ('love-ology for the herbivorous man') was first published in 2008.

8 'Porn Statistics 2024: Consumption Data, Demographics & Global Trends' [blog post], Merlio, 18 March 2025, <https://merlio.app/blog/porn-statistics-2024-analysis-trends>.

9 Hannah Jane Parkinson, 'Do Lesbians Have Better Sex than Straight Women?', *Guardian*, 9 July 2018.

10 David McCormack, 'Porn Study Had to Be Scrapped after Researchers Failed to Find ANY 20-something Males who Hadn't Watched It', *Daily Mail*, 12 January 2013, <https://www.dailymail.co.uk/news/article-2261377/Porn-study-scrapped-researchers-failed-ANY-20-males-hadn-t-watched-it.html>.

11 Julian, 'Why Are Young People Having So Little Sex?'.

12 The Rangaku (蘭学) or 'Dutch Learning' period refers to the era (roughly 1641–1853) when Japan, under the Tokugawa shogunate's policy of *sakoku* (national isolation), limited contact with the West to the Dutch trading post at Dejima in Nagasaki.

13 Danielle Knafo, 'Guys and Dolls: Relational Life in the Technological Era', Psychoanalytic Dialogues, *The International Journal of Relational Perspectives* Volume 25, Issue 4, 2015, pp.481–502.

14 Jane Wakefield, 'Sex Robots: Experts Debate the Rise of the Love Droids', BBC News, 22 December 2016.

15 Roland Kelts, 'Japan Leads the Way in Sexless Love', *Guardian*, 27 December 2011.

16 From a promotional ad for Gatebox. See: <https://www.youtube.com/watch?v=7mAwi-c9bB8>.

17 'Why I "Married" a Cartoon Character', BBC News, 17 August 2019; see also: 'What Happened to the Japanese Man Who "Married" Virtual Character Hatsune Miku?' *Mainichi*, 11 January 2022.

18 Pilling, *Bending Adversity*, p.69.

19 Henry Tricks, 'Into the Unknown', *Economist* Special Report on Japan, 20 November 2010.

20 First statistic from Matanle, 'Towards an Asia-Pacific "Depopulation Dividend"'. Second statistic from Richard Hendy, 'Yubari, Japan: A City Learns How to Die', *Guardian*, 15 August 2014.

Chapter 7

1 Holden, 'The Vacant City'.

2 'Deterrence failure' and 'counter-strike capabilities' are terms I picked up from Andrew Oros's lecture 'Japan's Greying Security Landscape' on 20 June 2023 at Temple University in Tokyo. Oros is author of *Japan's Security Renaissance*, Columbia University Press, 2017.

3 The JSDF are supposed to be 250,000-strong, but currently have only 226,000 personnel.

4 Demography is one regard in which North Korea has an advantage over its foes. In 2020, its fertility rate stood at 1.82, which makes it positively fecund by comparison with Japan and South Korea. Data from Andrew Oros's lecture, 'Japan's Greying Security Landscape'.

5 Mark Brazil, *Japan: The Natural History of an Asian Archipelago*, Princeton University Press 2022, p.89.

6 Brazil, *Japan: The Natural History*, p.168.

7 '100 Years Since the Great Kanto Earthquake, Urban Disaster Prevention and Preparedness for an Earthquake Under Tokyo', press briefing by Professor Takaaki Kato at Foreign Press Centre Japan, 22 August 2023.

8 Alex Kerr, *Lost Japan*, Lonely Planet Journeys 1996, p.49.

9 Brazil, *Japan: The Natural History*, p.130.

10 First statistic is from Pilling, *Bending Adversity*, p.145. Second statistic is from Gavan McCormack, 'Breaking the Iron Triangle', *New Left Review*, Jan./Feb. 2002.

11 Only with the First Imperial Constitution of 1917 was divorce made more difficult in Japan; the divorce rate fell dramatically the following year. Ueno, 'The Position of Japanese Women Reconsidered'.

12 Miki Tanikawa, 'Clubs Where, for a Price, Japanese Men Are Nice to Women', *The New York Times*, 8 September 1996.

13 Life Expectancy, WorldData.info, <https://www.worlddata.info/life-expectancy.php>.

14 Johanna Airth, 'What the Japanese Can Teach Us about Super-ageing Gracefully', BBC Future, 30 March 2020.

15 Paul Fradale, 'Resurgent Interest in Traditional Japanese Vernacular Architecture: Field Notes from the *Kominka* Boom', lecture at Lakeland University available to view at <https://www.youtube.com/watch?v=GYio9mUOVhE>.

16 Gavin Blair, 'Akiya Houses: Why Japan Has Nine Million Empty Homes', *Guardian*, 1 May 2024.

17 Miura, *The Rise of Sharing*, p.146.

Chapter 8

1 Schoolchildren means children in elementary and junior high school, which is to say between the ages of 6 and 16. 'No. of primary, middle school students in Japan down 1 mil. in decade', Kyodo News, 19 July 2022.

2 Toshihiro Menju, 'Population Decline and Immigration Policy – Making Japan a Popular Destination for Immigration', video report

for Foreign Press Centre Japan, <https://fpcj.jp/en/worldnews-en/briefings-en/p=99078/>.

3 Jeffr Kingston, *Contemporary Japan: History, Politics and Social Change Since the 1980s*, Wiley-Blackwell 2011, p. 57.

4 Japan Country Commercial Guide, International Trade Administration website, <https://www.trade.gov/country-commercial-guides/japan-pharmaceuticals>.

5 Mariko Oi, 'Japan Nappy Maker Shifts from Babies to Adults', BBC News, 27 March 2024.

6 Tricks, 'Into the Unknown'.

7 Todd Schneider, Gee Hee Hong and Anh Van Le, 'Land of the Rising Robots', IMF *Finance & Development* magazine, June 2018, <https://www.imf.org/en/Publications/fandd/issues/2018/06/japan-labor-force-artificial-intelligence-and-robots-schneider>; Tricks, 'Into the Unknown'.

8 Pilling, *Bending Adversity*, p.160.

9 First statistic is from '10% of Japan's 2070 Population', *Asahi Shinbun*. Second statistic is from Gabriele Vogt, 'Guest Workers for Japan?', *Asia Pacific Journal* Volume 5, Issue 9, 3 September 2007.

10 Kingston, *Contemporary Japan*, p. 42.

11 Amelia Hill, 'UK State Pension Age Will Soon Need to Rise to 71, Say Experts', *Guardian*, 5 February 2024.

12 Cabinet Office Annual Report on the Ageing Society 2021.

13 Charles Chau, 'Japan Approves Law Raising Retirement Age to 70', HRM Asia, 6 April 2021.

14 See: List of Countries by Government Spending as a Percentage of GDP, Wikipedia, <https://en.wikipedia.org/wiki/List_of_countries_by_government_spending_as_percentage_of_GDP>.

15 Pilling, *Bending Adversity*, p.127.

16 Pilling, *Bending Adversity*, p.124.

17 Pilling, *Bending Adversity*, pp.150–55.

18 Statistics are from Wikipedia article on Japan Post: <https://en.wikipedia.org/wiki/Japan_Post>. See, too: Pilling, *Bending Adversity*, pp.150–55.

19 Household Saving Ratio in Japan from 1994 to 2024, Statista.com, <https://www.statista.com/statistics/1235833/japan-saving-ratio-of-households/>.

Chapter 9

1 British farmers, who have an average age of 59, are not exactly spring chickens either. See: 'The Ageing Crisis Threatening Farming', BBC 2019, date unclear; see: <https://www.bbc.com/future/bespoke/follow-the-food/the-ageing-crisis-threatening-farming/>.
2 See: 'Vision for a Digital Garden City Nation', *Kizuna* (the official magazine of the Japanese government), 28 December 2021, <https://www.japan.go.jp/kizuna/2022/01/vision_for_a_digital_garden_city_nation.html>.

Chapter 10

1 The survey was conducted in 2006. Miura, *The Rise of Sharing*, p.167.
2 There is currently a Rural Revitalization representative in over a third of Japan's 3,229 municipalities.
3 Miura, *The Rise of Sharing*, p.187.
4 From 'Shrinking but Happy? Investigating the Interplay of Social and Individual-Level Predictors of Well-Being in Rural Japanese Communities', a talk by Dionyssios Askitis at the University of Vienna on 18 September 2019.
5 Miura, *The Rise of Sharing*, p.283.

Chapter 11

1 This is based on projections indicating a 50 per cent reduction in the population of women aged 20–39 (the core childbearing age group) between 2020 and 2050. See: 'The Number of Municipalities at Risk of Disappearing

Decreased? Future of National Land Without "Competitions for Citizens as Resources" Desired', Yano Research Institute, 14 May 2024.

2 Many JR lines have seen declines in passenger numbers of two-thirds or more since the 1980s. Not long after I passed through Hiroshima prefecture in the summer of 2023, the Japanese government announced that it would streamline the process by which JR companies close lightly travelled railway lines.

3 The crime rate rose in 2022, but this was probably a blip caused by the easing of lockdown restrictions. 'Reported Crime in Japan Increases for First Time in 20 Years', nippon.com, 20 February 2023, <https://www.nippon.com/en/japan-data/h01582/>.

4 Erik Herber, 'Crime Prevention in Japan Orchestration, Representation and Impact of a Volunteering Boom', *International Journal of Law, Crime and Justice* Volume 54, September 2018, pp.102–10.

5 Christoph Schimkowsky, 'Crime Prevention in a Low-Crime Nation: An Enquiry into Japanese Bōhan Initiatives', *Contemporary Japan* Volume 33, Issue 2, 2021.

6 The 9,888 offences they committed in 1988 rose to 48,605 in 2007. Kingston, *Contemporary Japan*, p. 60.

7 Sugimoto, *Introduction to Japanese Society*, p.90.

8 Shiho Fukada, 'Japan's Prisons Are a Haven for Elderly Women', Bloomberg, 16 March 2018.

9 Yuka Royer, 'Japan Contends with Record Number of Bear Attacks Amid Rural Depopulation', France 24, 7 December 2020, <https://www.france24.com/en/asia-pacific/20201207-japan-contends-with-record-number-of-bear-attacks-amid-rural-depopulation>.

10 Justin McCurry, 'Bear Snared after Three-Day Supermarket Standoff with Japan Police', *Guardian*, 2 December 2024.

11 Incidentally, Japan has several other national animals, including the dormouse, making it probably the only country to have a rodent as a symbol of the nation.

12 That figure does not include Hokkaido, thought to be home to just under 12,000 Ussuri brown bears, whose population has more than doubled since 1990. McCurry, 'Bear Snared after Three-Day Supermarket Standoff'.

Chapter 12

1 Amelia Hill, 'When 75 Is Time to Die: The Horrifically Plausible Film Imagining State-Run Euthanasia in Japan', *Guardian*, 8 May 2023.

2 Schad-Seifert, 'Coping with Low Fertility?'.

3 This is a literal translation of the ministerial title Naikakufu Tokumei Tantō Daijin – Shōshika Danjo Kyōdō Sankaku. The official English title is Minister of State for Gender Equality and Social Affairs. See: Schad-Seifert, 'Coping with Low Fertility?'.

4 'Japan's Marriage Market', East Asia Forum.

5 Tsuchiya Hideo, 'End of the East Asian Miracle? A Demographic Look at Asia's Economic Future', nippon.com, 24 April 2023.

6 Kleeman, 'America's premier pronatalists'.

7 Fertility rate for 2006 from: South Korea Fertility Rate (1950–2025), Macrotrends.net, < https://www.macrotrends.net/global-metrics/countries/kor/south-korea/fertility-rate>. Fertility rate for 2022 from: 'Fears for Future as South Korea's Fertility Rate Drops Again', Al Jazeera, 28 February 2024.

8 Carlo Martuscelli, 'The Populist Right Wants You to Make More Babies. The Question Is How', Politico, 11 September 2023.

9 Anthony, 'The Global Fertility Crisis'.

10 Stephen J. Shaw in discussion with Jordan Peterson, 'The Epidemic that Dare Not Speak Its Name'. Plus notes taken from Shaw's Q&A at Temple University.

11 Sheila Cadge, 'Roman Women and Children Part I – Fertility' [blog post], Vindolanda.com, <https://www.vindolanda.com/blog/roman-women-and-children-part-1>.

12 The Japanese expression was '*Umeyō fuyaseyō okuni no tame ni.*' See: Nemoto, 'Postponed Marriage'. Ironically, the interwar years were a time when contraception was not widely available, and many poor farming families in north-eastern Japan were reduced to committing infanticide to keep numbers down.

13 '*The Handmaid's Tale* author Margaret Atwood: "I have never believed it can't happen here"', CBS News, 8 November 2019. Atwood was inspired to write *The Handmaid's Tale* by the Islamic Revolution

that took place in Iran in 1978–79, following which a theocracy was established that drastically reduced women's rights and imposed a strict dress code very much like that of Gilead. In *The Handmaid's Tale*, a reference is made to the Islamic Republic in the form of the history book *Iran and Gilead: Two Late Twentieth Century Monotheocracies* mentioned in the endnotes describing a historians' convention in 2195. See Faye Hammill, 'Margaret Atwood's *The Handmaid's Tale*' in *A Companion to Science Fiction*, ed. William Seed, John Wiley and Sons 2008, pp.522–33.

14 'The Guardian View on Population Growth', *Guardian*.

15 See Mariarosa Dalla Costa, 'Reproduction and Immigration', first published in Italian in *L'operaio multinazionale in Europa*, eds. Alessandro Serafini et al., Feltrinelli 1974. It was translated into English by Silvia Federici and Harry Cleaver and revised by the author, and is available to view online at: <https://libcom.org/article/reproduction-and-immigration-mariarosa-dalla-costa>. See, too: Ueno, 'The Declining Birthrate: Whose Problem?', p.108.

16 Nemoto, 'Postponed Marriage'. See, too: 'Japanese Women Live on Their Own, and Like It', NBC News, 31 August 2004.

17 'The New Asian Family', *Economist*, 6 July 2023.

18 Ueno, 'The Declining Birthrate: Whose Problem?'.

19 Hannah Devlin, 'Scientists Create Mice with Two Fathers after Making Eggs from Male Cells', *Guardian*, 8 March 2023.

20 Approximately 397,000 dogs and 489,000 cats were bought or adopted in 2021, making for a cumulative total of 886,000. That year, 811,604 human infants were born. Paul Hansen, 'Urban Japan's "Fuzzy" New Families: Affect and Embodiment in Dog–Human Relationships', *Asian Anthropology* Volume 12, Issue 2, 2013, pp.83–103.

21 Dogs and cats currently outnumber children under the age of 15 by a factor of two. *The Sociology of Pets in Contemporary Japan*, Deutsche Institute Japan.

22 Hansen, 'Urban Japan's "Fuzzy" New Families'.

23 See George Lloyd, 'Kanno-ji: A Temple where Pet Lovers Pray for the Rebirth of Their Beloved Cats and Dogs in Paradise', Grape Japan, 23 January 2021, <https://grapee.jp/en/163426>. See, too: 'Can Dogs Be

Reborn in Paradise? Japan's Buddhist Funerals for Pets', nippon.com, 5 February 2019.

24 Ueno, 'The Declining Birthrate: Whose Problem?'.

25 'Precarity and Placelessness in Japan's Superaged Society', a lecture by Dr Jason Danely, Reader in Anthropology, Oxford Brookes University, 5 April 2023.

26 Lubman, 'Japan Confronts a Stark Reality'..

27 Lubman, 'Japan Confronts a Stark Reality'.

28 Lubman, 'Japan Confronts a Stark Reality'.

29 Matthew Hernon, 'Six Japanese Robots Working Where You'd Least Expect Them', *Tokyo Weekender*, 7 October 2017.

30 See Giulia De Togni, 'Hearts Meet Wires: Navigating the Ethical and Social Implications of Care Robotics', in *The Future of Humans and Emotional Machines: Narratives from Japanese Culture in the 21st Century*, eds. Elena Giannoulis and Berthold Frommann, Routledge 2025.

31 James Wright, 'Inside Japan's Long Experiment in Automating Elder Care', MIT Technology Review, 9 January 2023.

32 Hill, 'When 75 Is Time to Die'.

Chapter 13

1 Sam Holden, a keen observer of post-growth Japan, is no fan of the Chūō Shinkansen maglev project. He says that the company behind the project 'has been lying for years about the timeline and economic viability of the project and has now yoked the country to a fabulously expensive albatross that will cannibalize the Tōkaidō Shinkansen's profits, consume vast amounts of electricity, and worsen the fiscal position of the whole railway system as the population declines'. See: Sam Holden, 'Trains from the Past, Trains to the Future: Where Japan's Railways Are Headed in a Post-Growth World' [blog post], Substack, 10 October 2024.

2 Christopher Null and Brian Caulfield, 'Fade To Black: The 1980s Vision of "Lights-Out" Manufacturing, Where Robots Do All the Work, Is a Dream No More', CNN Money, 1 June 2003.

3 Lisa Thomas, 'What's Behind Japan's Love Affair with Robots?', *Time*, 3 August 2009.

4 Moonshot Research and Development programme, Japan Science and Technology Agency, <https://www.jst.go.jp/moonshot/en/program/goal1/index.html>.

5 In addition to AI, Altman has invested in several reproductive technology start-ups, one aiming to engineer human eggs out of stem cells, and another that screens human embryos for health outcomes. He is on record as saying, 'Of course I'm going to have a big family. I think having a lot of kids is great.' See: Kleeman, 'America's Premier Pronatalists'.

6 Larry Elliott, 'Robots Threaten 15m UK Jobs, Says Bank of England's Chief Economist', *Guardian*, 12 November 2015.

7 Arwa Mahdawi, 'What Jobs Will Still Be Around in 20 Years? Read This to Prepare Your Future', *Guardian*, 26 June 2017.

8 Hernon, 'Six Japanese Robots Working Where You'd Least Expect Them'.

9 'Softbank unveils "human-like" robot Pepper', BBC News, 5 June 2014.

10 ' "Pepper" the Robot Has a New Job', CBS News, 24 August 2017.

11 It is certainly a lucrative market: the Lovot retails at ¥498,000 (£2,502). If that is a bit steep for a lonely member of the precariat toiling away on a zero-hours contract, its manufacturers, Groove X, give customers the option of paying in monthly instalments. See: groove-x.com.

12 'The Guardian View on Population Growth', *Guardian*.

13 'Population Dynamics and the Future of Japan', a briefing by Miho Iwasawa, Director, Department of Population Dynamics Research, NIPSSR, at Foreign Press Centre Japan, 29 September 2022.

14 '10% of Japan's 2070 population', *Asahi Shinbun*. Between 2016 and 2018, the only prefectures in which the population increased were Tokyo and six other prefectures, and more than half of the new arrivals were foreigners. With the exception of Okinawa, the six prefectures that saw their populations rise are all highly urbanized. Three of them – Saitama, Kanagawa and Chiba – are satellites of Tokyo, while Aichi is dominated by Nagoya, and Fukuoka is dominated by the city of Fukuoka, the largest in Kyushu.

15 'Japan's Incremental Immigration Reform: A Recipe for Failure', nippon.com, 25 August 2023.

16 'Foreign Population in Tokyo Soars as Chinese Buyers Seek Condos', Japan Forward, 1 August 2024.

17 '10% of Japan's 2070 population', *Asahi Shinbun*.

18 Vogt, 'Guest Workers for Japan?'.

19 'Number of Potential Migrants Worldwide Tops 700 Million', Gallup, 8 June 2017.

20 Shimizu, 'Digital Transformation and Japan's Political Economy'.

21 Richard Miles, 'A Smaller, Wealthier Mexico Is on the Horizon', Center for Strategic and International Studies, 11 December 2017.

22 Stephen J. Shaw in discussion with Jordan Peterson, 'The Epidemic that Dare Not Speak Its Name'. Plus notes taken from Shaw's Q&A at Temple University.

23 This may be mitigated by vast increases in displacement and migration as a result of climate change, which, by some estimates, could run as high as 2 billion people by 2100.

Chapter 14

1 Akita has 15.5 deaths and just 5.4 births per 1,000 residents (data from 2017). Ying Zhou, 'A Deserted Akita Town Offers a Glimpse of Japan's Demographic Future', *Japan Times*, 12 July 2021, <https://www.japantimes.co.jp/news/2021/07/12/national/fujisato-akita-aging-depopulation/>.

2 Holden, *The Vacant City*.

3 Zhou, 'A Deserted Akita Town'.

4 The prime minister at the time of writing, Shigeru Ishiba, also seems to find the concentration of wealth and resources in Tokyo problematic. He is on record as saying, 'I have real misgivings about the capital getting more and more convenient at a time when the population is falling, the economy is not growing any more, and we need to come to terms as a country with over-concentration in Tokyo and the Tokyo region.' Cited in Holden, 'Trains from the Past'.

Conclusion

1 Masashi Kawai, 'Ultra-Aging Japan's "Issue of the 24th Year of Reiwa" – Department Stores and Banks Will Close Down and Local Governments Will Reduce by Half', Japan Foreign Policy Forum, 17 July 2019.
2 'Dentsu Institute and Doshisha University Announce 9 Distinctive Trends in Japan Revealed by Analysis of the World Values Survey', Dentsu Institute 22 March 2021.
3 'Elon Musk Warns Japan Will Cease to Exist if Birth-Rate Continues Decline', Kyodo News, 9 May 2022.

Index

*Entries with a * refer to footnotes*

Abe, Shinzo, 8, 26–7, 51, 250, 262
Abegglen, James, 12
abortion, 58, 225
Adachi, Toshihide, 231–2
Africa, xxiv, 265
ageing population in Japan, vii–viii,
    xix–xxi, xxvi; and abandoned
    houses, xxv, 7–8, 127, 144–5,
    147, 151, 199–200, 242–3, 276; in
    Akita prefecture, 269–77; boom
    in geriatric crime, 209–10; and
    contraception, 91; and dementia,
    235–6, 237, 238; development of
    care robots, 236–9, 250; economic
    impact of, xviii, xxi, xxii, 153–6,
    163–5, 166–70, 199–207, 214–17, 243–4,
    269–77, 285–6; future political
    impact of, 154–5; growth of
    grey economy, 153; healthy life
    expectancy rates, 5, 140–1; impact
    on farming, 166–70, 171, 181, 185–92,
    199–204, 211, 214–17; impact on
    innovation, xxii; and loneliness,
    xvii–xix, xxii, 146, 209–10, 235,
    273–4, 275, 282–3; 'marginalized
    settlement' term, 198; *meiwaku*
    ('trouble' or 'bother') concept, 244;
    and military strength, 128–9; and
    mountain communities, 200–6, 211,
    214–15, 269–77; as not newsworthy,
    4; and rural wildlife, xvii, 210–14;

    as warning to the world, xxiii;
    warnings over, xxiii, xxv, 4
Ajinomoto (food processing
    company), 258
Akiko (working mother), 48–51, 58–62,
    66, 226–7
Akita City, 270–5
Akita Partnership (NGO), 273–5
Akita prefecture, 194, 269–77
Allison, Anne, *Precarious Japan* (2013),
    76
Altman, Sam, 250–1
anime, 41, 67–8, 90, 93, 95, 113–15, 231
Aomori prefecture, 269, 270, 278–9
Aoshima island, 176–80
Apple, 40, 45
Arakawa, Kazuhisa, 54, 70–71
architecture/built environment:
    decay and dereliction due to
    depopulation, 148, 149, 151, 178–9,
    186–7, 230, 276, 278; Hiroshima Bay
    area, 198–9; and Kobe earthquake
    (1995), 63; mania for public works,
    131–3, 163, 184; of Matsudo, 115,
    118; public toilets, 4; renovating
    of empty properties, 186–7, 195;
    small post-war housing, 104–5;
    Tokyo's urban plan, x, xii–xiii, xiv,
    3–5, 6, 18, 23, 100; tourist-friendly
    infrastructure, 182–3; traditional
    rural houses, 187; ultra-modern

China, 44, 101, 110, 132, 250, 266;
  Chinese workers in Japan,
  8–9, 104, 171, 260, 262; Japanese
  hostility to, 45, 128, 157, 262; rise
  of in present era, 11; students
  from in Japan, xiii; tourists from,
  30, 180, 233
Christian missionaries, 117
climate, 103, 148, 161, 173–4, 184, 199;
  rainy season, 167, 179, 197, 215, 230;
  typhoons, 167, 173, 184, 199, 215, 230
Confucianism, 24, 240
'Cool Japan' brand, 41–3, 256
coronavirus pandemic, 19, 76, 142,
  182, 255
corporate/business sector:
  advertising, 27, 39, 41, 101–2, 153, 280;
  Big Pharma, 153; corporate culture,
  8, 13–17, 24–8, 31, 34, 38–9, 94, 106,
  172, 244–5, 264, 284–5; and culture
  of overwork, 24–8, 34, 38, 94, 244–5,
  284–5; employee stakeholders,
  12; export-led industrialization,
  11–12; female graduates in, 53, 55;
  female senior managers, 49, 51,
  168; and foreign workers, 8, 11,
  264; and Korean War, 12; lifetime
  employment system, 14, 15, 24–5,
  38–9, 55–6; and *mazakon* ('mother
  complex'), 38–9; and parasite
  singledom, 20
cowrie shells, 176–7
crime, 83, 206; boom in geriatric
  crime, 209–10; con men preying
  on the elderly, xvii, 209; crime
  prevention groups, 207–9;
  fraud and cyber-crime, 209; and
  immigration, 262; *Kaigo tsukare*
  ('care-giving fatigue'), 235; low
  rates of, xvii, 3, 207

daimyō (feudal lords), 86
Dale, Peter, *The Myth of Japanese
  Uniqueness*, ix
Dalla Costa, Mariarosa, 36, 226
Dawn Avatar Robot Café (Tokyo),
  248–9, 253
De Gaulle, Charles, 12
demographics, global: ageing
  populations of North-East Asia,
  128–9; Blue Zones, 140–1; and
  climate crisis, xxiv; falling fertility
  rates in developed nations, xx, xxii,
  xxiii–xxvi, 28–9, 223–4, 225–6, 285–6;
  falling fertility rates in developing
  world, xxiv, 129, 264–5; falling infant
  mortality rates, xxiii; 'human
  capital' and innovation as declining,
  xxii; impending population crash,
  xxi–xxii, xxiii–xxvi, 214, 285–6; mass
  ageing as not newsworthy, xxiv–xxv,
  4; past overpopulation warnings,
  xxiv; replacement level fertility
  rates, xx, xxiii–xxiv, 26, 62, 120, 177,
  200; rural depopulation in Europe,
  214; urban living and birth rate, 29
Denmark, 224
Dentsu (advertising giant), 27, 283
depopulation (shrinking of total
  population) in Japan, xx, xxvi; and
  falling economic demand, 153–4;
  fatalism over, 168, 190, 206, 269–70,
  273, 275, 277; foreign interest in
  difficulties, 166; government policy,
  26–8, 51, 59–60, 147, 154–5, 162, 163–5,
  167, 182, 221–7, 249–51, 257–64; and
  immigration, 8, 11, 17, 236, 257–65;
  optimism over, 154–5, 270, 271–5;
  population decline in Tokyo, 6–7;
  profound implications of, xxiv–xxv,
  154, 166; and rural communities,